BECAUSE THEY HATE

Praise for *Because They Hate*

"Part memoir and part analysis of the social, political, and religious factors that created the current situation in the Middle East, Gabriel issues a clear warning."
— *The Tampa Tribune*

"A compelling and captivating personal story with a powerful lesson about threats to freedom in our time."
—R. James Woolsey, Director of Central Intelligence, 1993–1995

"Brigitte Gabriel's story is at once intensely personal and possessing global significance. . . . the story of her family and her childhood encapsulates the threat that faces the entire free world today. Brigitte Gabriel's words should be read, and studied carefully, by all the law enforcement and government officials of the West—as well as by everyone who values freedom."
—Robert Spencer, author of *The Politically Incorrect Guide to Islam (and the Crusades)*

"Her writing is eloquent and her passion tremendous."
— *Publishers Weekly*

"Gabriel believes the West is complacent about the threat posed by radical Islam. She learned while growing up Christian in Lebanon that Islamofascists are serious—and if we want to survive we better take them seriously. She speaks with the passion of a survivor who has seen death and destruction firsthand—and doesn't want America to suffer the same future as Lebanon."
— *World Magazine*

"Brigitte Gabriel eloquently reminds America what is truly at stake in this struggle against terrorism: our families, our way of life, and our hopes. Ms. Gabriel's personal account of her own experience is riveting, compelling, and spellbinding. This is a must read for the entire American public . . . *Because They Hate* contains monumental revelations that will shock and disturb you. But it is also a story of an indomitable spirit—Brigitte's—that will move you."

—Steve Emerson, author of *American Jihad: The Terrorists Living Amongst Us,* executive director, the Investigative Project on Terrorism

"*Because They Hate* is powerful, passionate, and full of divine purpose."

—Dr. John C. Hagee, senior pastor, Cornerstone Church, author of *Jerusalem Countdown: A Warning to the World*

"*Because They Hate* should be read by all to understand radical Islam. . . . This book gives dire warning of what is to come if the democratic and Western world does not take responsible action to protect its people and societies. The United States is the primary target as Islamic radicalism attempts to spread its worldwide dominance."

—Paul E. Vallely, Maj. General U.S. Army (Ret.), FOX News Channel Military Analyst, and coauthor of *Endgame: The Blueprint for Victory in the War on Terror*

"[Brigitte Gabriel's] writing is a critical wake-up call to Americans as we face the threat of takeover by jihadists. We are glad to be able to help her share her story with God-fearing, patriotic Americans who care about the truth and want to learn about the threat every nation throughout the world is facing from radical Islam."

—Paul F. Crouch, Jr., vice president of administration, Trinity Broadcasting Network

"Gabriel makes her case, but also offers a sound and powerful program of what we have to do as a nation and as individuals to stave off defeat by radical Islam."

—*The Bulletin*

BECAUSE THEY HATE

❖

A Survivor of Islamic Terror

Warns America

❖

Brigitte Gabriel

St. Martin's Griffin ❦ New York

www.stmartins.com

Library of Congress Cataloging-in-Publication Data

Gabriel, Brigitte.
    Because they hate : a survivor of Islamic terror warns America / Brigitte
Gabriel.
        p.   cm.
    Includes bibliographical references.
    ISBN-13: 978-0-312-35838-9
    ISBN-10: 0-312-35838-5
    1. Terrorism—Lebanon.   2. Victims of terrorism—Lebanon.   3. Terrorism—
Religious aspects—Islam.   I. Title.

HV6433.L4 G33 2006
956.7204'4092—dc22
[B]
                                                                    2006013500

20 19 18

IN HONOR OF

My mother, Bahia, my father, Nicholas, and
all the victims of religious-bigoted terror.

DEDICATED TO

My pride and joy, Jessica and Virginia,
in the hope that their generation may live
under freedom and democracy.

CONTENTS

INTRODUCTION
TO THE 2006 EDITION

Radical Islam's modern war of world domination has been picking up momentum, with its universal rallying cry of "Allahu Akbar" accompanying each act of terror and destruction. It first began after the Arab nations that were artificially carved out after World War II settled into internal despondency under despots and monarchs appointed by the Allied powers. It slowly fermented through the 1950s and 1960s. By November 1979 it was well on its way when the Iranians took over the American embassy in Tehran.

But no one really noticed or cared.

I noticed when I was a ten-year-old girl in Lebanon, and Muslim rockets exploded in my bedroom on a November night four years before the American hostages were taken. With my life on the line, I really cared, while the rest of the world just watched. My problem was that I wasn't an American, the marines weren't coming to save me, and we Lebanese Christian—non-Muslim infidels—were being labeled the aggressors by the press. Muslims dominated and now control Lebanon. Christian infidels paid the price then; and for their indifference and shortsightedness, infidels worldwide are paying the price now.

The civil war in Lebanon was pushed off U.S. front pages by the hostage situation in Iran; the obsessive media exposure turned the 444-day captivity of diplomats and embassy workers into a nation-wide trauma and a national disgrace. Finally, the marines came to Lebanon and got bloodied, and the U.S. went away to lick its wounds. Despite extensive news coverage and obvious implications, the war in Lebanon and the hostage crisis were never recognized for what they were: declarations of war on Western civilization by radical Islam.

Today, radical Islam's war rages with varying degrees of intensity throughout the world, not just against Christians and Jews in the West, but also against Hindus, Buddhists, Copts, indeed all non-Muslim infidels. The radical Islamists' degree of zealotry even has them attacking other denominations within Islam itself. Islamic radicals are instigating and perpetuating terrorist campaigns, insurgencies, civil wars, minority suppression, and ethnic cleansing and/or genocide in Afghanistan, Algeria, Bangladesh, Belgium, Chad, Chechnya, Dagestan, Denmark, Egypt, Ethiopia, France, Gambia, Great Britain, India, Indonesia, Iran, Iraq, Israel, Kashmir, Kenya, Kosovo, Lebanon, Macedonia, Mali, Mauritania, Morocco, the Netherlands, Niger, Nigeria, Pakistan, territories administered by the Palestinian Authority, the Philippines, Qatar, Russia, Saudi Arabia, Senegal, Somalia, Spain, Sudan, Syria, Tanzania, Thailand, Tunisia, Turkey, the United States of America, Yemen, and Zanzibar. The rest of the world is held hostage to fear.

From Saudi-funded madrassas and mosques worldwide, to the parliament of Iran, to the cabals of al Qaeda and Hezbollah, radical Islamists have repeatedly declared and demonstrated that their goal is to impose Islamic rule throughout the world, by the sword or by the suicide bomb. Numerous radical Islamic "scholars" have declared that it is every Muslim's religious duty to dominate or exterminate all infidels.[1] What they write and say is what they are going to do. All we have to do is read and listen.

The United States has been a prime target for radical Islamic hatred and terror.[2] Every Friday, mosques in the Middle East ring with shrill prayers and monotonous chants that call down death, destruction, and damnation on America and its people. The radical Islamists' deeds have been as vile as their words. Since the Iran hostage crisis, more than three thousand Americans have died in a terror campaign almost unprecedented in its calculated cruelty, along with thousands of other citizens worldwide. Even the Nazis did not turn their own children into human bombs, and then rejoice at their deaths as well as the deaths of their victims. This intentional, indiscriminate, and wholesale murder of innocent American citizens is justified and glorified in the name of Islam.

And yet, there are still Americans who are unable or unwilling to recognize the nature or the extent of the threat presented by radical Islam. Whether motivated by naive wishful thinking or rigid political correctness, they assert that Islam is a "moderate," "tolerant," and "peaceful" religion that has been hijacked by "extremists." They ignore the repeated calls to jihad, Islamic holy war, emanating from the government-controlled mosques of so-called moderate Islamic countries such as Egypt, Pakistan, and Indonesia. They refuse to accept that in the Muslim world, *ex*treme is *main*stream.

American citizens have been murdered in this terror war for thirty years. However, America cannot effectively defend itself in this war unless and until the American people understand the nature of the enemy that it faces. Even after 9/11 there are those who say that we must "engage" our terrorist enemies, that we must "address their grievances." Their grievance is our freedom of religion. Their grievance is our democratic process. Islamic religious authorities and terrorist leaders repeatedly state that they will destroy the United States and Western civilization, and replace it with the only true religion, Islam. Unless we take them at their word, and defend ourselves accordingly, they will succeed. For the sake of our children and our country, we must wake up and take action. In the face of a torrent of hateful invective and terrorist murder, America's learning curve since the Iran hostage crisis has been so shallow that it is almost flat. The longer we lie supine, the more difficult it will be to stand erect.

Like the Christians in Lebanon, Americans today are not realizing the power of the Islamic call to jihad. The Islamic takeover of Iran and its subjugation of Lebanon were strategic victories in Islam's war for world domination.

This book is in part my personal story and my observations. It is written in the hope that Americans and the West will recognize this imminent threat to their way of life and make the correct philosophical, legal, governmental policy, and military decisions to protect themselves from suffering the same fate as the Lebanese infidels.

INTRODUCTION
TO THE 2008 EDITION

In July 2006, four weeks before the scheduled release of this book in hardcover, a bloody war broke out in Lebanon between Hezbollah and Israel. The history described in *Because They Hate* suddenly came alive. History repeated itself in the same South Lebanon towns I wrote about—the villages in which I grew up and experienced the Lebanese war between 1975 and 1982. In 1982 we saw Israel push into Lebanon, fed up with the rockets that had been raining down on Northern Israel; they invaded Lebanon in order to push back the the PLO and Syrians. Similarly in 2006, Hezbollah captured Israeli soldiers and again sent rockets into Northern Israel. The world was upset with Israel in 1982, but in 2006 the situation had changed and the international community gave Israeli forces time to hit Hezbollah before the UN Security Council called for an end to hostilities by unanimously adopting resolution 1701, on August 11, 2006. The resolution called for a permanent cease-fire to be based on the creation of a buffer zone free of armed personnel other than the UN and armed Lebanese forces.[1] The intervening twenty-four years of Muslim mayhem had knocked some sense into the world and altered its thinking and response to radical Islam. My publisher, St. Martin's Press, released *Because They Hate* two weeks prior to its scheduled date, so it was available for readers who wanted to understand the situation in Lebanon in terms of its underlying conflict and sources.

The tragic summer conflict opened the doors for me with the media and launched *Because They Hate* along with hundreds of media interviews. I was one of the most knowledgeable experts on radical Islam in Lebanon—not only was I a survivor who lived through the Lebanese war but I was also a journalist who covered the area in the 1980s.

As I travel worldwide, I have been overwhelmed with the love and appreciation I receive when I speak at churches, synagogues, business and political functions, and private organizations. I have met many thousands of Americans who are frustrated with the current situation and who are all supportive of fighting Islamofacism no matter what it takes. Many have told me that they have been made to feel isolated in their thinking and appreciate my clear presentation of the realities and danger of radical Islam. In the many and varied communities in which I have spoken, hundreds and thousands show up to hear me speak. I have seen people from different backgrounds and religions who have come together to form friendships and associations that support their involvement in fighting radical Islam—a movement that threatens our freedoms and way of life. These gatherings are very heartening and have inspired me even more to continue with my vision for American Congress for Truth (ACT for America), which is not only to educate millions of Americans about the threat of Islamofascism, but also to mobilize millions of patriotic citizens into a national grassroots force—to give power to "we the people" and empower every concerned citizen to become a voice affecting their community and our great nation. ACT for America (a 501(c)(4) nonprofit organization) is an issues advocacy organization dedicated to effectively organizing and mobilizing a powerful American grassroots citizen action network, and is committed to informed and coordinated civic action that will lead to public policies that promote America's national security and the defense of American democratic values against the assault of radical Islam.

ACT for America was founded to unify the voice of Americans who are not only concerned about the threat of Islamofascism but also understand that "political correctness" is causing government action—and inaction—that compromises American security, safety, and liberty.

ACT for America is now in the process of setting up chapters nationwide to network and organize citizens by empowering them and giving them the tools by which they can make a difference on their own level in their own community.

To be honest, I was not surprised by the positive reactions *Because They Hate* received. I had expected it. I have been an activist since 2002 and have been communicating since then with different groups and people through the activities and community on www.americancongressfortruth.org. I knew there were thousands of people nationwide who had become fed up with political correctness and were hungry to hear the truth regarding our enemy and our national security. Patriotic Americans were tired of journalists putting our country down, standing up for our enemy, and all the while sabotaging our government that was doing everything in its power to protect us and disrespecting our soldiers who were putting their lives on the line. The disdain, ridicule, and extreme posturing from the far left and some Congressional committee members toward General Petraeus during his Iraq report to Congress in September 2007 were typical of the uniformed position of the blind left. The whole performance was disgraceful to our country and helpful to our enemy.

But I knew there were readers out there who wanted the truth. One reader told me that when he went to a bookstore and inquired about "the book that is number one under terrorism on Amazon.com," the store clerk reacted in disgust and answered with a scowl, "The author did something recently on C-SPAN and we keep running out of stock."

Readers such as this one put *Because They Hate* on the *New York Times* bestseller list as the readers flocked to buy copies, pushing the number of copies in print to ten times the initial printing. C-SPAN, which aired one of my Washington, D.C., presentations at the Heritage Foundation, was so overwhelmed with requests for the DVD of the presentation that they aired the interview multiple times on multiple weekends. Because of book-related publicity, over twenty thousand people signed up and joined my organization American Congress for Truth, asking to receive our e-mails and action alerts.

I worked sixteen hours a day for twelve months (and counting!) either traveling to speaking engagements or giving radio interviews from my hotel room or office. On some days I would give fourteen radio interviews, starting at 7:00 A.M. and going until 11:00 P.M. Radio talk show hosts would thank me for my honesty and tell me after the interview that I made their phone lines light up like they have never seen before. It was clear that the American public was ready to speak and to hear the truth, and to be inspired to learn what they could do to protect their communities.

As I worked to publicize *Because They Hate,* I learned a lot about the state of our society and the place honesty and forthrightness hold. I discovered that many organizations wanted to have me as a speaker for major events because of the popularity and effectiveness of my message, but they were afraid and intimidated by the possible reaction of Muslims in their community. Some organizations canceled bookings out of intimidation from influential members who thought that my ideas would inflame the Muslims in their communities. Many times I was instructed before speaking to be politically correct and not to offend anyone. And so I agreed to give only the facts without inserting my political opinion—I let the news facts reported around the world about current events and terrorists activities and attacks speak for themselves. By the end of my presentations to many even leftist groups, my audiences agreed with me on 90 percent of my presentation. The only disagreements came from Muslim invited guests—usually doctors and respected members of the Islamic community—who passionately argued that Hezbollah is not a terrorist organization, that we do not have terrorists in our communities, and that their Islamic community was different and peaceful. It was laughable to say the least hearing these arguments in Toronto where sixteen local Canadian Muslims tried to blow up government buildings and behead politicians;[2] in Miami where many local Muslims have been charged with terrorist activities;[3] in New York where local Muslims were charged with a terrorist plot to blow up JFK;[4] in LA where a massacre was planned by local Muslims against two Los Angeles synagogues;[5] and in Australia where nine men were tried in a terrorist plot to blow up Australia's only nuclear reactor.[6] One organization flew me across the country to be their keynote speaker for their annual event, and then, after hearing my first presentation, instructed me to change facts reported in the news—I wasn't to offend people with the truth even if it meant I had to lie.

Discussing news events has apparently become a bigoted and racist activity because terrorists are Muslims. Discussing those facts may offend some people and so we must stay silent.

In all the presentations that I have done with crowds large and small at a variety of venues, I have not run into one Muslim who stood up and apologized for the murder and attacks that were perpetrated in the name of their religion. Whenever a Muslim stood up from the crowd, it was to argue that I was making Muslims look bad. No one stood up to call for reform in their religion or used the opportunity to ask other Muslims if they would like to join in a movement to publicly condemn terrorist organizations by name.

The Muslim community recognized quickly that my message had a welcome audience and that I present it effectively and without fear. And so they tried to organize to stop me from coming to their communities in the first place. They tried everything from intimidating and threatening me by phone and e-mail in detailed terms, to intimidating the groups who invited me to speak, especially universities. They knew that anyone who attended my lectures would walk away with a different reality than the one that has been perpetrated for the last thirty years by the PLO and presented by sympathetic media and "progressive" Muslims on campus.

Speaking boldly earned me passionate enemies and faithful supporters. When I was scheduled to speak at the University of Michigan in Ann Arbor, an e-mail originating out of an organization in California was sent to members in the Detroit community. The title of the e-mail said: "Islam-Basher Brigitte Gabriel to visit Ann Arbor on December 4" and the text included the following: "Muslims, Arabs, and their friends and allies should give Gabriel a proper welcome." College campuses I visited, occupied by deceptive, self-loathing Americans and Islamist sympathizers, became battlegrounds—in order to exercise America's right to freedom of speech, I had to be surrounded by an army of police officers insuring my safety. Extensive security, bodyguards, and K9 units at university lectures became the norm. Many times I thought that America's freedom of speech, much attacked and laying in an intensive care state, was in dire straits.

As Muslims (and what I am finding to be more surprising, some Jews) complained about this book from one continent to another, *Because They Hate* earned respect and admiration from world leaders and decision makers in business and politics.

I had the privilege of visiting England and addressing the British Parliament/House of Commons, as well as business leaders throughout the country, about the rise of radical Islam in Europe. Audiences were very receptive and shared their concerns and feelings of helplessness against the tsunami of radicalism swelling within their community. What was shocking and eerie especially in London was the evidence of a rise of anti-Semitism throughout Europe. This is a direct side effect of the rise of Islam and the brainwashing and intimidation by the swelling number of Islamic communities preaching hate in their mosques and Islamic schools. Jews cannot even go to their temples for prayer services without intense security to ensure their safety.

Since this book has been published, I have been invited to meet and work with the FBI in addressing counterterrorism strategies and educating agents on the mind-set of terrorists, how radicalism is spreading through the mosques in America, and what to do about it. *Because They Hate* was put on the reading list at the FBI Academy and was assigned as mandatory reading for Navy SEALs heading to the Middle East. I addressed the United States Special Operations

Command in Florida as well as the Joint Forces Command in Virginia. Standing in the presence of such heroes made me realize the greatness of America and the people behind the freedoms we enjoy.

But my proudest moment was September 10, 2007, when I addressed members of Congress on Capitol Hill after General Petraeus delivered his address to the House about the war in Iraq.

Being on Capitol Hill that day was a remarkable experience. As my assistant and I pulled into the Capitol under heavy security, we looked around in utter amazement as heavily armed SWAT teams with fully loaded M16s covered the Capitol and its surrounding streets with weapons ready to fire. One would expect to see this in Israel—but not in the United States. It was a chilling sign of the times we live in and a harsh reminder that we are at war with Islamofascists who are bent on killing us.

My presentation on Capitol Hill was one of the most important presentations I have ever given. The room filled quickly after the 9/11 ceremony on the steps of the Capitol. I began speaking at 7:30 P.M. There were no journalists, no cameras, and no C-SPAN. I was more candid than I have ever been in any public presentation. I knew I had only one chance to drive the point home to these influential representatives who make decisions about our country that impact our safety and our future. By the time I was done speaking and finished another hour answering questions, I was standing in the company of brothers and sisters who share the same concerns for the welfare of our nation, our children, and our grandchildren.

It was obvious my message was like a breath of fresh air. Our representatives hear from CAIR, Moveon.org, and similar organizations, but as many of them told me, there is *no one*—no other organization on the Hill—that carries the message I brought to them.

My presentation on Capitol Hill was the beginning of a partnership between American Congress for Truth (ACT) and those of our elected officials who are interested and are listening. They welcomed us to bring issues to their attention, and to become more involved in writing bills and resolutions to protect our country and its citizens. Finally, we are no longer working on the outside and hoping they hear us. We are working together, hand in hand on the inside.

I also had the privilege of visiting Australia on a speaking tour and speaking with Prime Minister John Howard, when I presented the keynote address at a dinner gala in Melbourne. It was surreal being escorted by security through the bowels of the Crown Palladium Grand Hotel kitchen as protestors screamed and shouted "Brigitte Gabriel and John Howard are Islamophobes." They held protest signs and chanted pro-Palestinian slogans in their attempt to upset and disturb people entering the hotel. Afterward, I had the opportunity to meet with key patriotic Australian businessmen and women and community leaders, one of whom was a member of ACT and who had flown from around Australia to meet me in Melbourne. Together we all sat in the living room of my hotel suite and strategized about mobilizing Australia and creating a branch of American Congress for Truth, the organization I started here in America. Out of that meeting Australian Coalition for Truth was born, an Australian grassroots movement to counter the Islamic threat within Australia.

Recent events around the world support the facts I discuss in *Because They Hate,* and about which I have been lecturing. Events are unfolding around the world fast and furious parallel to the rise of Islamic radicalism in every continent. On August 14, 2007, two journalists were kidnapped in Gaza—Fox News correspondent Steve Centanni and cameraman Olaf Wig—and were released only after being forcing to convert to Islam on their knees with their faces down as they recited the *Shahada.*

Muslims viciously attacked the Pope around the world for quoting in an academic speech a Byzantine Emperor on how Islam was spread by the sword and through forced conversion. The Pope's comments started a wave of global upheaval: priests in Islamic countries were killed, churches were burned, the Pope was burned in effigy as well, and a nun serving in a hospital was shot dead in the back by two gunmen in Mogadishu.[7]

But the most frightening developments have been from the terrorist activity rising from within England and America.

Our enemy is not an organization of people living overseas plotting to attack. Our enemies are the neighbors next door, the doctors practicing in our hospitals, and the workers who share our lunch break. Our enemies are terrorists driven by a dangerous ideology and clothed in deception who operate under cover and laugh about the advantages our sensitivity training, gullibility, and political correctness give them.

Who would have thought that in June 2006 the words "Those who heal you will kill you," spoken to an Anglican priest in Iraq by an Al Qaeda spokesman would come to haunt British citizens in their own cities.[8] Londoners woke up to hear that another attack on British citizens had come close to taking lives again. Luckily the terrorists bungled their first two attempts and authorities discovered the unexploded devices and disarmed them; the third attempt went off at the entrance to Glasgow Airport but injured no one except the terrorist himself. With amazing speed, Scotland Yard rounded up the terrorists and we all discovered the prophetic implication of the reported threat "Those who heal you will kill you." The perpetrators were all Muslim doctors.

I have always firmly believed that Islamic terrorism has nothing to do with economic position or status in life. This event in Britain reinforced these views as my heart went out to a nation of people facing days of fear and uncertainty. During the Lebanese war, doctors in Lebanon slaughtered hand in hand with the terrorists in the name of jihad. This is a very difficult concept for Western minds and especially Western intellectuals to accept and understand or even believe. I remember when I started speaking out about my experiences during the war, I would share how our neighbors—doctors and lawyers who we had known for years—became radicals overnight and started massacring us the next day. People looked at me with disbelief as if I were making things up just to make the Muslims look bad.

Both my experiences in Lebanon and the UK bombings planned by doctors strongly bolstered my opinion that Islamic terrorism is a religious, jihad doctrine–driven effort to murder or subdue and subjugate non-Muslims. The familiar arguments of Western liberals that "it's a class struggle" or "the West is bad and economically oppressive" no longer have purchase.

Not only did doctor terrorists shock the world, but radical Islam also turned parents into coldhearted terrorists bent on mayhem. What else could drive a mother and father with their six-month-old child to willingly carry liquid explosives onto an airplane, hiding the liquid in the child's baby bottle? This scenario unfolded in August of 2006 when police arrested twenty-four British-born and -raised Muslim citizens who had plotted to blow up as many as ten planes headed to the United States using liquid explosives. Officials say details of the plan were similar to other schemes devised by al Qaeda. Accounts such as these remind us of just how determined our enemy is.[9]

Back at home in America, a group of ten Islamic radicals conspired to kill U.S. servicemen at New Jersey's Fort Dix Army Base. The plot was disrupted thanks to the FBI infiltration of the terrorist cell. In January 2007, a vigilant video-store worker contacted the FBI after a customer brought in a DVD to be duplicated that showed ten young men in their early twenties "shooting assault weapons at a firing range in a militia-like style while calling for jihad and shouting in Arabic *Allah Akbar* (God is Great)."[10]

Within six months, the FBI had placed two cooperating witnesses within the terrorist cell, and they recorded meetings and phone conversations with the plotters. The terrorist cell reportedly surveyed Fort Dix, the Lakehurst Naval Air Engineering Station and Fort Monmouth in New Jersey, Dover Air Force Base in Delaware, and a Coast Guard building in Philadelphia. They also reportedly considered an attack timed to the annual Army-Navy college football game in Philadelphia.

One of the charged conspirators, Serdar Tatar, was familiar with Fort Dix because his family owns a pizzeria nearby and he delivered food to the base. He used his position as a pizza delivery boy to become a terrorist undercover agent committed to kill those to whom he brought food. The potential jihadists often viewed terror training videos, clips featuring Osama bin Laden, and a tape containing the last will and testament of at least two of the 9/11 hijackers. They also viewed tapes of armed attacks on U.S. military personnel and erupted in laughter when one plotter noted that a Marine's arm was blown off in one such ambush.[11]

Shortly after, on June 4th, a terror plot unfolded at John F. Kennedy Airport in New York. Three Muslim men living and working in the United States planned to blow up John F. Kennedy International Airport, its fuel tanks, and a jet fuel artery. One of the plotters was a former JFK air cargo employee.[12]

In all of these events, one striking similarity shines through: the terrorists' belief in an ideology that is based on the belief, faith, and teachings of Islam as it is written in the Koran. The common denominator within all the plots mentioned above is that these people were Muslims dedicated to becoming martyrs, to advance Islam, and to kill infidels regardless what country they came from, what culture they were raised in, what society there were living in, or what level of education they had.

Unless we understand the source from which this ideology of hate toward our Western cultures and nations is coming from, we will not be able to fight the cancer that is plaguing our international body. This cancer is called Islamofacism. This ideology is coming out of one source: The Koran.

What all terrorists are trying to achieve is the advancement of Islam and the establishment of an Islamic caliphate throughout the world ruled by *sharia* or Islamic law. Ayman Al-Zawahiri, the number two man of al Qaeda, repeatedly states that "Our cause is one cause, and we have the responsibility of unifying this *umma* (Islamic Nation), Allah willing, and establishing Allah's religion on his earth . . ."[13]

Polls taken around the world show that a majority of Muslims in large Islamic countries support the establishment of a *sharia*-based Islamic caliphate regardless of their approval of al Qaeda or any other Islamic terrorist organization.[14] Their loyalty is to Islam and not to any specific organization. This flies in the face of the image presented to us by leaders in the Western world that most Muslims are mainstream and do not share al Qaeda's convictions that have hijacked a peaceful religion and twisted it to serve their purpose. Our elected officials continuously ignore the jihad teaching of pure Islam. Our Western leaders continuously ignore the fact that most Muslim countries in the twenty-first century are moving more and more into radicalism in their culture, which oppresses women and minorities and is pushing to impose *sharia* law as it is written and instructed in the Koran.

In his September 2007 video address Osama bin Laden wanted you to believe the lie that it is our presence in Iraq and our foreign policy that is causing Muslims to be enraged worldwide and wage jihad on us, and that if we just withdraw from Iraq and repent of our evil foreign policy ways and convert to Islam we will all live peacefully ever after. What most people miss here is that Osama bin Ladin wants us out of not only Iraq and Afganistan, but also out of every base, every presence we have on Muslim soil regardless what country we are in. That means our infidel U.S. soldiers must be out of Bahrain, Dubai, and Saudi Arabia. He does not want any Western influence or any Western cooperation between us and most Muslim leaders whom he despises. This will give Al Qaeda the opportunity to topple those regimes which Al Qaeda considers not Muslim enough, and establish an Islamic caliphate linking the *umma* (Islamic nations) together as one. By asking the West to convert to Islam, Osama was following the teaching of the Koran. Muslims are mandated by the prophet Mohammad in the Hadith to invite the enemy to convert to Islam before you attack.

> Fight in the name of Allah and in the way of Allah. Fight against those who disbelieve in Allah. Make a holy war . . . When you meet your enemies who are polytheists, invite them to three courses of action. If they respond to any one of these, you also accept it and withhold yourself from doing them any harm. Invite them to (accept) Islam; if they respond to you, accept it from them and desist from fighting against them. . . . If

they refuse to accept Islam, demand from them the Jizya [the tax on non-Muslims specified in Qur'an 9:29]. If they agree to pay, accept it from them and hold off your hands. If they refuse to pay the tax, seek Allah's help and fight them. (Sahih Muslim 4294)[15]

There is no time for any more delusions. There is too much at stake. America needs to wake up from a gullible state of ignorant bliss and start learning Islamic history. We must expose the truth and must get involved in ensuring that our elected officials know that they have our support to throw political correctness in the garbage. We must clearly state that we are sick and tired of the lies and deception, that we want to know the truth about the enemy we are fighting and what we can do to win this war. Only then will we have a chance of winning this battle. Once our elected officials know that they can count on our support and they will not be demonized for stating the facts, they will be more courageous in coming out in the open and declaring war on our enemy.

I urge all of you to get involved in ACT for America (www .actforamerica.com) and become an active voice affecting your community and our nation. Because of the huge success of *Because They Hate,* I realized that there is a huge need for a citizen's action network, a national grassroots organization that will give power to "we the people." ACT for America has connected, mobilized, and organized concerned citizens into one of the largest lobbying voices on Capitol Hill focused on and dedicated to America's national security.

Join us in our defense of America.
—Brigitte Gabriel

BECAUSE THEY HATE

1.

PEACE BEFORE THE RAGE

It's 1978. I am thirteen years old. My family is in the third year of living in this bomb shelter, a tiny underground room that sits off to the side of a bombed-out pile of rubble that was once our beautiful home. Tonight the shelling is the heaviest it has been in two and a half years. The three of us, my elderly father and mother and me, sit in the dark on the corner of the bed.

We have been trapped in our shelter now for three days, and we are out of water. A shell hit near the entrance of our shelter, collapsing a wall of sandbags against our door and imprisoning us inside. We have given up trying to get it open.

No one knows we are trapped. For three days we have called out and screamed for help. But we are too far from the road for anyone to hear us amid the explosions. Besides, no one is going to venture outside in this heavy shelling. We don't talk about it, but we could die of thirst or starvation if this goes on much longer.

The shelling is so bad we can't sleep. If a big 155-millimeter bomb lands on our shelter, that's the end for us. I do not want to die. I only hope it will kill us quickly, just bang and nothing more, rather than wounding us so that we die slowly and painfully. There is no one to get us to the hospital or give us first aid. I've already gone through being wounded and buried alive in rubble. A direct hit from a shell would be better.

To distract me, my parents are talking about my childhood, telling me how surprised they were when I came into their life, how much joy I have brought them, how they regret that I must live through this nightmare.

I was born in the small town of Marjayoun, a once peaceful, idyllic Christian town in the mountains of southern Lebanon. For my first ten years I lived a charmed and privileged life. All that came to an end when a religious war, declared by the Muslims against the Christians, and tore my country and my life apart. It was a war that the world did not understand.

This book is a warning. It is a warning that what happened to me and my country of birth could, terrifyingly, happen here in America, my country of adoption. It is a warning about what happened to countless other non-Muslims in the Middle East and what should never happen again anywhere or to anyone else. It now is becoming a dire warning because I see increasing evidence that what happened to me in Lebanon is beginning to happen in towns and cities throughout America and the Western world. Watching the World Trade Center buildings fall in 2001, I was struck by the same fear that I experienced during the war in Lebanon. As I watched, words instinctively came from my mouth as I spoke to the TV screen: "Now they are here." I knew instantly why I had survived the suffering I experienced and what the purpose of my life would be. My being an eyewitness to the assault of Islamic jihad against non-Muslim Lebanese gives me a voice to help America and the West understand what is now happening to them.

But for you to understand anything about how the Middle East and Islamic jihad relate to the West, you must remember this: without understanding the past you will never understand the present and will have no idea how to plan for the future.

My country of Lebanon was much like America and the West are today. It was an island of freedom in the middle of an Islamic sea of tyranny and oppression. The majority of our citizens adhered to European Christian customs, traditions, ethics, and philosophy. Beirut, our capital, was commonly called the Paris of the Middle East. Our seemingly modern lifestyle, progressive thinking, democratic form of government, and schools of higher learning were a thorn in the side of the backward, feuding, feudal Arab world, whose Islamic customs and religious philosophies dominated other countries of the Middle East.

Lebanon is small, about 135 miles long and only about 25 to 50 miles wide. It is situated on the east coast of the Mediterranean between Israel to the south and Syria to the east and north. Lebanon has both pristine beaches and snowcapped mountains, and an ideal Mediterranean climate most of the time. Its coastal resorts and city nightlife were famous before the war. In ancient times, Lebanon was known as "the White" because of its distinctive snow-crowned inland mountain ranges.

My town, Marjayoun, lies between two beautiful green valleys, along the top of a long range of hills that runs from the border of Israel north into southern Lebanon. To the west is the Litani River valley. The hill slopes gently down to the river on the far side of the valley that runs along the bottom of steep cliffs that border its western bank. On top of the cliff stands the historic Beaufort Castle, once inhabited by a French nobleman who in the 1860s was sent by Napoleon III to intervene on behalf of the Christians in Lebanon being plagued by the Druze, a religious sect of Islam. The other valley to the east has many springs, which explains the name of my town: Marjayoun means "the valley of springs." Across this valley toward the east is a large Muslim town called Elkhiam. Beyond Elkhiam, rising over nine thousand feet, is Mount Hermon, which is usually snowcapped.

Marjayoun was a small, peaceful town, much like any small town in the USA, with about three thousand citizens. There were Catholic and Protestant churches and a cemetery. The church bells rang for services, prayers, weddings, and funerals. We had a town center where we did most of our shopping, and one movie theater, which doubled as a place for community activities and school stage productions. There was a Catholic school, a private school, and public elementary and high schools. Some people were farmers who worked the fields down in the valley. Some were businessmen who had hardware stores, grocery stores, clothing stores, beauty parlors, and restaurants. We had an elected city council and mayor. It was a close-knit country town that you might drive through in five minutes. It was a great place to live. While growing up as the only child born to an elderly couple, I always knew there would be a special meaning and purpose for my life. That meaning and purpose would be derived from the horror Lebanon and I would soon face, and are what this book is about.

My parents' house was located on the road that ran along the ridge of the hill connecting Marjayoun with another Christian town to the south called Klaia. Our majestic two-story stone house was set into the side of a hill and surrounded by beautiful gardens of fruit trees and flowers. My parents had been married for more than twenty years but were unable to have any children. In Arab culture, it is considered shameful when a woman is unable to bear children, and it is always considered the woman's fault. Thus, being childless had been a major source of frustration for my parents. They had prayed for a child year after year. Then, in the late summer of 1964, my mother, at fifty-four years of age, noticed a mysterious swelling in her abdomen. Her alarm increased as the swelling continued to grow. She began to believe that she was ill with cancer and about to die. Since she was a devout Maronite Christian, she prayed about her "illness" every evening at the altar of the Virgin Mary hanging on the wall of the living room. She would spend hours praying to Mary and Jesus for comfort, saying the rosary, burning candles, and crossing herself.

A visit to the doctor was in order. After a few tests the doctor had great news: she was pregnant. My mother's mouth dropped open. She couldn't believe her ears. "No! How can that be?" she asked. "At my age! And my husband is sixty!" Although the signs would have been unmistakable to a younger woman, she never imagined that she could become pregnant at her age.

Despite the potential difficulty and danger in having a child at her age, my mother was overjoyed. She couldn't wait to tell my father. Finally, their prayers had been answered. My parents would love me very much, and my birth would always be looked upon as redemption for my mother, and proof of God's love.

Although everyone was delighted with the news, my mother, with only two months left in her pregnancy, faced a new concern. Would her child be a boy or a girl? My mother was well educated for a woman in Lebanese society, and had a self-assurance and confidence few women could muster. She knew, however, that Arab culture praised the birth of a boy but condemned the birth of a girl. As her delivery day approached, this reality cast a shadow over her joy.

I had not yet been born, but the oppressive hand of Arab culture and society had already touched my life.

The nearest hospital that could handle deliveries was a two-hour drive away. When the day arrived, my father loaded my mother and her suitcase into a taxi and sent her off to the hospital alone. He stayed home. Men in Lebanon don't have much to do with delivering babies or taking care of children. They will take credit if the baby is a boy, and will shower him with attention, love, and praise. If the baby is a girl, usually there is neither credit taken nor attention paid. After delivery a woman will know immediately if it is a girl by the lack of excitement and congratulations by the doctor or nurses. In my mother's case, because of her age, she was congratulated on surviving delivery and giving birth to a healthy child.

However, even though I was a girl, people from all the surrounding towns and from every walk of life came to see us in Marjayoun because my father was a former government official, a successful businessman, and a pillar of the Maronite community. Indeed, he had raised the money to build the church in Marjayoun. So they came to pay their respects and to see and be seen, bringing with them the traditional birth gifts of gold jewelry, milk, and honey. The church gave a present of incense to my parents so that they could light a candle and burn it every night in thanks for my birth. I was told many times throughout my youth that the turnout for my birth celebration was "pretty good, for a girl."

My early childhood could be described as idyllic. As my parents' only child, I was lavished with all of their affection. They were also financially comfortable, so, along with their care and love, they could afford to give me lots of toys and material possessions. After retiring from his job with the Lebanese government in his late fifties, my father became a landlord and restaurateur. He built a restaurant on our property, as well as a few small homes attached to our main residence, which he rented out to other families.

Like most of the buildings in Lebanon, our house was constructed of light brown stone quarried from our mountains. Each room had high ceilings, and across the front of each story were the main doors and eight wide arched windows. My father's restaurant was located to the left and front of our property, facing the main road. A long driveway to the right of the restaurant went up the hill to our house.

My parents kept big, elaborate gardens bordered by jasmine bushes both in front and in back of our house. They planted strawberries, about ten different kinds of grapes, and every kind of fruit tree you could imagine: apple, orange, grapefruit, peach, plum, pear, persimmon, apricot, lemon, fig, and cherry. They also planted mint, parsley, and many types of vegetables: three kinds of beans, artichokes, squash, eggplant, cauliflower, green peppers, onions, tomatoes, cucumbers, lettuce, watermelons, and cantaloupe. In addition to fruit-bearing trees and bushes, they grew roses. In the springtime, all the trees and bushes would bloom in a variety of colors. We lived in a virtual Garden of Eden.

My day always started with a long breakfast, usually hot milk and eggs with both of my parents. Papa and Mama woke early, at six thirty. Papa would make his list of fresh restaurant supplies to buy for the day from the market while Mama made breakfast.

For me, every day was like a party. The people renting in our apartment complex became one big family. We were nine children all about the same age—within five years of each other—and we always played together. We might start the day outside or in one of the apartments, but since I had so many toys—and my own playroom—we usually ended up at my house. Our moms would also gather there each morning, bringing with them whatever they were going to fix for lunch. While preparing lunch, they would drink coffee, share news and gossip, laugh and cry.

When I turned four, it was time for me to go to school. My parents sent me to a private school, Le Saint Coeur, one of the most reputable Catholic primary schools in the country. Le Saint Coeur was on the edge of a tall hill from where we could look down and see the entire green valley and smaller hills covered with wildflowers. We had a breathtaking view of historic Beaufort Castle, as well as one of the most famous rivers in the Middle East, the Litani. The winding, sparkling Litani flows from Syria to Lebanon, supplying most of the country with water and hydroelectric power.

Our lessons were taught in both Arabic and French, and the teachers, especially the nuns, were strict and demanding. Homework was assigned from the very first day. But I loved school, and I wanted to be a "good girl," so I worked hard, learned quickly, and soon, I could read and write in both languages.

Our school day was finished at 2:00 p.m. After we were released, I would go home and eat lunch with Papa and Mama. In Lebanon, the midday meal is the main meal of the day. It's the time when family members gather around the table to eat and talk over the morning's events and their plans for the rest of the day.

It was always a joy to come home from school and find my parents standing outside on the balcony waiting for me. They would greet me with a big smile, a hug, and a kiss. Driving rain, summer heat, freezing snow—it didn't matter to them. In the wintertime, they would stand shivering in their coats or under umbrellas until I arrived. My mother would greet me by telling me all the special things she had done for me that day. She would say, "Look, I made you your favorite cake," or "You know what? The dress that I was sewing for you is finished. I can't wait for you to try it on." The house would always smell wonderful when I came home from school. Our meal would include fresh bread from the bakery and a variety of delicious fruits. I would proudly tell my parents about what I had learned in school that day, and then we would take a nap, as was customary. I remember the roads would be empty at that hour because everyone in town would be sleeping. Today, as a mother and businesswoman in American society, I really miss that custom.

Around three o'clock in the afternoon, Marjayoun would wake up from its community nap. Papa would go down to his restaurant to be ready when all the shops and businesses reopened at around four. On some afternoons Mama would take me along while she went to visit her friends. Some of them owned businesses, and we would walk to them and buy ice cream and visit. The wives worked alongside their husbands running the stores, as my mother helped my dad.

As much as I loved playing grown-up with Mama and her friends, my favorite afternoon activity was riding my bicycle from one end of Marjayoun to the other. This was no ordinary bicycle. It was painted red and yellow. Papa had put a light and a horn on it too, but I was never allowed to use the horn on the road. That would not have been polite or ladylike.

Whether I went with Mama to visit with her friends or riding on my bicycle, we would always end up at Papa's restaurant for dinner.

The air around the restaurant was filled with tempting aromas from the kitchen, and if the wind was right I could identify the evening's specialty a hundred feet away. Our restaurant was known not only for the best food in town and the best prices, but also for the beautiful view. People loved sitting out on the terrace facing majestic, snow-capped Mount Hermon across the boulevard.

At seven thirty, Mama would take me up to our house and tidy up or prepare for the next day while I studied and did homework. When Papa came home from the restaurant, they would both tuck me into bed and sit with me for a while. We would say our prayers and exchange endearments, and I would go to sleep happy, comfortable, and secure.

For my tenth birthday, October 21, 1974, my parents decided to throw a huge birthday party. My mother was sixty-five years old, and my father was approaching seventy. They invited all their closest friends and all of mine for an early sit-down dinner. Even my teacher, Mademoiselle Amal, was invited. About twenty adults and fifteen children came, including, of course, our entire housing complex's children and parents, plus Tante Madeline and Uncle Jamil with their sons Walid and Milad, and Tante Samira and Uncle George with their three girls, Rose, Violette, and Ghada. They dressed in their Sunday best and walked from the other end of town just to attend the dinner.

Mama spent the whole day chopping vegetables for tabouli, the traditional Lebanese salad, and making kebabs to cook on the *shish* that afternoon. She had been cooking for the previous two days, preparing stuffed grape leaves; kibbe, the traditional Lebanese meat loaf; humus; meat pies; a variety of Lebanese appetizers; and of course baklava. My father didn't go to the restaurant that day. Instead, he spent the morning cutting roses from our garden for the table. Since it was already fall, the sky was cloudy and the air a bit chilly, so the dinner was held indoors. Our dining-room table wasn't big enough, so my parents borrowed furniture from the restaurant. My mother got out her fancy embroidered tablecloths and arranged roses at both ends of the table. She was determined that everything would be just perfect. At three o'clock, I got dressed in a white-and-green dress that Mama had sewn just for the occasion.

Every inch of the main table was covered with appetizers, from cashews and almonds to every single dip and delicacy on the Lebanese menu. My parents were pleased and proud as their guests kept commenting on the delicious food and the wonderful decorations. Little did we know that this was going to be the last party for a long, long time. Indeed, it marked the end of my dream childhood. One month later, in November 1975, Lebanon's national nightmare began, and with it began the destruction of our lives.

The Arab World I Was Born Into

Lebanon is considered part of the Arab world. However, as a child I was taught that my people, the Lebanese Christians, are the descendants of the Phoenicians, who established independent city-states on the eastern shore of the Mediterranean in the late Bronze Age. The Phoenicians were of Aramaic (Canaanite), not Arabic, descent.[1] Their skill as mariners and traders was unmatched in the ancient world. Phoenicia flourished for centuries before it was swallowed by a succession of empires: the Assyrian, the Persian, the Greek, the Roman, the Byzantine, the Arab, the Ottoman Turk, and finally the French.

But the Phoenician people remained. Jesus preached among the Phoenicians, and Phoenicians were among the first gentile converts to Christianity.[2] By the time of the Arab Conquest in the seventh century A.D., the ancestors of the Lebanese Christians had already been living in the land known as Phoenicia, now known as Lebanon, for more than two thousand years. And the Christians of Lebanon have been resisting the Muslim onslaught ever since. Although Lebanese Christians practiced Arabic culture because it was the environment we lived in, we never considered ourselves Arabs. We held on to our Christian heritage and practiced Western culture too. Ours was the only country in the Middle East where Christian holidays such as Christmas and Easter were celebrated in the ways they are America and Europe, openly and gloriously. During Christmas stores would sparkle with decorations as shoppers set out to buy the latest in designer clothes straight off the runways of Paris and Milan. Christmas trees decorated homes and streets, and Christmas songs played on the radio and television. We sang "Jingle Bells," "Silent Night," and many more American Christmas songs, but with Arabic words. During Easter, Christian towns from one end of the country to the other would color Easter eggs, exchange chocolates, and ring church bells for midnight and early masses. Christmas and Easter were the two main holidays when families would travel across the country to visit and share big meals, as kids were out of school for the traditional extended seasonal vacations.

Although we are considered by the West as Arabs, we are Arabs only by language and not by blood. We consider ourselves Phoenicians who are simply Arabophones, meaning Christians who speak the Arabic language after being conquered by the Arab Islamic invaders. Even today our church services and liturgy are said in Aramaic, the ancient language of Jesus.

We have many Christian denominations in Lebanon. There are the Maronites, the Roman Catholics, the Greek Catholics, the Greek Orthodox, the Armenian Orthodox, the Syrian Orthodox, the Assyrian Nestorians, and Protestants of various denominations. (Similarly, there are numerous sects of Islam in Lebanon, including the Shia, the Sunni, the Druze, the Alawis, and the Ismailis.)[3] My family, like the majority of Christians in Lebanon, is Maronite. The Maronites get their name from the late-fourth- and early-fifth-century religious leader John Maron. His followers lived in the mountains of Lebanon, following his teachings and preaching the gospel.

When Lebanon gained its independence from France in 1941, its population was approximately 55 percent Christian and 45 percent Muslim. The Lebanese National Pact of 1943 created a unique democratic power-sharing arrangement between the religious communities.

Under this arrangement, the president of Lebanon was a Christian, the prime minister was a Sunni Muslim, and the speaker of the parliament was a Shiite Muslim.[4] Representation in the Lebanese parliament was established with a ratio of six Christian deputies to five Muslim deputies, to reflect their proportions in the country's population in the last census.[5] The cabinet, the civil service, and the army were composed of both Christians and Muslims. Posts in the cabinet, and positions of authority at all levels of the civil service and military, were assigned to representatives of each community.[6]

This unique balance had a parallel in the United States Constitution. In the debates on representation in the new country's legislative branch, the small states wanted each state to have equal representation, while the large states wanted representation to be based on population. In order to resolve this conflict, the Founding Fathers invented the bicameral legislature, dividing lawmaking power between two chambers: the U.S. Senate, where each state has two senators, and the U.S. House of Representatives, where each state was represented according to its population. Similar to the governmental structure created by the Lebanese National Pact of 1943, this democratic division of power represented each group fairly and equally. There was another significant similarity between the United States Constitution and the Lebanese National Pact. Like the Constitution, the Pact recognized the need to protect the rights of diverse religious communities, and institutionalized those rights in the structure of the government.

Lebanon's governmental structure under the National Pact certainly bore a closer resemblance to that of the United States than to those in the rest of the Arab world, where totalitarian government is the norm, and minority, civil, and religious rights are routinely denied, frequently with extreme brutality. Some Arab countries, such as Saudi Arabia, Jordan, and the states of the Persian Gulf, are absolute monarchies or family fiefdoms, although a facade of representative government may exist in the form of a powerless "advisory council" or a "legislature" handpicked by the ruling clique. Other Arab countries are ruled by military or hereditary dictatorships, such as the Assad family dictatorship in Syria, the presumptive Mubarak and Gadhafi family dictatorships in Egypt and Libya, respectively, and the former Saddam Hussein family dictatorship in Iraq.

We Lebanese Christians inherited the commercial skills of our Phoenician ancestors, who were renowned for their business savvy, and the budding democracy prospered. In no time at all, Beirut became a world banking capital. Lebanon was the only country in the Arab world where Arab and Western culture mixed comfortably. On Hamra Street, Beirut's equivalent of Fifth Avenue, young Lebanese women dressed in the latest fashions from Paris, Milan, and New York mingled with Muslim women shrouded in the black hijab. All of the oil-rich sheikhs and royal families of the Arab world would come to Beirut to lavishly indulge in the Western lifestyle that they prohibited and condemned in their own countries. They would be joined by jet-set tourists and celebrities such as Cary Grant, Sophia Loren, and Brigitte Bardot, to be entertained by the finest performing artists in the world, from Frank Sinatra to Joan Baez, from Nureyev and Fonteyn to Herbert von Karajan conducting the Berlin Philharmonic Orchestra. Beirut, like New York, San Francisco, and many other great American cities, was a cultural kaleidoscope, where different traditions from all over the world flourished side by side. This stood in stark contrast to all of the other Arab countries, where the openness and diversity of Lebanese society and culture were simultaneously envied and despised, but never replicated.

Although the rest of Lebanon was not as Westernized and cosmopolitan as Beirut, all of the people of Lebanon, Christian and Muslim alike, enjoyed the highest standard of living in the Arab world.[7] All of this came without the benefit of the oil resources that were pumping petrodollars into other Arab countries.

We as Lebanese prided ourselves on our multiculturalism and diversity. We were a canvas of different colors, from the dark skinned to the blonds with blue eyes. Because of Lebanon's geographical position on the tip of the Mediterranean, Lebanese blood was mixed with that of Europeans, as Lebanese merchants had brought Western brides with them, and with that of the Muslim Arab invaders who raped their way through the country. Just as America is a rainbow of different colors, we were that also. We did not, however, have any black people. We had bedouin tribes, Gypsies, Shia and Sunni Muslims, and a variety of Christian sects, people who wore different costumes, from authentic traditional bedouin clothing to Western clothing by Christian Dior and Yves Saint Laurent, from conservative to flamboyant.

Lebanon was a beacon in the Middle East for different religious and ethnic groups coming together and working together as Lebanese. We celebrated Christian holidays as well as Muslim ones. In our cities you could hear the church bells ringing in the morning as well as the mosques sounding their prayers from their towers. We had open borders through which people from the surrounding Arabic countries came in and out freely. We had the best universities in the Middle East, where prosperous Arabs sent their children to study. Just like America, we welcomed anyone seeking an education at our universities and were eager to learn about their culture and their tradition. Some Arab students remained to work in Lebanon because it was the prosperous business hub of the Middle East. We were renowned for our hospitality, good-heartedness, and generosity, just as America is known for the same qualities today.

Sadly, those same similarities were the cause of our destruction. We were so deluded with our multiculturalism that we did not realize the risk of losing the very culture we prided ourselves on having. We did not realize that the intolerant Islamic side of our culture was gaining strength on the back of our Western openness and pride in diversity. With our open-border policy, we unwittingly allowed what would turn out to be our enemy to infiltrate our society to plot and fight with radicals within to gain control of our government.

Beneath the surface, relations among Lebanon's diverse religious and ethnic communities were far from perfect. Despite Lebanon's prosperity, the nation's unique experiment in democracy was precarious because of ancient and persistent hatreds and rivalries that continued to simmer.

My parents were true Christians, not just in terms of ritual, but also in teaching love and respect for all people. That is what they taught me at home. In contrast, the Arab Islamic culture that surrounded Lebanon taught fear, mistrust, and hatred. The airwaves were filled with stories demonizing Israel, calling for its destruction. Conspiracy theories were the topic of the day, every day. There were even ghastly stories of Arab leaders ruling with iron fists. One I remember in particular was of Syrian president Assad killing twenty thousand Syrians in Hama who tried to rebel against him. Sunni and Shiite Muslims were taught to hate each other because of a theological disagreement more than twelve centuries old. Muslims in general hated the Christians over a theological disagreement even older, and the Christians hated the Muslims in return. The Christian clans mistrusted and feuded with one another, and the Druze were the odd people out. But everybody had one thing in common: we were all taught to hate Israel and the Jews. In the universal hatred that was preached against Jews, virtually no distinction was made between the Jewish religion and the Israeli state. In my Christian private school, we studied only the New Testament. I never saw the Old Testament, because it was considered the enemy's book. All I heard was "Israel is the devil, the Jews are demons, they are the source of all the problems in the Middle East, and the only time we will have peace is when we drive all the Jews into the sea."

However, as a little girl, I never met a Jewish person or even knew that they even lived in Lebanon. Where were the Jews who were causing all these "problems"? Lebanon's unique experiment in democracy was not threatened by Israel or some international Jewish conspiracy, as we were told by our leaders and Arab leaders in the surrounding Arabic Islamic Middle East, but by intercommunal enmity and strife between Christians and Muslims. Prosperity enabled the various communities and factions to suppress their ancient hatreds enough to tolerate each other, but differences in cultural standards, values, and customs between the Christian and Muslim communities may have made conflict inevitable. Perhaps the most critical difference was the value placed on education. Although Lebanon had one of the highest literacy rates in the Arab world, Lebanese Christians had a literacy rate twice that of Muslims.[8] The lack of emphasis on modern education in the Muslim community caused them to have higher levels of poverty than the Christians.

In addition, the Muslims' much higher birth rate began threatening the demographic balance reflected in the Lebanese National Pact of 1943. The Islamic birth rate was one of the major differences between Christians and Muslims. As Christians, we would marry one spouse till death did us part. We would have two, three, maybe four children. From the time children were born we started thinking about what school we would send them to and what education we would give them.

According to their religion, Muslims, on the other hand, are allowed to marry up to four wives at the same time. All a Muslim man has to do to divorce a wife when he gets tired of her is to say three times in a row, "You're divorced, you're divorced, you're divorced," and she's divorced. Meanwhile, Muslim men have many children with each wife. It is this cultural dynamic in the Muslim faith that increases the population. Thus, power shifted in Lebanon. By 1970 the Christians became the minority and the Muslims the majority. The most famous Muslim in the world today is Osama bin Laden. He is one of fifty-three children. He himself has twenty-seven children. Father and son have sired eighty children. That's not to mention Osama bin Laden's fifty-two brothers and sisters.

These demographic changes created political pressure to modify the structure of the Lebanese government. When the Muslims became the majority, they started demanding more power in the executive, legislative, and administrative branches of the government. The better-educated minority Christians started demanding more guarantees to protect the Christian political presence by insisting that the presidency remain in Christian hands. These inner Lebanese problems might have been worked out, and Lebanese democracy might have survived, if it had not been for the arrival of Palestinian refugees and Palestine Liberation Organization gunmen, who were mostly Muslims.

The Christians in Lebanon had always had differences and problems with the Muslims, but we never thought our neighbors would turn on us to kill and blow up our cities, towns, and villages. The problems started in 1968, shortly after Lebanon accepted its second wave of Palestinian refugees. The first wave came in 1948 and 1949, when Israel declared its independence and was immediately invaded by the combined armies of five surrounding Arab countries, including Lebanon. Arab governmental and religious leaders had urged the Arabs living in the fledgling state to flee temporarily, assuring them that they would return shortly and share in the spoils when Israel was destroyed. However, Israel won its War of Independence, and up to 180,000 Palestinian Arab refugees were taken in by Lebanon.[9] Our government and the United Nations Relief Works Agency (UNRWA) set up refugee camps in and around the major cities of Sidon, Tyre, Tripoli, and Beirut for the Palestinian refugees who were too poor to go anywhere else.

The second wave of refugees came as a result of the Six-Day War of 1967. As Arab nations around Israel placed their militaries in offensive readiness to invade and partook in media saber rattling, declaring their desire to wipe Israel off the map, Palestinians again fled to Lebanon and Jordan with the expectation that they would return when Israel was defeated and destroyed. These expectations were again dashed, greatly increasing the Palestinian refugee population of both countries.

Jordan had experienced great waves of Palestinian refugees in 1948–49 and 1967. The PLO set up a corrupt, terrorist ministate, and used Jordan as a base to conduct terrorist operations against Israel, drawing the inevitable Israeli counterterror response. In September of 1970, King Hussein of Jordan finally grew weary of the PLO agitating and destabilizing his country. He ordered his army to expel the PLO from Jordan, and it did so, killing thousands of PLO gunmen and thousands of Palestinian civilians in the process.

However, the survival of the Hussein regime and the expulsion of the PLO from Jordan was a disaster for democratic, Christian, tolerant, and open-minded Lebanon. In the wake of "Black September," the rout of the PLO from Jordan, Lebanon was the only one of twenty-two Arab countries that was willing to open its borders to a third wave of Palestinian refugees. These additional Muslims, combined with the higher Muslim birth rate and a high rate of emigration by Christians, caused Muslims to outnumber Christians in Lebanon. To this growing Muslim numerical superiority, the PLO gunmen from Jordan added brutality, arrogance, intolerance, and aggression. That's what tipped the scale toward civil war in Lebanon. Not only were Muslims the majority, but they felt empowered by the presence of the PLO and Yasser Arafat, who were well financed and backed by the Soviet Union and by the other Muslim countries.

The Palestinians' mission to "liberate Palestine" was mandated by pan-Arab nationalism and later infused with Islamist fervor in order to draw Lebanese Muslims over to their side of the struggle. The only value Lebanon had to the Palestinians was as a launching pad for attacks against Israel. The first thing that stood in their way was the Lebanese government and its democracy. Knowing that Lebanese and Palestinian Muslims now constituted a majority of the population, the PLO exploited the ancient hatreds and rivalries that had always simmered below the surface of Lebanese society. This is exactly what al Qaeda and radical Islamists are exploiting in America today in the African-American community, which is the largest community converting to Islam. They are using the race issue to attract converts, increasing the Muslim population in the U.S.

When Lebanese Muslims and Palestinians declared jihad on Christians in 1975, we didn't even know what that word meant. We had taken the Palestinians in, giving them refuge in our country, allowing them to study side by side with us in our schools and universities. We gave them jobs and shared our way of life with them. What started as political war spiraled very fast into a religious war between Muslims and Christians, with Lebanese Muslims joining the PLO fighting the

Christians. We didn't realize the depth of their hatred and resentment toward us as infidels. The more that Christians refused to get involved in the Palestinian-Israeli conflict and to allow the Palestinians to use Lebanon as a launching pad from which to attack Israel, the more the Palestinians looked at us as the enemy. Muslims started making statements such as "First comes Saturday, then comes Sunday," meaning first we fight the Jews, then we come for the Christians. Christian presence, influence, and democracy became an obstacle in the Palestinians' fight against Israel. Koranic verses such as sura 5:51—"Believers, take not Jews and Christians for your friends. They are but friends and protectors to each other"—became the driving force in recruiting Muslim youth. Many Christians barely knew the Bible, let alone the Koran and what it taught about us, the infidels.

We should have seen the long-simmering tension between Muslims and Christians beginning to erupt, but we refused to believe that such hatred and such animosity existed. America also failed to recognize this hatred throughout all the attacks launched against it, beginning with the marine barracks bombing in Beirut in 1983 all the way up to September 11, 2001. It was that horrible day that made Americans finally ask, What is jihad? And why do they hate us? I have a very simple answer for them: because you are "infidels."

When the Black September PLO gunmen first arrived in Lebanon, their only support from among the Lebanese people came from the Communist and leftist parties, because the PLO was a client of the Soviet Union. In 1970, the Left in Lebanon included both Christians and Muslims, but it was politically insignificant. However, with Soviet financial and material support and Arab oil protection payoff money, the PLO was able to lure significant numbers of Lebanese, both Christian and Muslim, away from their traditional religious and clan loyalties. With the arms that the PLO obtained from the Soviet Union, the leftist parties organized their new recruits into formidable militias. When hostilities broke out in 1975, the Palestinians and their leftist allies imposed a reign of terror on the people of Lebanon. Rape, murder, kidnapping, mutilation, and extortion were common occurrences.

Christian and Muslim sectarian militia groups formed and armed themselves for defense against Palestinian and leftist gunmen. Christians who championed the Palestinians' cause and fought for a greater Islamic presence in the government, thinking they were protecting the underdog and fighting for justice, were so blinded by their self-righteous attitude that they failed to realize they would become as much a target as we were. As soon as the Muslims and Palestinians got the upper hand in the war, they turned against the leftist Christians and fought them just as they fought the rest of us.

Between 1970 and 1975, the PLO launched numerous bloody terrorist attacks and innumerable artillery barrages from southern Lebanon into northern Israel. A favorite Palestinian tactic was to set up a couple of cannons or rocket launchers in a Christian village, fire a few rounds into Israel, and then quickly withdraw, knowing that Israel's return fire would fall on innocent Christian civilians. This created a double benefit in the eyes of the Palestinians: Lebanese Christians would die, and the Israelis would be vilified and hated even more. This has become a public relations ploy that has been authored and perfected by the Palestinians ever since. They use this ploy effectively to make precise targeted killing of terrorists in the Palestinian territories by the Israeli air force difficult. Precision rocket attacks on known Hamas leaders, bomb makers, and masterminds often kill other people too. The Hamas members' movements and their hiding among the population lead to collateral civilian deaths and the accusatory and inflaming headlines that invariably follow.

Today, Islamic terrorists throughout the world who fight against the West copy this tactic of hiding within civilian communities for protection. They change their location every few days and sometimes every day to escape pursuit. They know that Western liberals, trying to shape Western public opinion, will pounce and scream to high heaven on word of civilian deaths. They rely on Western media to blame the policy makers who approved such an attack, and the military's antiterrorism efforts, for the death of innocent women and children, when in reality it was the cowardly jihadists who placed themselves among civilians who brought death to those innocent victims. In reality, these terrorists are consciously making media martyrs out of the unsuspecting people they associate and hide among.

By the early 1970s Lebanon was divided into two camps. The conservative camp on the Right came to be known as the Lebanese Front. It wanted to maintain the existing structure of the Lebanese governmental system. At most it would allow the introduction of moderate reforms to that structure to recognize the new demographic realities, while at the same time protecting the rights of the various religious communities. Factions in this group wanted Lebanon to steer an independent course internationally rather than align itself with the rest of the Arab world. Some in the Lebanese Front had sympathy for the Palestinians, but felt that the burden of supporting the Palestinian cause should be borne by the Arab world as a whole, not by Lebanon alone. The Lebanese Front strenuously opposed allowing the PLO to have sovereign status within Lebanon, and allowing the PLO absolute freedom to attack Israel from southern Lebanon. The Lebanese Front was mostly Christian, but had Muslim adherents.

The leftist camp, which came to be known as the National Front or the "revisionist coalition," was mostly Muslim (including the Palestinians), but it also had Lebanese Christian elements and supporters. The National Front wanted to radically alter the structure of the Lebanese government and society, without regard to the impact on the rights of Lebanon's various communities. Internationally, the National Front sought to strongly align Lebanon with the rest of the Arab world. Not surprisingly, the Palestinian factions in the National Front supported the "right" of the PLO to have quasi-sovereign status in Lebanon and to attack Israel from anywhere in the world, especially southern Lebanon. The Lebanese Muslim factions in the National Front felt that it was their duty as Muslims to support the Palestinian cause and to allow the free use of Lebanon as a staging ground for attacks on Israel.

The incident that started all-out civil war occurred on April 13, 1975, when Palestinian gunmen opened fire on worshippers outside a

Maronite church in Beirut, killing four and wounding many. In response, Christian militiamen launched an attack on Palestinians. The violence spiraled out of control, first in Beirut, then in other parts of the country. Although the issues that sparked the civil war were not as simple as Muslim versus Christian, the conflict soon developed a brutal and vicious sectarian dimension. Lebanon's descent into hell had begun.

America has always prided itself on its multiculturalism and its multireligious communities, just as Lebanon prided itself on its multicultural, open-minded, and multireligious society. Today America's lack of sufficient immigration and border control, like Lebanon's, is allowing terrorists and other hostile individuals to come into our country at will. People who want to hurt us are mixed in with other Muslims who have no intention of becoming a part of our nation but are actually working to make America a part of their radical Islamic agenda.

Muslims have become a sensitive issue in our American society, with demands and expectations, and a group to watch out for and be careful with. There are barely 6 million Muslims in America today out of a total U.S. population of 300 million, yet their presence has been seen and felt throughout every state in America. Stories of Islamic terrorist cells, Islamic charities linked to funding terrorism, Islamic mosques, and Muslims demanding more rights and acknowledgment are beginning to dominate the news. Islamic communities are harboring terrorist cells within. Their mosques are teaching hate against infidels both Christian and Jewish. They are placing demands on American corporations to provide prayer time for Islamic employees on the job. Dell Computers has already caved in to the pressure put forth by the Council on American-Islamic Relations (CAIR) regarding this issue and now allows its Muslim employees prayer time on the job.[10] Our radio and TV talk show hosts are watching their tongues when criticizing even the radical Islamic element of the religion lest they be fired or sued, just as Michael Graham was fired from ABC radio for linking Islam to terrorism.[11]

The Islamic community throughout the world is outreproducing Christians and Jews almost seven to one.[12] It will be a matter of a few generations before they can get voting power to challenge state laws and change the Constitution of the United States. Islam is already the fastest-growing religion in Europe. Driven by immigration and high birthrates, the number of Muslims on the continent has tripled in the last thirty years. Most demographers forecast a similar or even higher rate of growth in the coming decades.[13] It is important to note that the world's fastest-growing Muslim populations are found in Europe and the United States, where they are the second- or third-largest religious communities.[14] This is the beginning of America's and the West's war with radical Islam. This demographic shift is an exact duplication of what happened in Lebanon and is already having a huge effect throughout Europe. People like me, who come from the Middle East and have seen how the radical Islamic agenda started and spread in Lebanon and ultimately destroyed equality among religions and changed the fabric of Lebanon, see and read the writing on the wall in America and the West today. Americans need to listen: their country is at stake. I lost my country of birth to Islamic fundamentalism and don't want to lose my country of adoption to the same fate.

2.

MY 9/11

As a young child in southern Lebanon, I was largely unaware of the political and religious winds and how they would blow and change our
lives. I noticed that we had stopped visiting our relatives in Beirut, but
my elderly parents didn't like traveling all that much anyway. Their re-
luctance to travel stemmed from something that people in the West will
probably be surprised by. In Lebanon everyone carried a national ID
card that identified not only our religion but also what sect of that religion we belonged to. It proved to be something that could mean the
difference between living or dying. Incidents were being reported of
Muslims setting up checkpoints and stopping cars to check IDs. Sometimes, if the Muslims saw that a car's occupants were Christians, they
would order everyone out of the car and then shoot them all. They
didn't kill us because they were Communists and we were capitalists.
They killed us because we were Christians. They would shout "Allahu
Akbar," "God is Great," as they sprayed Christians with machine-gun
bullets. These became known as "identity card killings."[1] News of such
atrocities spread fast, and fear along with it. Most Christians in the
county had stopped traveling by late 1974, becoming virtual prisoners
in their homes and villages.

Sensing increasing instability and a fearing a breakdown of social
institutions, my father had his savings withdrawn in cash from the

Bank of Lebanon. He hid the money in our beds at home. His plan was to use it to move us all to America and start a business if the need arose. That would have been in line with what happened to most persecuted Christians in other parts of the Arab world. When things get tough, leave. It is something the spread of Islam has relied on for centuries.

One cold, windy November night in 1975, as winter began taking hold on Marjayoun, there were no customers at the restaurant. Papa closed early, sent his employees home, and walked to our house fifteen yards up the hill behind the restaurant. In anticipation of his arrival my mother had already set the table in the family room and turned up the kerosene heater. The heaters used in Lebanese homes came in a variety of shapes and sizes, with a round metal reservoir for kerosene attached to the heater by a metal feeder tube. A knob on the tube allowed one to adjust the flow of kerosene much as a nurse controls the drip for an IV in a hospital. The kerosene simply dripped inside the stove and burned with a yellow-orange flame on the bottom of the heater. A metal chimney pipe about six inches in diameter went from the stove up through the ceiling. The stove usually sat in the middle of the room. In southern Lebanon, this is what passed for "central heating."

Because we didn't have central heating as most Americans know it, the family room became the center of our lives in winter. It served as the bedroom, dining room, living room, breakfast nook, and, since it was the room with the TV, the entertainment room.

My parents followed a nightly ritual. Since it was winter, and the heater would go out at night, they tucked me in between two wool blankets covered by a big heavy comforter and another wool blanket over that. They sat one on each side, and we said our prayers, thanking God for that day's blessings. I thanked God for things that happened to me at school, for my friends, for my parents, for our food, and for my health. Then they sang me a lullaby. I could smell Mama's perfume on her neck as I snuggled and gave her little kisses that made her hold me tighter. Her hair tickled my face as she moved, and I could hear the smile in her voice. I could feel Papa's big fingers running through my hair and the stubble on his cheek as he gently kissed me. Our nightly ritual closed with their telling me, "We love you higher than the skies, deeper than the oceans, and bigger than the whole wide world."

I felt no greater love could ever exist.

My parents then went into the family room, where they sat sipping arak, the traditional Lebanese liquor, and quietly discussing the restaurant business and the events of the day. An angry wind whistled through the grapevines outside my window. The TV signal faded in and out as the antenna on the roof swayed back and forth. For their evening snack, my father laid paper-thin pita on top of the kerosene heater, filling the room with the smell of toasted bread. The electricity would blink out for a few seconds now and then because of the high winds. As the room would go from light to pitch black, all you could see were little flickering lights on the ceiling from the design on the kerosene heater. Instead of being frightening, it added a cozy flair to the smell of toasted bread, the fragrance of freshly cut herbs, and the anisette aroma of the arak. All was right in the world, and I was becoming drowsy, about to drop off to sleep to the sound of my parents' voices. Their conversation went from how delicious our new batch of olives was, to the problem with the old patisserie refrigerator, to the new chandeliers my father was thinking about buying for the restaurant this coming spring as a part of the new decor he had in mind.

Suddenly, a very loud boom with a bright light shook our house as if lightning had struck our front yard. My parents jumped up in shock. Papa rushed through the living room and out the front door, with my mother right behind him, to see what had happened. He went to the edge of our long balcony and stood there, peering out in the darkness. He couldn't see anything, but the smell of explosives and burning was strong. Mama begged him to come back inside, but he refused to listen. Suddenly there was the muffled sound of multiple rockets being launched in the distance. Mama instinctively grabbed Papa by his shoulder, and they both ran toward the door.

They were barely inside the door when a rocket hit the balcony exactly where they had been standing. The force of the explosion picked both of them up off the floor and threw them across the room. Many more rockets exploded in quick succession in and around our house.

One came through my bedroom window. A deafening noise followed by fire, heat, and blinding light erupted in the bedroom. It was as if the gates of hell had opened wide and I was falling into the abyss of fire.

The explosion blew me out of my bed and into the corner. The blast was so loud and the flash so bright that I thought I'd never hear or see again. As my bedroom disintegrated around me, my mind was flooded with television images of explosions and destruction in Beirut and the rest of Lebanon. I remember thinking, "Tonight is Marjayoun's turn." This was a horrifying realization for a ten-year-old. I woke up from the dream of a perfect childhood and found myself in a hellish nightmare.

I was pinned in place, trapped under rocks and cinder blocks from a wall that had been knocked down by the explosion. I felt the iron grillwork of the window lying directly over my body, which was under the rocks. From where I lay on the floor, I could see fires burning around the room, including on the bed where I had been sleeping. But the air was filled with smoke and dust, and so it was mostly dark.

I couldn't feel my right arm or move the fingers of my right hand. I could move my left arm, which I had raised to protect my face from the explosion, but when I moved it, I felt as if I were in a shower, with hot water pouring over me.

My mind dissolved in unfocused panic. I screamed, and kept screaming for my mother, but I couldn't hear my own screams. The blast had numbed my ears. At first, all I could hear was a constant ringing, so loud it was painful. Like in a dream, slowly I began to hear myself screaming, as if the voice were coming from someone else far away, getting closer and closer. Then it was there—my own voice screaming, "Mama! Mama!" I didn't know if anyone could hear me. I kept wondering, "Who is pouring hot water over me?"

Finally, after what seemed an eternity, I heard my parents calling my name. They sounded frantic. I could hear Mama screaming: "God!

Please. Oh God, please." They kept yelling my name, asking where I was. I could only vaguely hear them. I tried to yell loudly enough for them to hear me, but I was exhausted. Half of my bedroom wall was sitting on top of my chest. I gathered all the breath I could and screamed, "Come help me. I can't move."

I don't know how long it took for my parents to get to me. It was very dark except for the flicker of flames burning in the rubble. We called out to each other until they located me in the corner of my bedroom. When Mama found me, she kept saying, "Stay put. Don't try to move." She called to Papa that she had found me. I could hear him saying, "I can't hear. I can't hear. I can't hear anything."

A long time went by as I lay there helpless in the darkness while Papa and Mama struggled to dig me from the rubble. Their voices were fading in and out, and sometimes I felt as if I were floating. It was as if I were there but not there at the same time. I had an unbearable taste in my mouth. I thought that it was probably from the hot, muddy water that I still felt pouring over me. It was in my eyes and in my nose. Sometimes I swallowed a big gulp of it, and it made me want to throw up. I think the nausea helped to keep me awake. My parents kept reassuring me, "You're okay. Everything is going to be okay." It was comforting to hear them say that, but I was still terrified.

When they finally succeeded in removing me from the rubble, my mother took my legs and my father lifted me from under my arms. They had to climb over more rubble to carry me out of the room. I screamed when I felt something poke into my back. They strained to lift me up higher. My father was seventy and my mother was sixty-five, and it was very difficult for them to move me, but they had to hurry because we had to get to a safe place before more rockets came.

They carried me to the dining room because it was the most secure room in the house, located in the center and somewhat protected by the surrounding rooms. While my father laid me on the cold floor, neighbors gathered around.

I was frightened by a sudden brightness shining in my eyes again like the bomb flash, followed immediately by my mother's screams.

I was even more frightened when I blinked and the brightness in my eyes turned from white to red. I thought the explosions were starting again, but the sudden light came from Papa's flashlight, and Mama's screams came from what that light revealed. My head and neck were covered in blood. My hair was matted with it. Papa's eardrums were torn, but his vision was intact. As he raised my arm searching for my injuries, blood gushed out of a gash in my forearm. One piece of shrapnel had entered my arm, and another had cut into my wrist. Blood spurted out of my wrist about six inches into the air. It wouldn't stop.

We had nothing resembling a first-aid kit at home. Even if we had, I don't know how they would have found it in the confusion and destruction. It was a miracle Papa found the flashlight. He went to the storage room and brought some kerosene to pour on my wound to make it stop bleeding. It was an old wartime remedy he had learned when the Turks occupied the country. I screamed as the liquid covered my ragged flesh. It felt cold and hot at the same time, and the fumes made the room smell worse. In the midst of their panic my parents did not think to put pressure on my upper arm to slow the bleeding. Even though the kerosene trick worked, my wounds desperately required medical attention.

We heard a soldier yelling nearby, checking to see whether anyone was critically injured and needed immediate transportation to the hospital. My father told him that I had been wounded but that he didn't think the injury was critical. The soldier then said he would get help later, when the shelling subsided. My father thanked him and waited eagerly for things to settle down so help would come and get me to the hospital. I guess he figured it would be safer, both for us and for the soldiers who would transport me, to stay put for a while instead of driving to the hospital under a rain of bombs. So my father waited patiently.

As I lay on the floor with my head on my mother's arm, I kept hearing her say that I was going to be all right. Someone had rolled fabric over my wrist to absorb as much blood as possible. I was getting very dizzy as the minutes passed. The rockets and artillery shells continued to fly back and forth between the Lebanese army outpost up the hill from our house and the Muslim position across the valley. Our neighbors had come up to what was left of our house, insisting on being with us. Everyone felt safer together, so we all huddled together on the floor behind the dining-room wall. I remember looking up at the sky and seeing balls of fire flying over us—there was no longer a roof over our heads. The sounds of explosions came so quickly that they reminded me of popping popcorn, except the pops were deafening. In the middle of it all, we lay helpless. I don't know how we survived the night in the cold and wind in the broken shell of our home.

By seven the next morning, soldiers had begun walking down to our house from the military base up the hill. When they saw my injuries, they sent for someone to take me to the hospital. I was afraid to go to the hospital because my traumatic experiences of being in a hospital after a car accident a year earlier were still fresh in my mind. But around eight thirty in the morning we were rushed into the emergency room, which was full to overflowing. My father carried me in his arms. I was crying, both from pain and from my fear of doctors and hospitals. Mama held my hand as they laid me on a bed. The doctor took one look at my wound and his jaw dropped. He couldn't believe that they were just now getting me to the hospital. He yelled at the nurses, who rushed to get scissors and the instruments needed to extract the shrapnel from my arm. He told my parents to hold me tight and not let me see what he was doing. I screamed as he cut my skin to the bone where the shrapnel was embedded. Without an adequate anesthetic, the pain was the worst thing I had ever felt in my life. Either the doctor thought there was no time to give me a general anesthetic, or he thought that dabbing some local painkiller on my arm would do the trick. It didn't. He didn't seem to hear my screaming as he worked to remove the jagged pieces of metal. Mama cried uncontrollably, as if she shared in the agony I was going through, as she held my head tightly against her neck. The only thing the doctors said to me was, "Another ten minutes and it will be over." I think I heard this about five times every ten minutes. Finally I was so weak I couldn't scream anymore, and I fainted.

I woke up later on a bed, with a needle in my hand and a bag of blood hanging over my head. The doctor had cleaned my arm and sewn it up. My parents were next to me. Mama brushed the hair from my forehead as Papa assured me that the worst had passed. He seemed to be talking a lot louder than usual. I was a bit relieved when he told me that the doctor had said I would be all right, but I cried and begged them to take me home immediately. I wanted to get away from that place. I was frightened whenever a nurse walked into the room to check the blood bag hanging over my head and connected to my arm because I had lost so much blood. I was afraid of anyone dressed in white.

The days in the hospital seemed endless. The doctors must have had me on some sort of painkiller, because I was always drowsy and slept a lot. Whenever I woke up, my mother was right there. She really did love me higher than the sky, and deeper than the ocean, and bigger than the whole wide world.

The destruction of our house was big news in town because we were the first victims of the war that had now come to southern Lebanon. Since my father was one of the most respected community leaders and spent much of his time at the hospital with me, my room was crowded with visitors coming to check on me and offer their condolences. From all the talk going on around me at the hospital we learned what had happened on that terrible November night.

The multiple explosions that had rained down on us were Katyusha rockets, launched from Elkhiam, the Muslim town across the valley. The Shia Muslims of Elkhiam were staunch Communists and allies of the PLO. We would come to know their Katyusha rockets well. The Palestinians and their leftist Muslim allies seemed to have an endless supply. Once primitive World War II–era rockets, these have developed over the years to become very effective in laying waste to large areas. Fired in rapid succession from multiple tubes on a single launcher, they carpet an area with high explosives in seconds, creating widespread devastation.

The first rocket the Muslims fired to check their aim that night hit its intended target, the army base up the hill behind our house. But the force of the rocket's firing tilted the launcher down a fraction of an inch, so the rest of the rockets fell fifty yards short, landing in and around our house. It was luck for our town that the Lebanese army base above my house didn't take the full brunt of the bombardment and was able to return fire. That was the only thing that prevented the combined forces of the PLO and the Muslims from overrunning Marjayoun that night. The Muslims' poor aim was good for Marjayoun, but bad for us. It changed the course of our family's life and my future.

I spent the next few days in a fuzzy, semiconscious state. I wanted to get out of the hospital and away from the doctors and nurses. I would carry an intense fear of hospitals and people in white coats for many years to come. After I threatened to run away if they left me there, my parents talked with the doctor, and arrangements were made for me to sleep at home at night and come back to the hospital during the day so the staff could check my progress and change my bandages.

Leaving the hospital was a relief, but I would not have been so happy if I had known what kind of life awaited us. Half of our once beautiful home was gone, and what remained was severely damaged. The living-room and family-room walls had collapsed. Blood from my injury was splattered all over my bedroom—on the walls, on the carpet, on the twisted metal of my bed's headboard. I had lost so much blood that it had dripped from the mattress onto the floor, covering an area half the size of the bed. The edges of my mattress were burned from the fire that accompanied the blast. The only part of the mattress that wasn't burned was the area soaked in my blood. It was a miracle that I was still alive. As we surveyed the house, we realized that my father would have been killed if my mother hadn't forced him to come back inside with her. Yet if they hadn't gone outside in the first place to check out what had happened, both of them would probably have been killed in the room with the heater. The table where they had been sitting was buried under rubble. For us to have survived at all could mean only one thing: there was some higher power out there that didn't want us to die yet. That was all my young mind could comprehend. The next seven years would be miserable, the days endless, and the fear of losing my life more real than the air I breathed.

To a ten-year-old, all this—the civil war and the attack against us—was bewildering. Just as people asked "Why do they hate us?" after 9/11, one evening I asked my father, "Why did they do this to us?" He took a long breath and paused, deeply concerned about what he was about to say. "The Muslims bombed us because we are Christians. They want us dead because they hate us." This hate was not because we had armies in the Middle East or because we supported Israel or for any of the reasons people easily turn to today. It was because we were Christians, infidels.

As a child, I was just too young to understand all the political implications, but I understood one thing: people wanted to kill me simply because I was a Christian. As I grew older I would discover more by watching television, and seeing the massacres, kidnappings, suicide bombings, and destruction inflicted by Muslims against non-Muslims worldwide. I would hear the hatred and bigotry espoused by mullahs in mosques televised throughout the Middle East and eventually throughout the world. Today I live on another continent eight thousand miles away from Lebanon. I sat watching television with my American children on September 11, 2001, crying as I heard the screams of family members looking for their loved ones buried under the rubble of the World Trade Center. It was my children who now looked at me and asked: "Mom! Who is Osama bin Laden and why does he call us infidels?"

Different generation, different nationality, different continent, twenty-five years apart. Same enemy: radical Islam.

3.

LIFE UNDER TERROR

By the time I returned from the hospital, every aspect of our lives had changed radically for the worse. My father had bought corrugated metal and used it to replace the walls that had fallen down in our family room. He put clear plastic sheeting on what was supposed to be a small window between the metal sheets. I lay in the family room on a torn metal couch. It was a very dark room. Winter made it gloomier, since we lived in the mountains and barely had a sunny day for three months in the wintertime. It was freezing cold despite running a kerosene stove in the middle of the room. The metal walls adopted the temperature of the cold mountains more than the meager warmth radiating from the little heater. The nights were scary, as the metal sheets would bang and rub against each other in the wind. The plastic sheeting on the window would breathe in and out depending on the flow of the wind. Perhaps the worst change was that now my religion was a matter of life and death. Most of the three thousand people who lived in Marjayoun were Christians, with a few Muslims living in their own neighborhood at the edge of town. However, in southern Lebanon, a large majority of the population is Shia Muslim, and the vast majority of the Palestinians were Muslim. Marjayoun was boxed in by Palestinian enclaves and hostile Muslim villages and towns to the east, north, and west. To the south was the Christian village of Klaia, numbering barely nine hundred inhabitants. South of Klaia was Israel.

Even before that first bombardment, relations with our Muslim neighbors were tense because of clashes between Christians and Muslims in other parts of Lebanon. Now the fear had hit home.

A lot of Muslims poured in from other Muslim countries, such as Iran, the founder and supporter of Hezbollah, one of the leading terrorist organizations in the world today. They also came from Somalia, Sudan, Syria, Jordan, Libya, Iraq, and Egypt. The Lebanese civil war was not between the Lebanese; it was a holy war declared on the Christians by the Muslims of the Middle East.

They started massacring the Christians in city after city. The Western media seldom reported these horrific events. Most of the press was located in West Beirut, controlled by the PLO and the Muslims. One of the most ghastly acts was the massacre in the Christian city of Damour,[1] where thousands of Christians were slaughtered like sheep. The combined forces of the PLO and the Muslims would enter a bomb shelter and see a mother and a father hiding with a little baby. They would tie one leg of the baby to the mother and one leg to the father and pull the parents apart, splitting the child in half. A close friend of mine became mentally disturbed after they made her slaughter her own son in a chair. They tied her to a chair, tied a knife to her hand, and, holding her hand, forced her to cut her own sixteen-year-old son's throat. After killing him they raped her two daughters in front of her. They would urinate and defecate on the altars of churches using the pages of the Bible as toilet paper before shooting and destroying the church. Americans just don't realize the viciousness of the militant Islamic fundamentalist. They refuse to see it even when they look today at video footage of churches being burned in Iraq or different parts of the world or synagogues being destroyed in Gaza.

I think the biggest disservice to the American people was the denial by the networks to air video of the beheading of Daniel Pearl, Nick Berg, or the many other hostages that were beheaded in Iraq. We as a society need to see the type of enemy we are fighting. People have been so sheltered in this country that they have not paid attention to what has been going on for the last twenty-some years. And today, even after the attack of September 11, people still cannot fathom that this type of barbarity could happen here.

As was common practice when Islamic terror prevailed, Christians fled. Any Christian who could move from Marjayoun did so. Unfortunately, when the bombs destroyed our home, they also turned my father's savings into ashes. With no money to move, we were trapped. As the Christians left, Palestinians and Lebanese Muslims flooded into Marjayoun.

At first we were protected by the Lebanese army base up the hill from what was left of our house. As long as the Lebanese military remained neutral in the civil war, we were safe. However, that did not last long. In January of 1976, the army began to disintegrate along sectarian lines. One lieutenant, Ahmad al-Khatib, broke away, announcing the establishment of the "Lebanese Arab Army" and urging all Muslim soldiers to mutiny and desert with their weapons. Lebanese army bases throughout the country were quickly taken over by sectarian militias, Muslims in most areas and Christians in some.

One morning shortly after al-Khatib's mutiny, the senior Muslim officer at the Marjayoun base called a meeting of the Muslims stationed there. When the Christians were told they'd better not be present, they knew exactly what was happening. While the Muslims met to plan the takeover of the base, the Christian soldiers quickly gathered as many weapons and tanks, and as much ammunition and equipment, as they could and dashed out of the base, south to Klaia.

With the army fragmented and the Christians soldiers gone, we were now at the mercy of the Muslims and PLO members who controlled the military base. And their mercy was not tender. With the military shift in power, the attitude and behavior of the Muslims living in our town and the surrounding area turned against us overnight. Even though not all of them became raging fanatics, the moderate voices of the less influential were silenced because of fear and intimidation.

The radicals started looting Christian homes and intimidating the owners. They would enter Christian businesses and demand products without paying or having any intention of paying in the future. Soldiers would enter my father's restaurant and demand that he prepare food for them even late at night when he was closing up. After a few months my father closed the restaurant because it wasn't worth the risk or the humiliation by the Muslims. We were nothing but *kuffar,* dirty infidel Christians, to them.

It was a shock to our sensibilities. We had always shown our Muslim neighbors kindness and respect. Many of the same Muslim soldiers had eaten at my father's restaurant before the war. Some of them had running accounts that Papa never collected because he knew they had no money. As I outgrew my clothes, Mama gave them to some of the Muslim families for their daughters. One of my friends through my five years of elementary school was a Muslim girl called Khadija, who lived in a nearby Muslim town. Khadija and I were inseparable. We attended the same Catholic school, shared the same classes, walked together on the playground, and sat together to have our lunch. I knew that her family remained in our area and was not involved in any evildoing against the Christians. There were plenty of these good-hearted Muslims, but they were subdued and silenced by the radicals. In a later chapter I will describe the far-reaching and dangerous implications of this ability of radical jihadists to subdue and influence moderate Muslims living in Christian communities.

At this point in the civil war the Communists were allied with the Palestinians. The only thing that saved our lives was Papa's friendship with a man who was a senior leader in the local Communist Party. This man had sufficient power to put us under his protection. He sent orders that our house was not to be looted and we were not to be arrested or abused. Although these orders were followed, we became prisoners in what was left of our home.

Meanwhile, the Muslims and PLO found another way to fill our lives with terror. By 1976 Klaia was the only town in southern Lebanon still under Christian control. It held out against Muslim attacks only because of the few tanks and cannons the Christian soldiers had taken with them when they had escaped from the military base. Klaia's conquest became the number-one priority of the Muslims. Since the Muslims and their Palestinian allies couldn't conquer Klaia immediately, they launched a campaign of artillery and rocket bombardment. The Muslims and PLO would set up their artillery and rocket launchers in our yard (or the yard of some other Christians who had been unable to flee Marjayoun), and they would launch a barrage of rockets or shells at Klaia or Israel. Then they would pack up and leave, knowing that we would absorb the brunt of the return fire. The Palestinians use this tactic today in Christian neighborhoods in the West Bank when attacking the Israeli army. The Christians experienced the same punishing results.

Even though our neighbors over in Klaia were still holding out in the last remaining Christian village, their situation was becoming desperate. They were under constant artillery and rocket bombardment, and running out of bombs and bullets with which to defend themselves. They knew they needed help fast, for their own sake and so they could come and save us. They knew our days were numbered and action was of the essence. For us in the south, there was no help coming from Christians anywhere else in Lebanon or the world. With nowhere to turn, the people of Klaia asked for help from the Israelis. Since they and we were facing torture and death at the hands of the Muslims, seeking help from Israel seemed to be the lesser of two evils. Under the cover of darkness, a few men from Klaia went to the border to make contact with the Israelis. This in itself was very dangerous because the Israelis were always on alert for attempts at infiltration by Palestinian terrorists. Fortunately, there were Arabic-speaking soldiers assigned to the Israeli border patrols. After a tense moment of flagging down a jeep full of soldiers with a .50-caliber machine gun ready to shoot infiltrators coming over the border fence, the men from Klaia were able to explain their dire situation.

The Israelis were well aware of the nature of the threat that faced the Christians, and they were willing to help for both moral and strategic reasons. The Palestinians had been launching terror attacks and artillery and rocket barrages against Israel from southern Lebanon for almost ten years. The Israelis knew that if the Muslims and Palestinians completely controlled southern Lebanon, the Christians could be slaughtered as they had been in other Christian towns and villages, and Israel would face even more terror attacks and bombardments. Accordingly, the Israelis offered to equip and train the Christian men so they could defend themselves and at the same time provide Israel with a buffer. They provided food and humanitarian assistance to the people of Klaia. This was the beginning of the South Lebanese Army, the SLA, led by Christian Major Sa'ad Haddad, who had defected from the crumbling Lebanese army to help protect Christians in the south. With the help of the Israelis, Christians from Klaia began formulating plans to come back and save us.

The Palestinians and their leftist Muslim allies, infuriated that the Christians in Klaia had sought and received help from the Israelis, increased the frequency and duration of their artillery and rocket attacks on Klaia and south across the border into Israel. This prompted the Israelis and the Christians to fire back at our town, where the shelling against them was coming from.

As the shelling intensified we started spending our nights in a small underground bomb shelter behind the restaurant. My father had had this shelter built with financial assistance from the Lebanese government, given to those in southern Lebanon to protect them from the "Israeli aggressors." Ironically, the bomb shelter my father had built with the encouragement of the Muslims in government to protect us from the Israeli enemy would be the same shelter that would protect us from being slaughtered by the Muslims. Papa, Mama, and I shared this tiny space, about ten feet by twelve feet, with Uncle Tony, Tante Terez, and their four daughters. Tony and Terez were not really my uncle and aunt, but that's what I called them. They were renting one of our houses in our complex at the time. Like us, they had nowhere else to go.

We lived in the shelter for three consecutive weeks, bombarded by shelling. One night it was particularly bad. We huddled in terror, sure we would not survive the night. Just before daybreak the shelling stopped, and was replaced by an eerie silence. The silence lasted for about half an hour, and then we heard a commotion on the road in front of the restaurant. Papa peeked out of a small window and saw gunmen fleeing north on foot and in jeeps and trucks. After fifteen minutes, the commotion subsided and the silence returned. We didn't know what was happening, but we were too terrified to move.

Suddenly, we were shaken by the rumbling of a tank pulling up next to our bomb shelter. Papa jumped to the window to see what was happening. Five men carrying machine guns climbed down from the tank and began walking toward the entrance to the bomb shelter. Papa gasped in fear, and then he started to laugh and cry at the same time. "They're wearing crosses," he said. "They're Christians, come to save us!" We all rushed out of the bomb shelter crying with relief and joy. The Christians had finally been able to expel the Palestinians and Muslims from Marjayoun. We felt as if we had returned from the dead.

In a short time, Major Haddad and his volunteer army of civilians and ex–Lebanese soldiers were able to extend protection to three small enclaves in southern Lebanon. However, although Marjayoun was now back in Christian hands, the danger was far from over. In fact, it became even greater. Now death could come out of the sky at any time, without warning. We were still surrounded on three sides. The Palestinians and their Muslim Communist and leftist allies held forti- fied positions in the mountains on our east, north, and west. It was the perfect setting for them. No matter which way they shot, they couldn't miss. Their largest artillery base was located across the valley to the east in the Muslim village of Elkhiam, where the rockets that bombed my home had come from. Their big guns were aimed straight at us. You could be sitting in your kitchen, or walking down the road, or vis- iting with friends on the porch, and suddenly there would be a loud explosion, and you could be dead or wounded. If you heard the rushing *zoom-whoosh* of a shell flying through the air, you were lucky, because that meant it would explode someplace else, giving you time to run to the bomb shelter before the next round landed.

And then there were the snipers. Elkhiam was so close that they didn't need binoculars to see us walking down the street. They could shoot with either small-caliber rifles like the AK-47, or big machine guns with bullets that could go through thick metal and still take your head off. We could hear the hiss of bullets zipping by before hearing the sound of the shots being fired. Because of the echoes created by the hills and valleys, we couldn't tell where the shots were coming from. They were bombarding or sniping at us most of the time, making us prisoners in our tiny shelter.

Our bomb shelter had one small window, which we blocked with marble tiles that my father had originally bought to decorate our living room. Now we strategically placed the tiles to stop shrapnel. Although no sunlight could get through that window, somehow a freezing wind found its way in. We covered part of the door with a big block of cement that had been a public bench next to Papa's restaurant. A long plastic tarpaulin was hung over the remainder of the opening to partially stop the cold wind.

It's a good thing that we were already very close to Tony, Terez, and their four daughters. All nine of us had to share the small space, deprived of any privacy. We slept on the floor almost on top of each other. The women and girls slept on one side and the men on the other. With our long hair, sleeping on a damp floor, it was not long before Mama, Tante Terez, and all five of us girls developed an infestation of lice. Mama and Tante Terez put kerosene on our heads to get rid of them. I remember getting dizzy from the fumes, but I had to put up with it. It worked, and it was better than itching.

We lived on the southern edge of town in an isolated no-man's-land between Marjayoun and Klaia. Few people walked by, because doing so would have made them easy targets for snipers across the valley. Anyone who drove by would zoom down the road as fast as he could to avoid being hit. Every time I heard a car coming I wished so hard that it would stop, so we would have someone to talk to and tell us what was going on. But knowing they were being followed in someone's gun sights across the valley, drivers pushed the gas pedal even more. Days would go by without seeing anyone other than my parents and Uncle Tony's family.

I remember our first Christmas Eve in our new wartime surroundings. We stayed up until midnight singing Christmas hymns around the fire. Our parents told stories about Christmas when they were growing up. They asked us to close our eyes and imagine that we had a beautiful new dress laid out next to us, so when we woke up Christmas morning we could wear our new clothes to church. But that Christmas Eve it was hard to dream beautiful dreams while hearing artillery shells exploding every two seconds. That's what our militia later estimated had fallen on us during that long night. It was a Christian holiday, and the Muslims were not going to let us enjoy it in peace.

Morning ushered in a very sad Christmas. We had no gifts to exchange and no electricity. Because the shells continued to explode, we had to stay inside. We ate our breakfast by candlelight and then just sat there for the rest of the day. We didn't have much to celebrate. It was Christmas, but for us it was just another day in a war. We had no way of knowing how long it would last, or how long *we* would last.

Later that week, Uncle Tony told my father that he had been looking for rental homes and that he had found an underground house at the other end of town where his family could live. It would be safer, and they would have more room. He had tears in his eyes as he told my father that they had to leave. It was very hard for us to see them go. If we had been able to move away from the front lines we would have done it too, but we couldn't just leave our home, since we were the owners. Uncle Tony could just take the same amount of rent he was paying my dad and pay it to someone else and move. We had lost our money and had no monthly income, so we couldn't afford to pay rent anywhere.

There was no shelling on the day they moved. My mother helped

Tante Terez pack dishes, and my father helped Uncle Tony carry the furniture to the truck. No one said a word. We were as gloomy as the day was dark and cloudy. The sun refused to come out. By three o'clock in the afternoon everything had been packed, and it was time to say good-bye. Tony had rented from my parents for fourteen years, since before I was born. I didn't know life without them. As we cried and hugged each other, the rain began. It mixed with our tears and ran down our faces. To me, it seemed as if even the skies were crying because we were separating. Now it would be just Papa, Mama, and me alone at the edge of town.

There was nobody living in the few houses around us. The only people I saw were the Christian militia soldiers manning a checkpoint nearby. Even the military base was deserted: a huge empty structure where the wind blew at night, making noises that added to the spooky explosions of shellfire. My father was now seventy-three years old, and he seemed helpless without Uncle Tony. Tony had been someone that my father could depend on to take care of us if something happened to him.

However, now we had a little more space, so we made a few improvements. We had all been sleeping on the floor on thick blankets. Now we had room to move two beds from our ruined home into the shelter. Mama and I slept on one bed and my father slept on the other. We also brought down one chair from the house, and for a dining-room table we used a big plastic 7UP box with a tray on top of it. The bomb shelter was so small that we had to sit on the edge of our beds to eat. The other corner of the shelter was our bathroom. It consisted of a big metal oil container with sharp metal edges. We had to be careful how we squatted over it so we wouldn't cut ourselves.

My parents stocked the bomb shelter with dried food brought down from our home. We had beans, rice, whole wheat, potatoes, onions, garlic, and dried greens, and oil for cooking. We could seldom leave the shelter to go downtown to buy food, so we had to be able to eat from what we stored in the shelter. We had no electricity, no heat, no bathroom, no shower, and no running water.

Our days were filled with a mixture of fear and boredom, accompanied by extreme discomfort. The Muslims had cut off the public water mains to our town. Thank God we lived in Marjayoun, "the valley of springs." In between the shelling, but still under the snipers' sights, my mother and I would take plastic containers and crawl carefully down to one of the many nearby springs. It was normally a five-minute walk from the house, but since we had to crawl in the ditch along the road to elude snipers, sometimes it would take us hours to reach the spring, fill our containers, and get back to the shelter. The pool at the spring hadn't been cleaned in a long time. My mother had to put nylon stockings over the tops of our water containers to filter out the dirt, worms, and rocks that came out with the water. Each of us carried two containers. Papa couldn't go with us because of his arthritis. Also, if the shelling started he wouldn't hear it and wouldn't be able to get back to the shelter fast enough. Because getting water was such a major undertaking, we strictly rationed it. We would drink only when we got very thirsty, and limited ourselves to one quick sponge bath per week.

Sometimes on those long trips crawling to and from the spring I would wonder about the snipers. Knowing that someone is actually looking at you ready to pull the trigger, trying to kill you personally, not just at random, is a surreal experience. I would wonder if the sniper was a young boy or an old man. Was he a teenager? I sometimes thought that maybe, if it weren't for the war, we would be in the same school (the Muslims went to the Catholic schools also, as the education was better than public schools) and visit in the courtyard together, maybe even dance at school parties. Instead, he was trying to murder me. I wondered if he would feel satisfaction watching me as I fell down after his bullets hit me. What would he say? Would he brag about it? Would he call his friends and boast, "Hey, I killed the girl with the long brown hair and the yellow water container. Come look, she's dead." I wondered if he ever thought I was pretty or ugly. I wondered if he had sisters or daughters my age. I wondered if he hoped to kill me first, or my mother. Which would have given him more joy?

Watching my mother cry desperately while she struggled to drag me back to the shelter after I got hit, or watching me cry desperately trying to save her?

When you live in silence and isolation you have a lot of time to think—and imagine the many possible ways you will meet your own death.

Food was, of course, just as much a concern as water—but even harder to come by. Mama and I would sneak out of the shelter, avoiding the snipers, to gather some green grass and weeds that grew in our garden and around the shelter. Sometimes the only vegetables we had to eat were grass and a variety of weeds. Mama would rinse the weeds and put them in a pan with some minced garlic, olive oil, and a drop of lemon juice. It's amazing how delicious they could be, especially dandelion mixed with garlic. We actually developed a taste for certain weeds, and would look forward to dinner with real excitement when we found them. We thought of these favorites as our "gourmet grass." Certain weeds tasted lemony; others had wide leaves that could be used as lettuce. Some grass we ate green with olives, and some with lentils.

Our lives fell into a pattern around our chores. During the day we would clean the kerosene lantern we used at night. Because the light burned all night, by morning the glass would be black from the soot and smoke. We had to clean it and trim the cotton wick so it would burn again the following night. The other chore was to take the potty outside, dump it, and clean it. Once these two things were done there was not much else to do.

About four o'clock one morning, Mama needed to go to the bathroom. When she put her feet down from the bed, she discovered she was standing in water up to her knees. She picked up our kerosene light and saw that an underground spring had broken through to the surface and flooded our bomb shelter. Papa ran outside under an artillery barrage to get a bucket so we could bail out the water. The shelling slowed and the rain stopped about an hour later. We brought more blankets from the house and put them on the floor of the shelter to absorb the water from the spring, and then we evacuated to a little room under our balcony that we had used as a chicken coop before the war. Until our bomb shelter dried out, it was the safest place to be.

We felt vulnerable in the room under the balcony because it was completely exposed. A shell could easily come through the ceiling. If one exploded nearby it would blow the front wall in. But we had no choice. We had nowhere else to go. We spread out our blankets and sat with each other by candlelight. I looked at my parents; they looked very old to me. I was thirteen. My mother was sixty-eight and had developed high blood pressure, and Papa at seventy-three was suffering from arthritis worsened by the humidity in the shelter. It took three days for our shelter to dry out enough to be livable again. In the meantime, we huddled together each night, fearing that the next shell was going to land on our roof.

When we returned to the shelter on the fourth day, it was all white inside. Because the sun couldn't enter the shelter, the walls had developed a fuzzy white snowlike mold in the humidity. It was as if we lived in a cotton room. The damp moldy smell combined with the smell of the toilet to create an unbearable stench.

To make matters worse, I had come of age and was having terrible cramps and crying from pain. My mother gave me a piece of black tire rubber to bite on when the pain became overwhelming. We still had a few bottles of fancy liqueur and wine in the shelter left over from my father's restaurant. These bottles now became our only pain medication—there was no going to a pharmacy. So my father would open up a bottle of Johnnie Walker, fill a cup, and hand it to me. He would say, "Now, honey, in one sip, just drink down the whole cup." I hated the taste of that stuff, but I would force myself to drink it, and within a few minutes I would go into a daze that would last for hours. For three days every month, this became my other nightmare.

Radio Monte Carlo, the only radio station we could get in the bomb shelter, became our only connection to the outside world. Its hourly news briefs helped us predict what our next hour was going to be like. For instance, if we heard that Christians in Beirut had bombed the PLO refugee camps in retaliation for a PLO terrorist act against them, we knew that life was going to be hell that night. If we heard that some Muslim headquarters in another part of Lebanon had been hit, we knew that in about two hours the shelling was going to rain down on us in response.

Sometimes the radio had good news, such as an announcement of a cease-fire agreement and how long it would last. These periodic cease-fires were important because at these times it became a bit safer for us to fetch water from the spring nearby. Not entirely safe, however. Cease-fires would stop the shelling, but not the snipers. Even during cease-fires, they felt free to shoot at anything in our town that moved.

Periodically, Caritas, a Catholic relief organization, would send supply boxes filled with rice, beans, dried milk, tuna, oil, flour for bread, and sometimes blankets. When Caritas held a distribution at a church or some other location, a cease-fire would be called, in some elaborate arrangement involving the UN. The distribution would be scheduled a week in advance so all parties would know.

On distribution days, my father and I would go to the distribution center, take a number, and stand in line. Unfortunately, many of the young men would shove and push until they got to the distribution door, grab a box, and leave. When people have to fight for survival, the stronger will always walk over the weaker. Papa was old and weak, and his feet hurt. He would stand to the side, leaning against a wall, waiting for his number to be called. Most of the time we were left until the end.

It tore my heart to see my father being treated this way. As a girl in an Arab culture I could not command respect, and I didn't have big brothers to fight for me. I painfully remember one day when Papa and I went to one of the Caritas relief giveaways held at the community center in town. We had taken a number and were standing in a long line on the street in front of the building. There were no walls for my father to lean on that day. So many people forced their way into the line ahead of us that when our time came we were told, "You are going to have to come again tomorrow." My father said, "Please, I can barely walk. I stood here in line for three hours." But the man shut the gate in his face and said again, "Sorry, you are going to have to come back tomorrow."

Seeing my father, with tears in his old wrinkly eyes, being turned away, I exploded. I started banging on the gate and calling the gate-keeper "a bastard without a heart" and all sorts of names. "Screw you and your donations!" I shouted. "That man," I said, pointing to my father, "donated the money to buy the ground you are standing on, before you were even born. We don't need you. You can shove it!" I yelled as I tore our number into little pieces. I threw it at the gate, and the scraps flew all over. My father grabbed me by the arm, telling me to stop crying. "Why did you do that?" he said. "Now we won't get any food."

Both angry and ashamed, I hung on to him as we walked slowly back to the shelter.

My mother spent the rest of that afternoon massaging my father's legs, which ached from having been standing up all morning. After dinner that evening, my mother and I sat on our beds talking. Papa was very quiet. He tried to get up to walk to the bathroom, but got only a few steps toward the door. His legs were shaking so badly that he lost his balance and fell down. As Mama and I helped him get up, he looked toward the oppressive ceiling of our shelter and, like Job of ancient times, screamed, "God, how could you let something like this happen to me? I am the one who served you all my life."

At one point we heard that we would be having two days of cease-fire. We decided to take the time to make our bomb shelter more protected. Papa went downtown and had men bring back sand for sandbags to fortify our shelter. For the next two days we worked fever-ishly, filling sandbags and using them to create a wall in front of the shelter that would stop the shrapnel. We also spread sandbags on top of the shelter for more protection. It was a good thing we did. When the fighting resumed, it was fiercer than ever. Big artillery now entered the picture—155-millimeter cannons, which fired an explosive shell about six inches in diameter.

One spring evening, after dinner, it was warm enough that we didn't have to make a fire. For a moment, the familiar sound of crickets in the garden made the world seem peaceful and normal. We knew that the shelling would probably pick up again around ten o'clock. But we had been listening to the news earlier, and there had been some talk about a peace proposal, so we went to sleep hoping that the warring factions would agree on something soon and that our nightmare would come to an end.

The enemy forces started shelling with the big 155s at around eleven that night. Each shell that landed felt like a volcano erupting, and would dig a crater into the ground six feet deep and eight to ten feet wide, lifting up rocky dirt and throwing it as far as a hundred meters. I was terrified. A direct hit would kill us instantly.

My father got out of his bed, which faced the door, and sat next to us on our bed. We prayed to God to have mercy on us. Five minutes later, a bomb landed just outside in front of the bomb-shelter door. At first we thought the bomb had exploded inside, because the room was lit up as if the sun itself had landed on us. I was shrieking and crying hysterically. Smoke filled the room. As we regained our senses we gradually realized that we were still alive and uninjured. We just sat there holding each other tightly.

The morning came and with it the realization that somehow the door had become blocked, and we were trapped. It was so dark we could barely see. In a lull in the shelling that morning, my parents tried to determine what had happened. All they could see was that the cement block, which took three men to carry, had fallen sideways on top of the door under all of the sandbags. There was no way that the three of us—an old man, his old wife, and a small thirteen-year-old girl—were going to move it. We tried anyway for about two hours until we became exhausted. We were kidding ourselves. We couldn't loosen it or move even a single sandbag. The only way we would be freed was if someone dug from the outside. Papa attempted to comfort us by saying, "Don't worry. A soldier will pass by and see this without a doubt. We will be just fine." But I knew it would take some real luck for that to happen, because our shelter was hidden behind my father's restaurant building, about twelve yards off the road. No one driving or walking by could see it.

Since the shelling had been so heavy during the past few days, we hadn't had a chance to go to the spring in a week. Only one and half bottles of water remained. We figured that the water would last us two days if we conserved it. Our stock of dry food was also low. We ate breakfast and decided to sit silently all day to conserve energy. If we heard someone walking by, then we would scream for help. Nine hours of silence went by with no sound of anyone passing. By the afternoon of the second day, we decided we had to try again to free ourselves. We worked for about an hour trying to move the block, but finally gave up, overcome by exhaustion. We hadn't been getting enough sleep because of the shelling, and were hungry and thirsty because we were rationing food and water. By the third morning the fear of death was there in the dark tomblike room. We prayed for help.

We were out of water, but we did have some rice and lentils left. Our plan for water if no one found us by the following day was to drink the urine collected in the can.

We tearfully embraced and began to say our good-byes to each other. As we sat together on the edge of the bed, my parents told me how much they loved me, how much joy I had brought them, how deeply they regretted that I had to go through this. They told me stories about when I was a little girl, the things I used to do and songs I used to sing. Once again, they told me they loved me higher than the sky, deeper than the ocean, and bigger than the whole wide world.

In that moment, I wanted more than anything to take away my parents' fear and worry. I told them that I knew that we might die, and that it was okay. "At least we are dying together without any pain or torture," I told them. "I would much rather die this way than be slaughtered in front of your eyes by the Palestinians."

We got very little sleep that night because the shelling was so heavy. By morning, just as we were falling asleep, we heard a car stop nearby and a door shut—we could barely hear it, so we weren't even sure if that's what we had heard. We got up and started screaming. I stood on the bed closest to the small window and yelled as loudly as I could while my mother took a chair and started banging it on the cement floor. We continued our desperate noisemaking for about fifteen minutes. Then we stopped to listen for whether someone outside had heard us.

There was no sound. Nothing. Complete silence. I fell on the bed crying. My brave resolve from the night before had vanished in the instant that a muffled car sound offered a slim hope. "I don't want to die. I don't want to die. Please get me out of here."

My mother grabbed me and shook me. "You aren't going to die, Brigitte. I swear to you that I will do anything to keep you alive. Someone is going to find us and get us out of here." Then my father said loudly, "Stop. I hear something." We stopped breathing. Then we heard steps on top of the shelter and a voice, muffled, calling, "Is anybody there?"

My father cried, "Help!" I joined him, screaming, "Help, we're trapped!" My mother resumed banging the chair against the cement. We heard feet running quickly toward the entrance, and then a man's voice saying, "Don't worry. I know you are there. Is anybody injured?" We shouted, "No!" as loudly as we could. Then we heard him say, "I will be right back with help. I need to get some men to help me remove this sand and rubble."

Our rescuers used a break in the shelling over the next few hours to remove the sandbags and move the cement block. Finally free, we ran outside and hugged our rescuers. Tears of happiness poured from our eyes. Even the young men who had dug us out began crying. There were three of them: Chuck, Bassam, and Eli. It was a beautiful day in May, about ten o'clock in the morning. The sky was clear and blue, the bluest that I had ever seen.

I ran to the base of the apricot tree in front of the shelter, put my hand around it, and started running in circles, screaming, "We're alive! We are going to live!" The whole world looked different to me. The garden was blossoming and there were buds on the trees and bushes. My God, I thought, I can't believe I hadn't noticed this before. I am sure they came out at least two weeks ago. I also noticed butterflies—it seemed like tens of thousands of them, of many colors, bright yellow, dark orange, pink, and brown with black stripes—flying all over the garden and fluttering above the flowers. I noticed the sun. I hadn't felt sunshine on my skin in at least a week. I just wanted to sit in the sun and let it warm me. Life took on a whole new meaning.

We sat down in the front of the shelter talking excitedly with our rescuers. Chuck, the young man who had found us, was an eighteen-year-old Christian militia fighter from our town. He was on his way up to the military base to meet friends. He told us that when he first passed our shelter he thought he'd heard something but ignored it, assuming he was imagining noises because he had been at the front lines all night. But about fifty meters past our place, he felt guilty. He thought, What if there is somebody there?—I better go back and check. And that's how he heard us the second time.

After our rescue, every week or so Chuck would stop by to make sure we were all right. He was five years older than me, about six feet tall, very well built and very masculine. His hair was curly and black. He had big black eyes and eyelashes any girl would die for, let alone a thirteen-year-old hungry for contact with the outside world. He would sit and have coffee and give us an update on what was going on. Since he was in the militia and toured the town, he knew what was happening. He would tell us who had died, who was injured, which houses had been destroyed. Chuck would stay for an hour or two and then excuse himself. My parents would always send their regards to his parents.

After three years of isolation we were no longer alone.

4.

HOPELESS EXISTENCE

It's hard to imagine we have been living like this for three years. It's now 1978. But time doesn't really matter or mean much anymore. There is no reason to keep up with time or days or holidays. There is no change; there are no events to look forward to: no time I have to be in school, no time to be at a doctor's appointment, no time to be at a social event. About the only thing time can tell us is when the shelling will begin, and it might be our time to die.

In theory, the Lebanese civil war ended in October 1976, with the Six Parties Summit. Delegates from Syria, Saudi Arabia, Egypt, Kuwait, the PLO, and, oh yes, Lebanon, represented by Syrian puppets, met in Riyadh, Saudi Arabia, and then Cairo, Egypt. They conveniently forgot to tell the people shelling us.

The Six Parties agreement "ended" the Lebanese civil war by validating Syria's virtual control over Lebanon. The agreement created the "Arab Deterrent Force," a thirty-thousand-man army, to maintain order and establish peace in Lebanon. The Arab Deterrent Force was made up of twenty-seven thousand Syrian troops already in Lebanon, and small contingents from Sudan, Saudi Arabia and the Persian Gulf states, and Libya.[1] The Six Parties also reaffirmed the Cairo agreement of 1969, which gave the PLO virtual sovereignty and freedom of action in southern Lebanon.[2]

The Six Parties ended the Lebanese civil war only in their own minds. They didn't end the violence we were suffering. They just gave Syria the authority to control the violence. In southern Lebanon, Hafiz al-Assad, president-for-life of Syria, controlled the violence by facilitating it. Despite the buffer zone protected by our SLA militia and Major Haddad, PLO artillery and rockets were still within range of communities in northern Israel, and certainly within range of us in Marjayoun. The PLO would fire artillery and rockets into southern Lebanon and Israel from positions within the United Nations Interim Force in Lebanon (UNIFIL) zone. Neither the UN troops on the scene nor the UN itself did anything to stop them. We who could benefit from the UN's taking action felt that they were all show and no go. The UN troops appeared to be some form of international effort to solve a problem, but they were actually making the situation worse. While not stopping the PLO from shelling us and Israel, they would become remarkably protective and indignant when either Israel or the SLA fired back at the PLO. The Six Parties may have fooled the world into believing that the Lebanese civil war had ended with their "agreement," but for us, the war went on.

The war forced us into a daily routine. Everything we did was influenced by the constant thought of keeping alive. Don't get shot by snipers, blown up by shells, maimed by mines, suffocated by carbon monoxide from our coal heater, frozen to death by the cold, or weakened by lack of food or water. If there was anything else to fear, I guess it was being bored to death. Other than the war, there was nothing else going on. There were no people to visit, no school, no movies— nothing that would attract a large gathering of people. The fear was too great that a shell would hit and kill a lot of people located in one place. The Muslims and PLO had a random shelling philosophy: traumatize the general Christian population by randomly shelling the civilian areas. It was a constant form of terrorism. You never knew when you would die from a shell from the sky.

We were being shelled every day. Our nights in the shelter under heavy shelling were like sleeping through a huge thunderstorm. The explosions, like the lightning that hits your house or a tree in your backyard ten times over, would jolt us upright out of our sleep in terror or never let us sleep at all.

Chuck came over one day with good news of a new and exciting development. Our elders had decided to reopen the schools so we could continue our education, something central to our culture and values. We would go during the morning when the fighting usually stopped or slowed down dramatically. What a relief from our boredom. It had been two years of sitting in our bomb shelters without studying or learning anything other than how to stay alive. Now living in no-man's-land would not be so bad. Not only would I get back to my studies, but I could see and socialize with my friends in town.

It was fun getting ready to go to school again. We would try to keep from being killed or wounded at night; then I would get up in the morning to go to school. Being able to take a shower would have helped a lot, since I had only two decent school uniforms in the shelter and alternated them every day; but we looked clean and well put together despite our lifestyle. Besides, come shells or high water in the shelter, we were going to continue our education. More important than anything else to our parents and leaders was that we be educated.

Our classes were held on the first floor of a three-story building so the floors above would give us added protection. Many days, just an hour after we got to school, the principal stormed into our class and informed us that shelling would start in fifteen minutes. He would order everybody to evacuate the classroom into the hallway. Some of the teachers who had cars would fill them up and drive us home to our bomb shelters. Many days I had to run home, sometimes crawling in ditches to avoid the bombs falling all around me. I used my books to protect my head from falling shrapnel. We missed many days because of heavy shelling, but we were determined to get an education.

I have to say that our quest for knowledge was tempered a bit by our circumstances. I would save studying for a test until the night before the test because I didn't know if I was even going to be alive to take it anyway, so why bother? This was the attitude of all my friends.

In March 1978, six months after school started, the fighting began to worsen. We stayed in our shelter for six days straight. Finally there was a cease-fire, and we went up to the house to shower and change our clothes. Our morale was very low because of rumors that the Palestinians, with the help of the Syrians and Iranians, had been fortifying their bases and planning an attack on the town. We were terrified that our exhausted troops were too weak to protect us and that our town would fall into the Palestinians' hands if they attacked that night.

I was washing my face when I heard Chuck's voice in our house. He was in a hurry. It was about three o'clock in the afternoon. He had stopped by to inform us that we were going to be attacked viciously that night in an attempt to take us over. He said, "Make sure you wear comfortable clothes and running shoes in case you have to flee. And if you flee make sure you run straight toward the Israeli border." He comforted me, saying he would be back the next day as soon as he could to check on us, if he stayed alive. Then he added: "But if we are all to die tonight, I wish us all a merciful death." And he left.

We were alone again. The silence that followed Chuck's disappearing footsteps made us feel that death was in our midst. Fearing we were going to be slaughtered that night, I didn't want strangers to see some poor dead girl in wrinkled old clothes who would be dumped in a hole. I wanted to look pretty when I was dead. Knowing that there would be nobody to prepare me for burial, I asked my mother if I could put on my pretty Easter dress. They might rob me of my life, but they would not rob me of how I wanted to look before I was gone forever. My dress was light blue with white roses all over it and beautiful lace around the neck and arms. I stood in front of the mirror crying as my mother combed my long hair and tied a white ribbon in it that matched the roses. I pleaded with her: "Please. I don't want to die. I'm only thirteen." My poor mother. Here was her only child, whom she had waited twenty years for, and all she could do was help grant her last wish to have some dignity in death. The sense of hope-lessness and fear in my pleading must have been breaking her heart. She asked me to stop crying and assured me that Jesus would take care of us.

Here I was in the pretty dress that I had worn to happy occasions and Easter services, and now I was shaking in fear sitting in the dingy bomb shelter with the crashing and exploding noises outside. We huddled in the corner on our bed. Mama and Papa prayed to God to protect us. All I could do was cry.

This was the explosive opening of what was going to be a long night. How long would be determined by whether the Palestinians reached us and how long our troops could hold out. Papa said, "Brigitte, you are young. We have lived a long life. We are old and are going to die soon anyway. We can't run if they come to kill us. But we will create a distraction while you run toward Israel and never look back." I started crying harder and said, "How could you say that? How can I run and leave you? I have nobody but you. Why do I want to live if you are gone?" My father begged me to listen to him. I just prayed that it would never get to that point. We spent the night dread-ing that we would take a direct hit or that death would come bursting through the door to slit our throats.

Daylight finally arrived, and the bombardment quieted down. The quiet after a battle is always the most agonizing time for those who do not know what is going on. It can be good or bad depending on who won the battle. Soon we could hear the rumbling of a long column of tanks and trucks heading north. Heading north was good. South meant bad. After years in the bomb shelter, we could tell the differ-ence between a tank, a truck, and an armored car just by the sound of their engines. We'd never heard so many sounds before, and they were different. My mother and I decided to poke our heads through the door to see if we could tell who was riding in these vehicles. There was a lot of activity. We saw tanks that we had never seen before and soldiers in uniforms we didn't recognize. The soldiers didn't look hostile, not like they were out looking for people. Another tank passed and I spotted Chuck sitting on the back. We knew we were going to be fine. The worst had passed, at least for a while.

The only reason we stayed alive that night was because Israel came into Lebanon and drove the Palestinians away. Like the Christians of southern Lebanon, the inhabitants of northern Israel had been forced for many years to spend long periods of time in bomb shelters because of artillery and rocket bombardments by the PLO and its Muslim allies in Lebanon. In addition, Palestinian death squads repeatedly attempted to infiltrate across the border into Israel to conduct terrorist attacks. Sometimes they succeeded, with deadly results. The incident that broke Israel's patience happened on March 11, 1978, when a squad of Palestinian terrorists from Lebanon hijacked a bus on a highway south of Haifa, on Israel's northern coast. They drove south toward Tel Aviv, brutalizing the bus passengers and firing indiscriminately out the windows at passing cars. Dozens of Israelis were murdered and scores were wounded before this Palestinian tour of terror was halted. Fed up with the incursions, on March 15, 1978, Israel launched Operation Litani.

This operation had two purposes: first, to bring the incessant bombardments of northern Israel to an end by driving the Palestinians out of artillery and rocket range, and second, to relieve the beleaguered Christians of southern Lebanon and assist the Lebanese army leader Major Sa'ad Haddad, who commanded the Christian soldiers when the Lebanese army disintegrated. With his help Israel could establish a security zone where his South Lebanese Army could protect the local inhabitants and keep the PLO from reoccupying the area and hitting Israel.

Although the Palestinians were full of swagger and arrogance when they bullied unarmed Lebanese Christians, they fled in panic before the Israelis. Most of their Muslim leftist allies threw their militia uniforms away, hid their AK-47s, and blended back into the population of Elkhiam and other Muslim towns and villages in southern Lebanon. In a few days the Israelis achieved their first goal, driving the Palestinians

north of the Litani River. The Israelis withdrew from Lebanon three
months later after achieving their second goal of strengthening the
South Lebanese Army. By the time Israel withdrew, the area protected
by Major Haddad had expanded from three small enclaves to a continuous strip of land along the Israel-Lebanon border.

The Lebanese Shia sect of Islam had not yet been infected by the
radical pan-Islamist fundamentalism that would sweep the Muslim
world in the wake of the Iranian Revolution one year later. Although the
main Shia militia, Amal, supported the National Front/revisionist coalition politically, it did not participate in the opening stage of the war.

Israel negotiated an agreement with the United Nations under
which the United Nations Interim Force in Lebanon was to take a position between the PLO and the SLA security zone. (In practice,
UNIFIL was to prove less than helpful.) The UN troops ended up
with a halfhearted policy in dealing with PLO or Muslim terrorists
trying to get into the security zone and Israel. If they caught a terrorist
trying to pass through their area they would take his gun away and return it to his militia leader. All he had to do was get it and try again. I
don't think he was told to go stand in the corner unless it was for failing his mission in the first place. If he had a bomb, the UN would keep
that but let him go without any form of detention or punishment. The
UN troops seldom ventured outside of their bases unless they were in
a supply convoy or relocating. None of them wanted to be killed in
someone else's war.

As a result of Operation Litani, life became a little easier. Although
there were still occasional rocket and artillery attacks (most of which
originated from the area "controlled" by the United Nations), the
shelling was not as bad as it used to be. You could still be killed by the
occasional shell falling out of the sky, but at least the snipers were
gone. Life could return to something that resembled normal. School
was much safer to attend now. But I would no longer be attending the
private one I had gone to all my life. My parents could not afford to
send me there anymore. Now I would be going to public school.

Money was scarce, as I was finding out. I had some idea that we had money in a bank but were unable to get to it because of the fighting. What was obvious was that Papa was not working. The restaurant was closed and no one was renting apartments. I did not know that we had no income from the government because Papa had collected his retirement all at once. I thought that it was not coming because of the war and problems in our government.

I came home one day to see a strange man in the room with my parents. My mother was handing him a handful of gold teeth and bracelets. The man handed her cash in return. I realized my mother was selling the gold fillings in her teeth and whatever jewelry she had left to help pay for food and the books and other things I needed for school. I now understood why she and my father had gone to the dentist the month before and got all their teeth pulled out and decided to wear dentures. After the man left I asked her, "Why are you doing that?" She told me that we were getting low on money. I couldn't understand what had happened to all the money we had in the bank. I knew we were wealthy. After all, we had servants before the war and lived a good life. The little money that had survived was gone. That's when they told me about what had happened to my father's life savings: that it had burned when the house was bombed. I was shocked and frightened when I heard their words. I realized we had no hope. I couldn't get a job even if I wanted to, at least for six more years. My father was seventy-four years old now and deaf, and he had difficulty walking after four years of sitting endless hours in the humid, wet shelter. I realized I was going to have to take on more responsibility in the family.

We continued our bare existence with Israel's help and support. The opening of the border created needed commerce for many in the security zone. The crossing became known as "the Good Fence." The Israelis set up an office to process daily visas for the Lebanese who started going in for business and work. Many people from the security zone went to work inside Israel in many fields, including agriculture, hospitality, and the service industry. They were able to make a living, earn shekels, and revitalize our own little economy by spending their earnings in town. A few people became businessmen importing Israeli meat and chicken and selling it in the stores. Some entrepreneurs became money changers, or chauffeurs driving people to the border and back. My parents and I, however, couldn't take advantage of this work opportunity. They were very old and I was still too young. My only comfort was knowing that in case of any medical need we could turn to Israel, which was our only lifeline. Israel had opened its hospitals free of charge to any Lebanese in the security zone that needed medical help. Some people had open-heart surgery, brain surgery, and many other procedures that they otherwise would not have been able to get. As my parents were older and had no financial resources for medical care, Israel was the rock we could lean on. Most of us couldn't even go to any other hospital in Lebanon no matter the severity of the illness, because if we got out of the security zone, the Muslim militias would kill us as traitors.

While Israel created opportunity and breathed life into our existence, the combined forces of Muslims and the PLO suffocated any type of normal life. Because of their bombardment of our area, the major employment centers, such as the bank, the hospital, the electricity plant, the water plant, government offices, business offices, and the movie theater, were closed.

One technological development of the West that would influence and become a major factor in my life was television. Before the war I had always hated it when my father would get engrossed with the news in the evenings. Nobody could talk and nobody could change the channel. Now TV was a welcome diversion, a major form of entertainment, and a source of information. During our long days and nights in the bomb shelter we operated a small TV on a car battery. It was my window to the world. It was also my comparative window to cultures and societies in the Middle East. The greatest thing it showed me was the differences between how people and governments treated people in their countries.

On Israeli TV I saw people from the government visiting with schoolchildren my age and talking with them as if they were concerned about their well-being. I never saw anybody from my government come and visit with us. I sensed a greater equality between men and women in Israeli society than there was in Arab societies. Women seemed to be working side by side with men. I did not realize how the influence of television would eventually affect my opinions and then my behavior. As I slowly became Westernized in a society that lived according to Middle Eastern customs, I was setting myself on a collision course with my Arabic culture.

Whenever we were lucky enough to get a couple hours of electricity, I would watch not only the news but American programs such as *Dallas* and *The Love Boat* that ran on Israeli and Jordanian TV. I fell in love with the people, the language, the culture, and the music. There was an opulence on *Dallas* that was another world compared to the one I was living in. The romance and glamour of *The Love Boat* swept me far away from the regimented and restrictive nature of Middle Eastern courtship between men and women. What I really came away with was a determination to learn English. I knew that if I ever wanted to leave Lebanon and go to America, I had to speak the Americans' language. I considered it my ticket out of hell. I knew I would have to be ready with knowledge of the language so when the opportunity presented itself I would be able to use it.

TV became my English tutor. All the American shows were in English, with Arabic subtitles at the bottom of the screen. I would write the Arabic subtitles on the palm of my hands and then a phonetic rendering of whatever English word was spoken when the subtitle appeared. My second language, French, came in handy, helping me link subtitles in Arabic with what I heard. Since we were low on water and didn't shower daily, I would build up a big vocabulary on my hands and up and down my arms. Since there wasn't much to do during the day, I would study and practice the words and phrases on my "notebook" in my hours of endless boredom. I never got any real practical experience talking in English, but I had it all in my mind, ready to go. I got to the point where I was comfortable listening to the English dialogue and understanding a lot of it without reading subtitles. Despite the hopelessness and difficulty of the situation, I had a vision for my future and the will to figure out how to prepare for it.

As a result of the military support and social services provided by the Israelis, our way of life began to improve somewhat. We were getting electricity for about two hours a day now and water for about two hours every other day. However, the presence of the Israelis in southern Lebanon also meant more targets for the enemy. Now the Israelis were even closer to them, in their land, on their roads, and in their cities. Shelling attacks from the Islamic and Palestinian fighters began to increase as they adopted new tactics. Before, their barrages had been predictable. We would know when the Palestinians were going to attack, and an announcement could be made to alert the town. Shops and schools would close, and we would be able get to shelter before hell fell out of the sky. But now, everything would be peaceful, and then all of a sudden the world would explode. An attack might last for days, and then, just as suddenly, everything would go back to normal.

Just before Easter, 1982, we went without any shelling for twenty-two days. It gave us a glimmer of hope that perhaps we could prepare for a normal holiday. In Lebanon, Easter is the biggest holiday of the year for Christians, as big as Christmas is for Christians in the West. Mama was sewing me a velvet dress for the holiday—actually, modifying one of hers to fit me. As I stood in front of the mirror, trying it on so Mama could see where to adjust it, all I could think about was what Chuck would think when he saw me wearing it. Chuck and I had become very close. I was seventeen years old and he was twenty-two. We cared about each other a great deal. It wasn't love with goose bumps, but the kind of feelings that made me think about him all the time and worry about his safety. I would constantly pray for him. He looked out for me and cared about my parents.

In this year when normalcy seemed to be returning, I was able to be deeply involved with the church and again sing in the choir. We practiced every day for a whole month before the holidays. After choir practice we would hang out with the priests and the nuns. We teenagers would eat, joke around, bake cakes, and prepare gifts for the needy. Chuck was Greek Orthodox, and he also sang in his church choir. After his practice, he would meet me at my Maronite church, and then we would walk home together.

The week before the holiday, everything felt different. Since we hadn't been shelled for twenty-two days, we started getting used to living normally. We felt free and happy to be alive, appreciating every minute of those days of calm. I don't know what it was. Maybe because spring was in the air. Maybe it was something about being seventeen. Maybe it had something to do with my special friendship with Chuck.

Chuck and I met every day that week, without arranging it. It had become a routine. He would walk with me to my church up the hill about fifteen minutes away, and we would talk and laugh—he had a great sense of humor. He would pick flowers from the side of the road and give them to me. We weren't in love, exactly, but we knew that there was something deeper that we couldn't explain. We liked flirting with each other, knowing it was safe. We knew we cared a lot about each other and that we wouldn't do something stupid that would mess up our relationship. As we walked back every night, we would talk about school and our dreams, what our plans for the future would be if we stayed alive. It's funny—we always included the possibility of death in our plans. Death was a part of our lives. Chuck would talk about how he would like to finish college if he stayed alive, and I would tell him about how I wanted to become a doctor if I survived the war. This type of conversation seemed very normal to us.

I had sung a solo at Saturday's midnight mass. Afterward, Chuck came over to praise me for my singing. I noticed he wore a blue-and-yellow-striped Christian Dior sweater and brand-new pair of Pierre Cardin pants. I complimented him on his appearance. He kindly thanked me and told me how much he was looking forward to seeing me the next day all dolled up for Easter.

With a newfound sense of self-confidence I told him that he was going to like the way I looked. Chuck took my hands, looked deep into my eyes, and told me that his church service would be finished by twelve o'clock, and invited me to eat lunch at his house. I convinced him that we should be with my parents, since I was an only child. He accepted, and left with a big grin on his face, saying, "Looking forward to seeing you tomorrow."

"Me too," I replied.

The next day was beautiful—the perfect Easter Sunday. I woke up at seven o'clock. Mama and Papa were already in the family room having their coffee and milk for breakfast. I kissed them and wished them a happy holiday. They hugged me. That morning, I think, I was the happiest girl in the world. I drank my milk really fast because I wanted to get dressed and go to the church for an early rehearsal. My parents were going to follow an hour later.

I put on my dress. As I stood in front of the long mirror, fixing my hair, a few rays of sunshine made their way through the curtain and shone straight on my face. The dress showed my figure very well. It fit tight across my breasts, and highlighted my thin waist and beautiful legs. My long black hair fell down my back, stopping at my hips. I felt beautiful, perhaps for the first time in my life. All I could think of was Chuck. I imagined the look on his face when he saw me in this dress. I knew he would ask to kiss me. I just knew it. I could feel it. Chuck would want me to know that he was falling in love with me. I could just tell, especially after all that had been happening between us for the last week. I looked in the mirror for the final approval and left for church after kissing my parents good-bye.

The church filled up very quickly. Everyone wore new clothes. Fresh flowers were in abundance. The altar was beautifully decorated. The mass was perfect. But toward the end of the service, I noticed that a lot of men were talking to each other and then leaving the church in groups. I thought, Oh my God, here it comes. We are going to be put on alert. I thought the shelling was going to start again, but the priest didn't say anything. He usually interrupted mass to inform people of an alert to give us time to run to shelter.

When the service ended at twelve o'clock, everyone stood around

the front of the church talking. I went out hoping that Chuck had finished at his Greek Orthodox service early and would be in the crowd
waiting for me. He would know what was going on. I looked for him,
but he wasn't there. While I was going back inside the church to see if
he was looking for me there, I overheard a couple of people standing
by the door talking about the terrible explosion at the border of town.

"What explosion?" I asked. They told me that Group 8—Chuck's
group—had received a tip that the Palestinians, knowing that this was
a holiday, were trying to sneak into the back of town to attack. So the
young men had left church, got into their tank, and headed over to the
edge of town to see what was going on. The tank had gone over a land
mine planted on the side of the road, and the mine had exploded.
Three of the group were killed immediately and four others were
wounded. My heart stopped.

I tried to control myself as I asked if they knew the names of the
men who died. They said, "We heard Eli and Bassam were killed." Eli
and Bassam were Chuck's best friends, the ones who helped him free
my family when we were trapped in our bomb shelter. "And," they
added, "also Chuck . . . but nobody really knows for sure who's dead
and who's alive."

By the time they finished their sentence, the blood had stopped
pumping into my face. Chuck couldn't be dead. I ran to the street,
where Tony, a friend of ours, just happened to be passing by in his car.
I stopped him and asked if he had heard anything about Chuck. I told
him what I'd heard and suggested we drive to the Good Fence, the
border with Israel, because I had heard that the wounded were being
transported to Israel for treatment. I saw Mama before we left and
told her what had happened, and that I would be home for lunch. I
asked her to wait just another half an hour for me.

I hopped into Tony's car and we drove to the Good Fence, which
was about a ten-minute drive south. When we arrived, the ambulance
was in the process of unloading bodies. We got out of the car and walked
toward the ambulance. It was horrifying. Blood was everywhere. I was
able to recognize the two bodies lying in the ambulance as Eli and

Bassam. Eli had lost both of his legs and one arm, and the top of his head was gone. Bassam had lost one leg, two arms, and his stomach area. The four who had been wounded were being taken to the hospital. Chuck wasn't in the ambulance with the other two bodies, so obviously he wasn't dead. Thank God, I thought; being wounded is better than dead.

We ran to the doctor to see where Chuck had been sent. The doctor said he was still in the ambulance. We said, "No. Only the dead bodies were there, and Chuck wasn't there."

The doctor replied, "Yes he is," and turned his face away.

Tony and I looked at each other, puzzled, and ran back to the ambulance, where soldiers were bringing boxes for the bodies. We looked inside the ambulance after they pulled out Bassam and Eli, but there was nothing left but a big plastic bag. The soldiers pulled a third box up to the ambulance. As they slid the plastic bag into the box, I saw Chuck's name written on its side. And as they pulled the bag over, a human finger fell from it. Without thinking, I bent down, picked it up, and put it in the box with the rest of him.

And then I began to scream so loudly that it hurt my throat. I was hysterical. Tony had tears in his eyes and held my hand until we got to the car. We drove back home without saying a word.

Tony dropped me off at my parents' house and continued on to Chuck's house. When I told my parents, they began to cry. As we sat at the table to eat, we looked at the empty dish that was intended for Chuck. Mama had prepared the table before she left for church that morning.

The funeral was set for two thirty that same day, about an hour from the time we got the news. They wanted to bury the dead as fast as possible because in response to the attack, shelling was scheduled to begin at four thirty that afternoon.

The coffins were sealed because the bodies were so badly mangled. The boys' mothers screamed in agony, banging on the coffins, pleading to see their sons one last time.

That beautiful Easter had turned into a day of unbearable sorrow.

A few hours before, these three young men had been singing in the choir of the same church where their funeral was now being held. When they had left the church on their mission, they were still in their holiday clothes. They left, died, and within hours came straight back to church for their burial ceremony. The church was still decorated with flowers and white satin cloth, inside and out. People were still dressed in their holiday clothes; little girls, looking like little angels, still wore their traditional white satin Easter dresses.

I stood there in my velvet Easter dress next to Chuck's coffin for our last good-bye. I told him that I hadn't realized that morning when I put on my lovely new dress—the dress I couldn't wait for him to see—that I was dressing for his funeral. I cried bitterly as I leaned over his casket, holding on to it so tightly that I could hardly breathe. The funeral was over by three thirty in the afternoon. Then everyone left for their shelters for what turned out to be the beginning of a week of agony, bombing, and despair.

That night, I sat on my bed in the corner of the shelter, numb, listening to the explosions of the artillery shells and thinking about Chuck. My parents kept talking about how Chuck would always check in on us and look out for us. They recalled how Chuck and his friends had saved our lives. Now all three of our rescuers were dead. "How sad," I remember Papa telling Mama. "The old people who have lived a long life are still here sitting in a bomb shelter, and the young ones are dead. Why didn't God take us, and let them live?"

I looked at the flickering dying candle trying to burn just a little longer to maintain whatever small glow and thought how similar we were. I had tried to hold on to hope in those few peaceful weeks we had enjoyed, thinking I had a chance to live, to learn, to become something, and to enjoy life. But when I could touch hope, hope vanished in the midst of hate, violence, death, and intolerance. Just when I thought peace was possible I was robbed of my innocence in the most gruesome way. Hope was dying along with my dying candle.

5.

A LIFE-CHANGING
EXPERIENCE

The war had been raging now for seven years as the Western world watched. No one realized what the Christians in Lebanon were going through except the Israeli Jews. They had been facing this force of hatred ever since their inception. Just when I was about to give up on life, when hope died and despair overcame me, fate stepped in to alter my destiny and give me the drive and reason to fight for the life I wanted, desired, and deserved.

Our militia was so angered by the Easter attack that it launched an all-out retaliation attack against the Muslims and Palestinians and their villages. The Muslims fired back with renewed vigor. That's the Middle East: revenge upon revenge, and it's usually the civilians who pay the price.

For the next three months things were very uncertain. The fighting had escalated to an unprecedented point. The Palestinians were getting stronger and more aggressive with their attacks. They would start shooting when we least expected it. They would fire a barrage into town at seven thirty in the morning when kids were riding to school and parents were buying food and running errands.

At the same time the Israeli army had set up an artillery base on the hill across the valley from our town. We knew something was up just by looking at the massive construction and listening to the heavy artillery barrages that the Israelis launched. This artillery base was our main defense against the Muslims and the Palestinians. Israel had brought in 155-millimeter cannons that shook our house when they fired. This was the same type of weapon that the combined forces of Syrians, Muslims, and Palestinians had been using against us for four years. We knew things were not going to get better any time soon.

At least after seven years the shelter had become a home of sorts. It was equipped with a radio and the small black-and-white battery-operated TV. Papa used it mostly to watch news programs. There were other things we could do to pass the time and create an atmosphere of normalcy. We had yarn for knitting, thread for crocheting, and old magazines and a few books to read. My father would scavenge wire from telephone poles that were blown up and strip out the smaller colorful wires inside. I would use them to weave baskets and plates using the different colors to create designs. We could play cards and backgammon, which the Lebanese call *tawle*. And, most important, we weren't starving. We had enough dried meat, beans, rice, and dried fruit to survive. Mama made it a point to prepare one major meal a week, after church on Sunday, and we looked forward to it because there would be some sort of meat served. Sometimes, if the weather was nice and bombs permitting, we could emerge from the shelter and sit on the porch of our ruined house.

Israel was finally fed up with the low-intensity war of attrition that the PLO and Syrian proxy militias were waging from southern Lebanon across the border into northern Israel. In 1970, well before we began living in a bomb shelter, the communities of northern Israel started digging and building their own bomb shelters. Now Israel decided that there needed to be a more thorough effort than 1978's Operation Litani to protect its northern border. A plan to drive the PLO all the way to Beirut and to expel it from Lebanon was put together. The PLO had been terrorizing not only northern Israel, but the entire population of southern Lebanon. In addition to fighting the SLA, made up of both Christians and Shia Muslims, the PLO had been engaged in bitter, open warfare against the Shiite Amal militia for most of the last three years for control of Lebanon. If the puppet Lebanese government, the Syrian puppet master, and the UN's worthless UNIFIL "peacekeeping force" would do nothing to stop the PLO reign of terror, Israel had to.

For its efforts to protect itself Israel would be bitterly criticized around the world and on the floor of the UN General Assembly. In Lebanon, the majority in both the Christian and Muslim communities rejoiced, but especially among the Christians.

For many in the West, June 6, the anniversary of the beginning of the liberation of Europe from Nazi domination, has a particular significance concerning the overthrow of oppression. For us, June 6, 1982, would come to share a similar meaning. It was the day Israel launched Operation Peace for Galilee, pushing PLO and Muslim forces north toward Beirut. Out of range of their artillery, we were free to come out of our bomb shelters and back to rebuilding our lives.

It began as a typically beautiful Mediterranean spring day, except for the war. We were serenaded by a choir of birds, interrupted occasionally by the sound of shelling somewhere off to the northwest. We'd been trapped in our shelter for three days, and the night before, the shelling had been particularly bad.

Since we'd gotten no sleep because of the shelling, I slept in until almost nine o'clock. By the time I got out of bed, both Mama and Papa were out of the shelter. Mama was making breakfast on the stove in her old kitchen, and Papa was sitting on the porch, having coffee in the sun and listening intently to Radio Monte Carlo, which was reporting large numbers of Israeli troops and equipment massing along the border as if to invade Lebanon. I began to say, "Maybe that's why the shelling stopped this morning," but I was interrupted by the blast of a 155-millimeter shell exploding fifty meters away from the house. Before I had a chance to start another thought, a second shell exploded in the backyard, and then it just started raining bombs. I screamed and dragged my father inside the door. Mama was already huddled on the floor. Shrapnel was flying everywhere. The three of us crawled on the floor to the hallway, but we were not safe there, either. We had to make it back to the shelter. We decided that my father should run first, because he could not hear, and he was the weakest of the three of us. I followed next, and then Mama. Two shells exploded ahead of me next to Papa as we ran for the shelter. I tackled him and threw both of us down in the dirt as shrapnel flew in all directions. I dragged Papa to his feet and held him up by his arm as we resumed our desperate dash for the shelter. I had lost track of Mama. As Papa and I reached the shelter door, I pushed him inside and turned to look for Mama. I could not see her in the smoke and dust, so I yelled for her to hurry up. Between the explosions I heard her say that she was coming. I turned to tell my anxious papa that she was on her way, but before I finished my sentence a shell exploded just in front of the shelter. The impact picked me up from where I was standing just inside the door and threw me on the bed. I thought that the explosion must have killed Mama. I picked myself up off the bed, ran to the door of the shelter, and started calling her name, but there was no answer.

Mama was outside somewhere in the smoke and flying shrapnel. I completely ignored the shells exploding everywhere and ran out of the door to look for her. I found her stretched out on the ground using her arms to pull her body toward the shelter one arm length at a time. She was covered in blood and leaving a bright red trail behind her in the dirt. I grabbed her arm and dragged her the rest of the way, pulled her through the door, and laid her on the bed. Blood was gushing from a deep wound in her left shin. I tore the sleeve off my pajamas and tied it around her leg to stop the bleeding. Then I checked the rest of her body, but I could find no other wounds.

Mama started to faint. Shock was quickly setting in. I tried to talk to her to keep her awake, but she couldn't talk anymore. She was losing too much blood, too fast. I was afraid that she had pieces of shrapnel lodged in her leg. I told Papa we had to get her to a hospital. I wanted to run outside to get us help. He refused to let me out of the shelter, saying, "I don't want to lose both of you at the same time. You stay here until the shelling stops and then you go outside." He started crying and hugging my mother. He kept repeating that we would take care of her and that we loved her.

Again I told Papa I was going for help. I had to try. I told him not to leave the shelter until I came back, no matter what happened. Mama tried to take my hand to stop me from going outside, but she was so weak she could barely move. I went back, took her hand, and kissed it. I told her I couldn't just sit there and watch her die. As I dove through the door and into the dirt and began crawling across the yard, I heard my father's voice cry out from the darkness inside the shelter, "Please be careful. May God protect you."

I made my way down toward Papa's restaurant. When I reached the ruined restaurant I pressed my body up against the broken walls for whatever shelter they could offer. Shells were exploding everywhere and the air was filled with shrapnel and debris. One shell exploded nearby, picking me up and banging me against the wall. Through the noise of the blast I heard a tank approaching at high speed. I struggled to my feet and ran around the building to the side of the road and started jumping up and down screaming for help. The tank roared by so fast that no one saw or heard me.

Over the next hour I found cover from the shells and ran out for the five or six tanks that passed by, but the result was the same each time. I was falling into despair. Sad thoughts were going through my mind. I was thinking about Chuck and his death. I wondered if he could see me or knew what I was going through. If he were still alive, I knew, he would come and take care of my parents and help me. But he was gone. Nobody came and checked on us anymore. Why did I have to live like this? Why didn't I have brothers or sisters to help me through this? Why did the entire burden need to be on my shoulders with nobody to help? And now my mama had been injured. Maybe it was my turn, now, here, in the middle of this shelling. There was no happiness in life.

I was about to crawl back to the bomb shelter to check on Mama and Papa when a battered car drove up in front of the restaurant. A young soldier jumped out and started running up the shortcut past our shelter toward the militia base. As the car was about to race off, I leaped in front it, waving my arms and crying. The driver blew the horn and skidded sideways, almost hitting me. The driver emerged from the car, and the young soldier ran back down the hill. I was re-lieved and hysterical at the same time. I told them my mother was se-verely wounded and she needed to get to a hospital. Before I finished explaining the situation they were running for the shelter.

When we entered the shelter, Mama was unconscious. The two men carried her to the car to take her to the hospital. I told Papa to stay put until I returned. I promised him that as soon as I learned something I would let him know. I told him God must have sent these two soldiers to save us and therefore everything would surely be okay.

As we approached the hospital in Marjayoun we could see it was be-ing shelled. This was not unusual. Even though it was well known and well marked as a medical facility, it had been a favorite target of the Muslims and PLO since early in the war. As a result, it was barely func-tioning as a hospital. It was vacant with the exception of a few nuns who lived in one undamaged wing and provided rudimentary nursing ser-vices. Since 1979 the Israeli army had stationed a doctor and three or four medics there. In between barrages, these Israelis looked after our general health, and supplied us with medication and prescription drugs. When the shells and rockets started exploding, they could provide emergency treatment, but the hospital was just not equipped to take care of seriously wounded patients. Anyone who required complex or extended care had to be transported south to a hospital in Israel.

As we drove up, the Israeli doctor and some nurses were working feverishly on two other casualties that had arrived shortly before us. When we opened the car door to get my mother out a medic took one look at Mama and shouted over his shoulder to summon another medic. Then he pulled a bandage out and applied direct pressure on the gash in Mama's leg while he asked me if she had any other injuries. By the time I told him I didn't know, the two medics were carrying her toward the sandbagged entrance to the hospital. I followed right be-hind. They carried her quickly and gently as one held the bandage on her wound and the other examined her for further injuries. I was amazed at how well they moved together and calmly worked together while shells were still exploding all around us. It was almost as if they were doing a delicate dance amid the chaos, a ballet of life choreographed to a symphony of death.

The Israeli doctor knew immediately that all they could do was stabilize her and send her to Israel. I couldn't let her go to Israel alone. But I was still dressed in my pajamas with one sleeve torn off, and one of my slippers was missing, lost somewhere in the dash to the hospital. I asked the doctor how soon she would be sent to the hospital. He told me that the ambulance had just left for the border, and by the time it was back in half an hour Mama would be ready to go.

I was able to beg a ride back to our bomb shelter. The shelling had calmed down a little, but Papa was still inside. He was overjoyed to see me, crying and hugging me as I walked in the door. He was sure Mama and I had been killed. I hurriedly changed my clothes and packed a bag for Papa. I told him that I was going with Mama to Israel, and that he could stay with a friend in town who would look after him for a few days. He started to protest, but he was too weak and tired. He pulled sixty lira (about fifteen dollars) out of the mattress and said, "Here is some money in case you need it." This was the first time I had ever touched money. We'd lived in the bomb shelter since I was ten. I'd never had any occasion to use it.

By the time we dropped Papa off and arrived back at the hospital, Mama was already loaded in the ambulance. I jumped in and we started the ten-minute drive south to the border with Israel. I was relieved to see that the driver was a friend of the family, named Kamal. As soon as we arrived at the border I went into the control office to get visas to enter Israel while Kamal and Israeli soldiers switched Mama to an Israeli ambulance. This took less than five minutes. Our friend Kamal walked to my side and asked me if I had any money for the ambulance fee. An innocent teenager who knew nothing about money or fees, I took out the bills that my father had given me and asked him how much it cost. He looked at what I had in my hand and took half. I was left with only thirty lira to live on and pay for whatever other expenses Mama and I might have. I had no idea what to expect. Tearfully I thanked him for driving us, and then I climbed into the Israeli ambulance.

The drive to the hospital inside Israel took about an hour. I felt alone and afraid and I didn't know if Mama would live or die. She was fading in and out of consciousness and moaning from pain. The ambulance driver was a middle-aged soldier. To my surprise, he spoke to me in Arabic, soothing me and reassuring me that Mama would be okay. He listened to the radio news reports and explained to me how the war was going in Lebanon. He told me he had a daughter my age, and she was worried about him too.

When we got to the hospital in Zefat, it was around two thirty in the afternoon. As the Israeli medical orderlies carried Mama into the hospital on a stretcher, I walked around the ambulance to pay the fee to the driver. I took what remained of the money out of my pocket, sure that it would not be enough. If the ten-minute drive from the hospital in Marjayoun to the Israeli border had cost thirty liras, I was sure, this ride had to cost much more. I held the money out to him and asked how much we owed. He looked at me with surprise and said, "You don't owe anything. The ambulance ride is free, a service from us to you. Keep your money. You'll certainly need it. I hope everything goes well with you. I wish your mother a speedy recovery."

I thanked him from the bottom of my heart and thought: What an honest and ethical man! He could have taken my money, and no one would have known the difference. Then I thought about the Lebanese driver Kamal, supposedly a friend of my family, who had taken my father's money. And the ambulance wasn't even his: it had been given to the Lebanese by Israel. Yet, he had taken advantage of Mama's injury to take our money. I was struck by the contrast between his behavior and that of the Israeli ambulance driver, a total stranger to me. This was the first of many lessons I learned about the compassion, generosity, and morality of the Israelis. I stuffed the bills back into my pocket and ran to catch up with Mama.

All of my senses were assaulted by the scene that greeted me inside the hospital. Even seven years of war in southern Lebanon had not prepared me for such an awful spectacle. The emergency room and the corridor leading to the rest of the hospital were overflowing with wounded people: Israeli soldiers; Lebanese, both Christians and Muslims; even Palestinians. There was blood everywhere. The air was filled with the screams of the injured, the shouts of medical personnel, and the *whoop, whoop, whoop* of helicopters landing outside with more casualties.

As I hurried across the room to where Mama was lying on a gurney I looked around to see the others receiving care. I was amazed that the Israelis were providing medical treatment to Palestinian and Muslim gunmen. I could understand why the Israelis would help Lebanese Christians. We were their allies. But these Palestinians and Muslims were sworn, mortal enemies, dedicated to the destruction of Israel and the slaughter of Jews. Yet, Israeli doctors and nurses worked feverishly to save their lives. Each patient was treated solely according to the nature of his or her injury. The doctor treated my mother before he treated an Israeli soldier lying next to her because her injury was more severe than his. The Israelis did not see religion, political affiliation, or nationality. They saw only people in need, and they helped.

When I reached Mama's side, my fear for her life pushed these thoughts out of my mind. The doctor examining her saw me approach and said something in Hebrew. When I didn't respond he asked in English, "Is this your mother?" I nodded my head, and he shouted something over his shoulder, again in Hebrew. A nurse hurried over and in perfect Arabic asked my name. I told her and she said, "Brigitte, my name is Lea. I'll find out how your mother is. Don't worry. We'll take good care of her." The doctor spoke to her in Hebrew for what felt like forever but was probably no more than twenty seconds. Then she translated for me. In addition to losing a great deal of blood, my mother had suffered serious damage to the blood vessels and nerves of her leg, and her thighbone might be cracked or broken. Her injuries were serious but not immediately life-threatening. She would have to remain in the hospital. Depending on her progress, she might be able to go home in four or five days. Nurse Lea told me she was assigned to the case so she could translate for the doctors and keep me informed of Mama's progress.

The doctor turned his attention to another patient, and they took Mama off in one direction for X-rays. Lea told me that I couldn't stay with her because the X-ray area was already too crowded. She said she would take me to Mama's hospital room and that Mama would be there within a half hour. Suddenly, in the midst of the chaos, I burst into tears. Lea hugged me and said, "Don't worry, Brigitte. Your mother will be all right."

Mama's room was on the fourth floor. It was already occupied by two Lebanese ladies, one Muslim and one Druze. Lea introduced us and sat me down in a chair next to the one empty bed. She told me she was going to check on Mama, and that while she was gone I should sit back in the chair, close my eyes, breathe slowly and deeply, and try to relax.

I followed her orders, except for the part about relaxing. I was exhausted and terrified, somewhere between hysteria and delirium. Images of the day kept ricocheting around like shrapnel inside my head. I worried about Mama. Then I worried about Papa—how could I have left him in the middle of that hell? And then I worried about Mama some more. I hurt everywhere, inside and out. After twenty-five minutes that seemed to be another eternity, Lea walked through the door to my side and put her hands gently on my shoulders. She whispered in my ear, "I told you. She's going to be fine," as they rolled Mama into the room. If Lea had not been holding my shoulders, I would have fallen out of the chair. Mama didn't look fine to me. She was almost as white as the sheets that they laid her on, and these were the whitest sheets I'd seen in seven years. Lea sensed the panic she saw in my eyes as I looked at Mama, who seemed to have needles and tubes stuck in her everywhere. Lea gently massaged my shoulders and explained, "This one is a blood transfusion and this one is a saline solution, and this one is an antibiotic and this one is for pain." In my hysteria looking at my Mama, it sounded like a bizarre nursery rhyme.

I broke out crying again, but this time not from fear and uncertainty, but because of the compassion and love being bestowed upon me. For the first time in my life, I experienced a human quality that I knew my culture would not have shown to its enemy. I experienced the values of the Israelis, who were able to love their enemy in their most trying moments. Lea didn't even know whether I was a Lebanese Christian or a

Muslim, or a Palestinian. I realized at that moment that I had been sold a fabricated lie by my government and culture about the Jews and Israel that was far from reality. I knew for a fact, as someone raised in the Arab world, that if I had been a Jew in an Arab hospital, I would have been lynched and then thrown to the ground, and joyous shouts of "Allahu Akbar" would have echoed through the hospital and the surrounding streets.

I took Mama's hand and gave it a little squeeze. I may have imagined it, but I thought I felt her give my hand a weak squeeze in return. For the first time since the shelling had begun that morning, I thought we both would live, at least a little while longer.

The doctor had said Mama might have to be here for four or five days. I knew that as long as we were in this hospital we would not be bombed or shelled. This, in and of itself, had a psychological effect that is impossible to describe. After seven years I had forgotten what is was like to live without war. The threat of imminent death had been my constant companion, physically, mentally, and emotionally, since I was ten years old. Every thought of life was shadowed by the fear of death. To have this shadow suddenly removed, even if for only four or five days, would be a relief. But I was simply too numb to enjoy it yet.

I thought about Papa, still in Lebanon. I knew he would be out of his mind with worry about both of us. I had to find a way to let him know that we had made it to the hospital. From this point on I was confident that Mama would be okay. The Israelis would feed her and take care of her. I wasn't so sure what I was going to do for myself. I was tired, dirty, and hungry. I had not brought any food with me. I had no change of clothes. I didn't even have a comb or a toothbrush. I had only thirty lira left, and I thought I would need that for the trip back to Lebanon. But I figured I would be able to scrounge something, and besides, I thought five days was not such a long time to go without eating.

Thoughts of the day again filled my mind, but the memory of explosions and blood were slowly replaced by reflections on the compassion and generosity that I'd seen the Israelis exhibit over and over, all day long. My mind kept returning to the realization that the Israelis were providing lifesaving medical services to Palestinian and Muslim gunmen who had been injured in the process of trying to kill Israelis. It suddenly dawned on me that the efforts of the Israelis were not just isolated, individual acts of compassion. Individual Israelis drove the ambulances and performed the medical services, but this was possible only because the Israelis, as a state, as a society, as a culture, made a conscious, deliberate decision to devote precious resources to saving the lives of their enemies.

I was stunned at the implications of this revelation. I recalled all of the horrible things that I had heard about Jews in general and Israelis in particular as I was growing up: they were greedy, brutal, and treacherous; they were the cause of all misery in the world. I had seen with my own eyes that nothing could be further from the truth. I was to learn this lesson many times while Mama was in the hospital.

I also learned about hatred, intolerance, and bigotry. The Muslim woman who was in the room with my mother had stayed in the hospital for about twelve days. And even after ten days, when the doctors left the room after changing her bandages and checking on her in their morning tour, she said, with an evil, hate-filled look on her face, "I hate you all. I wish you were all dead." And for the first time in my life I saw evil. I realized that this Muslim couldn't love the Jews even after they had saved her life. And when you are unable to be grateful to the people who saved your life, you have no soul. When humans become devoid of compassion, a sense of forgiveness, and open-mindedness, when they surrender their humanity to hate, they become an evil force of darkness that is irreconcilable with hope, love, and peace.

Because of her weakened condition after living in a bomb shelter for seven years, Mama did not heal as quickly as she should have. After four days with no improvement in her condition, the doctors decided she needed an operation. By this time, I was desperate with hunger. I hadn't had a thing to eat except for a few scraps that Mama left on her food tray. While I waited for her to return from the operating room, Lea came in and asked me if I would like something to eat. I was ashamed to tell her how hungry I was, so I told her that I had been buying food in the canteen. She said that she had asked in the canteen and they had never seen me. Caught in my lie, mortified by shame and weak with hunger, I burst into tears and admitted I hadn't eaten in five days. She put her arm around me and said, "I thought so. Come on. Let's go get something to eat while the doctors fix your mother's leg."

As she led me toward the staff cafeteria, all of the floor nurses greeted both of us by name. She asked me how they knew me and I explained that I'd been acting as an unofficial translator between the patients and the doctors whenever there were no other translators available. The patients would speak to me in Arabic, and I would translate what they said into the English I had learned from American TV shows. She looked at me with mock sternness and asked, "Brigitte, are you trying to take away my job?" She could tell from the look of horror on my face that I didn't know she was kidding, so she hugged me and told me she thought it was wonderful. Not only that, she said she would add my name to the list of official hospital volunteers so I would be able to eat in the staff cafeteria three times a day. All of that watching television and writing on my arm was paying off.

When we got back to the room, someone had set up a small cot at the foot of Mama's bed so I wouldn't have to sleep in the chair anymore. This made me happier than my newly full stomach because that chair had been was the most uncomfortable one I had ever sat in. Then I saw a small bag sitting under the cot. Inside the bag I found a toothbrush, toothpaste, a comb, a hair clip, four new pairs of underwear, and a set of clothing: a skirt and a blouse. Outside of my own family, I had never seen such thoughtfulness and generosity.

As it turned out, Mama was in the hospital for almost three weeks. During that time I learned a great deal about the ethics and values of the Israelis. There were also constant reminders of the differences between the Israelis and the Arab world. After the mercy the Israelis showed their enemies, the thing that impressed me the most was the respect with which women were treated. I loved to watch the Israeli women, particularly the young women in the army. Some of them were only a year or two older than I. I was amazed at how assertive and self-confident they were. I did not yet understand the language that they spoke, but I could tell from their tone of voice and the way that they carried themselves that they felt accepted and respected by the men. Some of them were even officers! This was such a stark contrast to the Arab world in which I had grown up. No Arab soldier would take an order from a woman. In the Arab world, women were property. We were owned by our parents, and then we were reowned by our husbands. Israel was truly a different world.

As my mother's condition improved, and the time to leave the hospital approached, I became very depressed. I was very happy about Mama getting better, but I hated the idea of going back to Lebanon, the bizarre world of death and uncertainty. When the day arrived, I went to the nurses' station to check us out. Lea was there. She had tears in her eyes as she filled out Mama's papers and handed them to me. She took me in her arms and gave me a big hug, saying, "Don't forget about us, now." I looked at her and said, "I could never repay you. How could I ever forget you? Thank you for everything." The phone rang and she had to go back to work. As we turned away from each other, tears were running down our cheeks.

The one-hour ride back to the border was pure torture. The closer we got to the border, the more I tried to convince Mama that we should stay in Israel. I said we could sell our house and restaurant and bring Papa to live in Israel. She told me that was crazy, that no one would ever buy our bombed-out property, and Papa would never leave anyway. I knew she was right. I was racked with guilt over not wanting to go back to Lebanon. I knew that Mama and Papa could not make it on their own. It was my responsibility to take care of them.

I knew that, for now, I had to leave Israel. I also knew that someday I would come back. As we crossed the border back into our personal hell I realized that our stay in the Israeli hospital had not only saved my mother's life, but had changed mine.

6.

REBUILDING OUR LIVES

Papa was delighted when we returned from the hospital in Israel. He had missed us terribly, and we had missed him just as much. For the next few days the shelling stopped and our house was packed with people from ten in the morning till ten at night. It seemed as if the whole town came to visit my mother and check on her. The days went by fast for me because I was so busy serving coffee and cake to all the people who visited. Even though it was wonderful seeing so many old friends and being one family again, I felt much sorrow and emptiness over missing my new friends in Israel and the exciting and different lifestyle I had experienced for a few weeks. From now on I would compare everything that happened to me in Lebanon with what I had experienced in Israel. War and peace, fear and tranquillity, bias and tolerance, close-mindedness and open-mindedness, inequality and equality ... now that I was back in Lebanon, many nights I cried myself to sleep.

For a while, there was no more fighting in our region, no more shelling and no snipers to hide from. Israel had pushed the Palestinians and their few remaining Muslim allies all the way to Beirut, so their rockets and artillery could no longer reach us. Mama had been injured by the last barrage from the town of Nabatiyah on the second day of Israel's Operation Peace for Galilee. When Mama and I returned home, the Israeli siege of Beirut was in its third week. In southern

Lebanon we were relatively unaffected by the turmoil up north. As a result of the Israeli military presence, roads opened up all over southern Lebanon. It was now safe for us to travel without being kidnapped or killed at Muslim checkpoints.

We came out of the shelter and began to rebuild our lives. Living in our house instead of the bomb shelter immeasurably improved the quality of our life. We were now able to cook a variety of foods with our gas stove, and have coffee any time we wanted to. More important, we could now bathe and go to the bathroom whenever necessary. It is amazing how the little things in daily life that most people take for granted have an impact on how we feel and our outlook on life.

The frequent shelling had taken a huge toll on our utilities. Electricians worked every day fixing the cables, transformers, and poles so that electricity could be restored. When they finished, electric power was available for only a few hours a day. Electricity was rationed between towns because there was only one functioning power station in the area. Repairs were made on the water system so the pipes could deliver water to our houses for household chores such as cleaning, bathing, and washing dishes. However, it was six months before the water system could deliver water that was good enough for drinking. During that time, we still had to go down to the spring for drinking water.

We thought the war was over, or at least we hoped so. Papa started fixing the window shutters ruined by shrapnel. He bought cement to fix the cracks in our walls. However, hope that the war was ended was not strong enough to convince him to replace the glass in our windows. Plastic sheeting would keep out the wind and let in some light, but glass would turn into shrapnel if the bombs came back.

My mother's leg was getting better, slowly but surely. She could now move around in the house, water her plants, and do a little laundry. The injury on her shin had left a big long scar. It hurt my mother to see her shin look like that. In Lebanon older woman do not wear pants, so Mama could not cover the scar, which was above her ankle and visible no matter what she wore. Even though the scar was obviously not her fault, she felt great shame.

The economic situation in town improved as people emerged from their shelters. There was a whirlwind of weddings, and all of the new-lyweds started looking for houses to rent. Papa, old and weak as he was, worked himself to exhaustion repairing our three apartments so they could be rented. They soon filled up. Papa also rented the restaurant to a husband and wife who returned to Lebanon from Kuwait, where they had lived since the beginning of the war.

My days were sad and my heart was broken because I missed the friends I had made in Israel. I spent most of my time looking at their pictures and the other reminders that I had brought back with me: clothes, books, lipstick, a pair of sunglasses. These were simple, every-day things, but each one represented a separate thought, a separate gesture of generosity from an Israeli to a stranger.

After the electricity was restored for four hours per day, we were able to watch the news on TV. The images and lies regarding the Is-raelis were shocking, and couldn't have been further from reality. The Palestinian and Muslim propaganda PR machine had launched a full-blown attack against Israel.

The Palestinians and Muslims were eager to offer theatrical perfor-mances in front of the TV cameras. They would beat their chests and wail about Israeli bombardment of their homes. Even Muslims who had received lifesaving medical treatment in Israel cursed the "bar-baric" Israeli enemy. The Palestinians screamed and yelled about Is-raeli "theft" of their "homeland." They swore in the name of Allah that they would destroy Israel and slaughter the Jews.

The blind hatred and victimhood mentality of the Palestinians to-ward Israel was so obvious that any educated and experienced Western journalist should have been able to see through it in a second. How-ever, journalists, both Lebanese Muslims and Westerners, broadcast to Lebanon and the rest of the world the Palestinians' distorted version of the war without checking its validity or accuracy, or even its relation-ship to reality, although that is their responsibility. The Christians of southern Lebanon barely had any media attention. Few journalists came to the security zone to interview any of us. When they did they referred to the SLA in derogatory terms, hardly a neutral journalistic position. No journalist visited any Israeli hospitals and interviewed any of us there. There was no mention whatever in broadcasts of the incessant cross-border artillery and rocket bombardments and terrorist infiltrations which provoked Israel into entering Lebanon. There wasn't a word about the Israeli humanitarian aid to the Lebanese. There was no mention of the Israelis giving lifesaving medical treatment to wounded Lebanese and even Palestinian gunmen in Israeli hospitals. There was no mention of the unprecedented mercy and compassion that the Israelis had shown to a relentless, brutal enemy. Every media outlet that we heard blamed Israel for protecting itself, painting Israel as the aggressive monster bent on killing and inflicting pain on the poor Palestinians living peacefully and suffering in their refugee camps along with the Lebanese population.

Their bias was shocking. The media reported a one-sided story, focusing only on the Palestinians and Muslims whose lives had been destroyed by Israel. I thought, What about our lives, which had been destroyed by the Muslims and the PLO? What about the massacres, slaughter, rape, and torture of Christians and the destruction of our churches by Muslims shouting "Allahu Akbar"? What about Lebanese democracy now under the thumb of the Syrians? What about the people of Lebanon, who were so open-minded, tolerant, and fair? What about the hatred, intolerance, and bigotry of the Palestinians who were given refuge in Lebanon, and then destroyed and terrorized what was once the beacon of culture, education, and modernity in the Middle East?

While the Arab channels were broadcasting a hatefest demonizing Israel, Israeli television was showing the humanitarian aid that was given to the Lebanese. We were able to watch Jordanian, Lebanese, and Israeli newscasts one after the other. The Israelis aired interviews of officials talking peace and the initial negotiations with Lebanon over a peaceful coexistence. Even though they also aired stories about their bombing of Palestinian camps, they never gloated about their successful attacks, as Arab news anchors did, as they smiled when reporting

Israeli casualties. They reported balanced news that showed Israel in both a good and a bad light. The Israelis also showed positive stories of Lebanese rebuilding their lives, reopening their stores, which had not been in business in years, and resuming their daily lives. Israel showed stockpiles of weapons given to the Muslims and Palestinians by Iran, the USSR, and Syria.

Two momentous international events had occurred during the seven years that my family and I lived in the bomb shelter. First was the Israeli-Egyptian peace agreement of 1979. In exchange for full withdrawal from the Sinai, which Israel had captured in the 1967 Six-Day War, Egypt "normalized" relations with Israel. Although it has turned out to be a very cold peace between the two countries, the accommodation between Israel and the most populous and powerful state in the Arab world effectively eliminated the possibility of a major war between Israel and the Arab world.

The second event, which had the most profound effect on Lebanon and the world, was the Iranian Islamic revolution of 1979. Prior to this time, although there was friction and sometimes fighting among the various religious communities in Lebanon, they all saw themselves as Lebanese. After the Iranian Revolution, Muslims throughout the world began to see themselves only as Muslims, with a religious duty to wage a holy war, a jihad, to make Islam supreme over the entire world. Fundamentalist hate ideology began to take hold in different parts of the world, inspired by the Iranian mullahs. Islamic terrorism began to escalate around the world. According to these radical Islamists, any civilization or culture that did not submit to Islam must be destroyed. In Lebanon, this led to the decline of the moderate Amal Shia militia and the rise of Hezbollah, the modestly named "Party of God." Hezbollah is made up of Lebanese Shia Muslims, but it is financed and supported by Iran and Syria. From its inception in 1982, Hezbollah has been as dedicated to the destruction of the United States as it has been to the domination of Lebanon. With the rise of Hezbollah, the turmoil in Lebanon mutated from a civil war over the future of Lebanon into one of the fronts in the worldwide jihad of radical Islam. Hezbollah today is one of the most lethal terrorist organizations in the world, with insurgent training centers spinning off terrorists worldwide.

Throughout Lebanon, talking politics was the national pastime. I watched men visiting my dad talk and noticed how they disagreed, and I compared their behavior to what I had observed in Israel. In Lebanon, the more people disagreed, the more they shouted and yelled and called each other insulting names, as if that were going to make their point more valid. I would contrast that with conversations I heard at the hospital between Israeli families who disagreed on many issues. Even though they passionately disagreed, they never called each other degrading names.

The more people visited us and the more I heard them talking, the more I realized how shallow and uninformed they were about Israel and Western culture. Of course, the main conclusion of every conversation was that the Lebanese war was an American-Israeli conspiracy, and if America wanted, it could stop it in three days. Both the Christians and Muslims believed this. This belief was repeated over and over by politicians at every opportunity in the Arabic media. The people believed it because they had no other perspective, as I'd had in Israel. The irrationality of the belief in conspiracy theories and lies presented by leaders and governments with hidden agendas is important to understand. People's subjective reality is far from the real situation. They believe ridiculous ideas, and logic simply isn't part of their thinking, which is why Western liberal reasoning isn't going to work.

As days passed, I became more disgusted with my culture. I began to compare my place as a female in Lebanese society to that of females in Israeli society. I recall a day when my cousin's husband, Shahine, came to drive my mother to the hospital, since we did not have a car. I was determined that I was going to have a good day. I was wearing a pair of shorts that Lea had given me, with a matching T-shirt and sandals. I felt beautiful, loved, and privileged to have met people like her. When Shahine walked through the door, I welcomed him with a big smile and told him how much we appreciated his help in driving us to the hospital. I asked him if he would like a cup of coffee before we left, and he said, "No, thank you. I have to get going."

I called my mother, who was already dressed, and informed him that we were ready. He looked at me with shock and said, "Aren't you going to get dressed?"

I said, "Oh no, I don't feel like dressing up today. We're only going to the hospital. This is cool and comfortable."

"I think you should go change." He said it like an order.

I said, "No, I am comfortable, I am not going to change."

"I will not drive you to the hospital looking like a slut. Go put something on that will cover your legs."

My mother intervened at that moment and asked me to go change. I said, "No way. If you don't like how I am dressed, you go to the hospital by yourself. I don't think I look like a slut. I wore this for three weeks in Israel. Nobody treated me like a slut."

Shahine screamed, "This is not Israel, this is Lebanon! If they don't have any morality over there, we have some."

This supposedly educated, not religious, middle-aged Arab man, and a family man at that, had decided I was not worthy of respect just because I wore shorts that showed half of my legs. Rather than worry about important things like my education, my values, my intellect, my character, and what I was going to accomplish in life, he was concerned with ancient tribal ideas of our family's honor, which depended on my sexual propriety. My poor mother was embarrassed and hurt. She insisted that I change because she needed me with her at the hospital. She was almost begging.

Feeling angry and degraded, I walked into my room to change my clothes. I started crying. If not for my mother, I would never have given in. Is it any wonder that Americans have gone to the moon and Israel became the strongest, most intelligent country in the Middle East? Arabic lack of development is because of Arabs like Shahine who spent their time worrying about nonsense. I swore that I would leave Lebanon as soon as I could, especially after the victory smile on Shahine's face telling me that now I looked worthy of respect. I couldn't understand how somebody could be judged on her appearance instead of her intelligence and what she had to offer her country and the world.

During the first few days I was in the hospital in Israel I earned the respect of everybody who came to know me. I helped many people by using a language that I had taught myself in a bomb shelter while watching TV programs. I checked people out of the hospital, translated for doctors, ran errands, changed people's clothes, and took them to the bathroom, none of which I had ever done before. People respected me for what I had to offer, for the attitude I had, and for going out of my way to help others, even my enemies the Palestinians.

I did not belong in Lebanon. I had no fond feelings toward the country. The more I thought about it, the more I realized I felt more at home in Israel, the place that had given me a glimpse of Western civilization. I related to the people there and the way they respected each other. Civilization can exist only where both culture and society respect and protect the rights of individuals, where self-improvement is encouraged, and where mutual respect is demanded, regardless of gender, religion, or ethnic identity.

Civilization is a collection of behaviors that people live by. It is a respect for education, for human beings. It is the desire for the improvement of self and the broadening of the mind without differentiating between a woman and a man. Civilization is the result of citizens who have been nurtured and encouraged to reach the ultimate goal of bettering themselves and others at every level. I did not feel civilization in Lebanon. The people there respected the shrewd, con artist businessman who made his wealth taking advantage of others. Bullies and corrupt politicians were respected, put on a pedestal as powerful. One thing that both Muslim and Christian cultures shared was their lack of respect and equality for women. A girl was never encouraged to continue her studies and have a career of her own if she chose to. Five friends of mine dropped out of college during their third year because they got married. It was time to have children and be wives. They would never be able to work, so education served as only a good addition to increase their value on the marriage market.

One of my friends wanted to become a doctor. Her brothers and family would laugh at her when she started talking about it. And we Christians considered ourselves an educated and sophisticated society because our boys went to the Sorbonne or Oxford to finish their education. We thought we were civilized, but we were acting like any other society that strongly discriminated against women.

Life in southern Lebanon improved greatly for us. The Israelis were able to drive away the radicals and bring peace to the areas they invaded. However, the PLO was turning Lebanon into a terrorist base, as the Taliban would do in Afghanistan in the mid-1990s. The world was not thanking the Israelis then, as no one thanked the Americans for driving out the Taliban from Afghanistan and giving people back their lives. No one thanked the Israelis later when they took out Saddam Hussein's nuclear plant in Iraq in 1982. And people don't think Hussein had any plans for nuclear WMD? Thank the Israelis for cutting that effort short. Now the same nuclear efforts are being made in Iran. Whenever Israel had the foresight to see what was happening concerning terrorist activity and did something about it, the whole world got upset. If the world had paid attention to the Islamic terrorists that Israel has been fighting for over fifty years, the whole world would not now be plagued with acts of terror against innocent civilians.

The Israeli siege of Beirut went on for ten weeks while the United States conducted negotiations between Israel and intermediaries in contact with Yasser Arafat. Arafat agreed to the expulsion of PLO gunmen from Beirut on condition that the thousands of Palestinians left behind in refugee camps would be protected by an international military force. The first contingent of the UN Multi-National Force (MNF), 350 French troops, arrived on August 21, 1982. The remainder of the MNF (800 Italian troops and 800 United States Marines) arrived August 25, and the expulsion of Palestinian gunmen from Beirut was completed.

On September 14, 1982, newly elected Lebanese president Bashir Gemayel was assassinated by a massive truck bomb. As a spontaneous act of retaliation against the PLO, Christian forces attacked the Palestinians.

Two of the most publicized massacres in Lebanon is the massacre at Sabra and Shatila. The notorious Sabra and Shatila camps were havens for all the terrorists on earth. From the Baader-Meinhof Gang to the Japanese Red Army Brigade, every terrorist organization at that time had some connection to Sabra and Shatila. In addition, kidnappers, drug dealers, and all sorts of criminals found refuge inside the camps. Lebanese were terrified of just the names of these two places.

The massacres during the Lebanese civil war were horrible. But mentioning Sabra and Shatila alone—about four hundred dead, not thousands—without mentioning the tens of thousands of victims of the Lebanese civil war is unjust and cruel to the memory of the dead Lebanese. One hundred thousand civilians were killed, 60 percent of those in massacres perpetrated against Christians. Palestinian militiamen started the killings in 1975, long before the 1982 Sabra and Shatila massacres. Beit Mellat, Deir Achache, Damour, Saadiyate, and many others were peaceful cities and villages where hundreds, if not thousands, of Lebanese were killed on their own land in their own country by armed foreigners, mostly Palestinians and Syrian Muslims. Of course those poor villagers could not afford the millions or billions of dollars that the PLO was paying for worldwide propaganda. So their tragedy remains mostly unknown, except among their families, their fellow citizens, and members of the local Lebanese news media.

The crimes perpetrated against unarmed civilians in Sabra and Shatila should not be excused. But then why not mention the "War of the Camps" of 1985–86, when for more than six months, armed Shiite elements from the Lebanese Amal militia supported by Shiite units of the Lebanese army surrounded Sabra and Shatila, then populated mostly by civilians with few armed elements. The Shiite militias bombarded the camps with heavy artillery and tanks, cut off power and water, and prevented food and medical help from reaching the camp population. It was far crueler than the 1982 attack. So where is the Palestinian and Arab outrage? Why ignore these abuses, which actually lasted much longer, and with more victims and more tragedies, than the 1982 ones?

Is it because the perpetrators were Shia Muslims? So crimes against humanity are now forgiven?

Meanwhile in Beirut the MNF would grow to a force of 5,200 French, Italian, British, and American troops. The United States government continued to conduct negotiations between Israel and the newly elected government of Lebanon.[1]

While the negotiations between the Israeli and Lebanese governments were progressing, Hezbollah, the newly formed radical Islamist militia supported by Iran and Syria, introduced a tactic that has become a worldwide plague. Although Yasser Arafat was the father of modern terrorism, it was Hezbollah that pioneered the use of suicide bombers.[2] On April 18, 1983, the driver of a truck packed with explosives detonated his vehicle in the driveway of the United States embassy in Beirut. Sixty-three people were killed and a hundred were wounded. This was Hezbollah's salutation to the United States.[3]

On October 23, Hezbollah struck again, this time both the barracks of the United States Marines and the headquarters of the French MNF contingent, with simultaneous suicide truck bombs. These attacks killed 241 marines and 58 French soldiers. Although the MNF remained for four more months, it was clear that it was not going to be able to maintain order and bring peace to Lebanon. The MNF left Beirut on February 26, 1984.

The fate of Lebanon was left in the hands of power broker Syria. The Islamic world was taking notes on how the mighty U.S. military, having been bloodied, had packed up and left. The lesson was not lost on one Osama bin Laden. America and the civilized world have failed repeatedly to understand the players and the cause of the Middle East conflict. When I heard President Bush speaking after September 11 about the Axis of Evil that included Iran and Syria, I wondered where the American government had been for the last twenty-some years. It was Iran that set up and financed Hezbollah and Syria that protected it. These events in Lebanon laid the groundwork for the war on terror we are fighting today. It sent a clear message to the terrorists that

America was blinded by its apathy. Because America was indifferent in dealing with Syria and Iran twenty-five years ago, today we're trying to stop Iran from developing a nuclear bomb and Syria from allowing insurgents into Iraq, not to mention Syria's possibly harboring Saddam's nukes. According to the number-two official in Saddam Hussein's air force, General Georges Sada, Iraq moved weapons of mass destruction into Syria before the war by loading the weapons into civilian aircraft in which the passenger seats were removed. "There are weapons of mass destruction gone out from Iraq to Syria, and they must be found and returned to safe hands," Mr. Sada said. The flights—fifty-six in total, according to Sada—attracted little notice because they were thought to be civilian flights providing relief from Iraq to Syria, which had suffered a flood after a dam collapse in June of 2002.[4]

As the exportation of Islamic fundamentalism from Iran began taking hold in Lebanon, I knew that I had no future in the country of my birth. My only hope to escape from the seemingly endless hell of Lebanon was to concentrate on my studies, especially English. I signed up for a typing course to learn how to type English so that I could get a job with a company that dealt with Israelis or Americans. I looked forward to my lessons two hours a week at the YWCA downtown. With each keystroke, I felt I was getting closer to my dream: to work in a company where I would meet people who were going to respect me for my character, for my abilities, for my mind and what I had to offer the world, not for my looks, my clothing, or the shallow "honor" between my legs.

As I matured, I occupied my mind and kept busy by becoming involved in the community and my church. I was a member of the art club and acted in two plays. I was in charge of eighty Scouts, girls and boys aged ten to thirteen. I supervised their involvement in the festivities in town during the holidays, and trained and directed them during the parades and community events. I was one of the founders of the Red Cross in our region. With the help of two people in the choir, we recruited and organized a volunteer force for Red Cross headquarters in Marjayoun. I also graduated from high school. But I had no chance to go to college. As the only child of aging parents, I could not leave them to travel to college in Beirut. And there was no money— every lira had been spent on helping me attain my high school degree.

As I started evaluating my life and the two others that depended on me, I decided to take a one-year business administration course in the business school at the YWCA. Three of the board of directors of the school respected my parents and knew our financial situation, so they gave me a break on the tuition. I enjoyed the course tremendously. My days were spent in school and my evenings at the church.

I graduated from my business course on June 15, 1984, and brought my degree home and showed it to my parents, who were very happy for me. They hoped that I would find a job (and a husband) at the same time. That week I was consumed with thoughts about my limited options in Marjayoun. I decided to go up to the army base and speak to the Israeli general who was in charge of the security zone, and apply to be his secretary. I had heard about him from our neighbors who worked at the army base. His name was Shlomo.

It was a crazy thought for a girl in my culture to go into to the heart of a military fortress alone and ask to speak to the general. How absurd! But I had no other choice. If I wanted to do something with my life, I had to take charge, be creative, and explore all the possibilities, no matter what. In the middle of a war and being in Marjayoun, the options were few. I figured the worst thing he could do was laugh at me and ask me to leave. So I got up one morning and worked up the courage to go see him.

I started walking up the hill to the army base. The route Chuck had used was now a regular shortcut used by the soldiers. Even though it was only a hundred yards from my house, because of the shelling it was the first time I had been there in eight years. The hill was a mess, with barbed wire all over the place. Even with the path, I had to find my way. Tanks and jeeps were parked on both sides of the entrance. I walked straight to the Israeli soldier guarding the gate. He looked at me and did not know what to think. I asked if he spoke English. He smiled, which encouraged me, and answered, "Of course. How can I help you?" I told him, "I am here to see General Shlomo." A bit shocked, he nevertheless politely guided me in the direction to the general's office.

I was on my own and out of my element. I was the only woman in the army base and the recipient of all sorts of looks from the military personnel. I was nervous. My only strength was derived from the thought of my old parents. I thought of their lives, their health, and how proud they would be if I got a job working for the general. When I got to General Shlomo's office, I took a deep breath and said a prayer. The door was just a hair open. I knocked on it twice, and heard a voice say *"ken,"* which is "yes" in Hebrew. I opened the door and said in English, "Is this General Shlomo's office?" Surprised, he replied in English with a smile, "Yes. How can I help you? I'm Shlomo." He was by himself sitting behind a big desk covered with papers. On the side was another desk attached to his with telephones and electronic devices. I asked him if I could come in.

He invited me in, gestured to a seat in front of his desk, and asked, "What can I do for you?"

I said, "My name is Brigitte Gabriel. I heard you are the general of this army base. I wanted to see you about the possibility of working for you as your secretary. I can write, read, and type English, French, and Arabic." I stopped talking and waited for his reply.

He said, "Brigitte, where are you from?"

"From here. I live in the apartment complex down the hill from this army base."

He said, "You must have incredible courage to come up here to see me and ask me for a job."

I did not know what to make of this comment. I said, "General Shlomo, I am an only child. My parents are in their seventies. We lost everything during the war and I have to support them. I am good and I learn fast. If you hire me for any position, I promise you that you'll never regret it."

He looked me in the eye for what seemed a lifetime, then said, "Brigitte, I admire your courage, but as you see, we don't have ladies in here. My secretary is a soldier. I will not be able to use your services. But if I ever need a secretary, I will keep you in mind."

Then I asked him about the hospital. He said they were not hiring at that time, but assured me that he'd keep me in mind for that, too. I thanked him for talking with me, since I'd arrived unannounced. He said, "You're very welcome. I hope you do find something."

In the following weeks I applied at the UN headquarters for our region, met with the general there, and got the same answer General Shlomo had given me. I also applied at a television studio in my town being built by Middle East Television. They were in the beginning stages and not yet hiring. I knew I was not going to find a job easily, but I knew I had better credentials than anybody in our area, as not many people spoke English, and no one else knew how to type it. I was the only one in school who took the English typing course. Everybody else took the French one, because there were more French companies in Lebanon than English or American ones.

One day when I arrived home, my parents told me that General Shlomo had sent a soldier looking for me. He asked to see me at the military base.

I knocked at the door. I heard Shlomo's voice say *"ken."* I opened the door and said, "Hello. You asked for me?" He looked at me and smiled a big smile. He said, "Finally you are here. I need you to do some work for me." He told me that he was hiring Lebanese doctors to work in the hospital. He needed me to type their contracts.

I typed papers that evening until about six thirty. We resumed the next day. I found out that the whole area reported to him; Israeli and Lebanese commanders had meetings with him that Friday. Israeli and Lebanese men would walk by his office and glance at me working beside him. Nobody understood how a Lebanese girl could be working with Shlomo at the military base. My presence there was a mystery, and I am sure the talk of the army base. I worked without asking him a word about payment or a position at the hospital. I just did whatever task he gave me, the best that I could do it.

I was down to my last two contracts that Friday afternoon. Shlomo was getting ready to return to Israel for the Sabbath. As I picked up the last piece of paper and slid it into the typewriter, I saw my name. It was my contract for a position of administrative secretary. Shlomo looked at me, smiled, and said, "You will be the best secretary that hospital ever had. This is my gift to you. I am finishing my term here and will be leaving Lebanon for good. I wish you the best in your life." I thanked him with tears in my eyes, shook his hand, and left.

My work at the hospital was a learning and enjoyable experience. The administration office, where I worked, was huge. My desk was to the side of the director's desk. Across from our desks were conference chairs because that's where the doctors held their meetings and lounged on their coffee breaks.

My position and location gave me further experience in comparing Arabs and Israelis. It was an opportunity to observe and socialize with Arab and Israeli doctors. Listening to their conversations and discovering their interests gave me deeper insight into the differences in cultures.

The Israeli doctors lived in the doctors' quarters at the hospital, and came from different parts of the world. I met doctors whose backgrounds were Russian, Polish, French, and Swiss. It was intriguing listening to them. They would talk about the books they were reading. They would discuss the story and the author's writing style and the effectiveness of the delivery of details. Sometimes they would discuss art. One of them loved oil painting, and art filled his time after his shift at the hospital. They consistently had good things to say about the nurses and the Lebanese doctors. They commented on the good work the nurses did, and how great the doctors were. They spoke about the nice favors that some of the nurses did for the patients, and made sure they complimented the nurses on their work.

I looked forward to when the Israeli doctors would come for a break. Out of politeness they tried to speak as much as they could in English, since I did not speak Hebrew. It was their behavior that taught me how to show respect to others from a different society.

When the Lebanese doctors got together, they talked about politics of course, and about the doctors they worked with. Each one of them criticized the others about something behind their back. There was no honesty in their relationships with each other, and none of them trusted the others. They would talk about the nurses in a most unflattering way. Not about their performance, mind, or ability, but about their looks, clothing, and social behavior. Then they would discuss how respectable Mr. So and So was because he was such a bully and he deserved the money he got because he knew how to use the system. Power and money bought titles for people without ability or experience, and that was to be admired. The Lebanese doctors had the highest respect for the biggest jerk or crook depending on his situation or title. People were shown respect because of their title no matter how unworthy a human being. I used to wonder how they talked about me after I left work in the afternoon.

My work in the small hospital put me at the center of what was happening in the area. The emergency room was just a few doors down the hallway. I could hear the sirens of the ambulances and the screams of the mothers meeting their wounded soldier sons or younger children in the emergency room. I used to go in and have a look at who had been brought in to find out if it was one of my friends, or simply to learn what happened. It was depressing seeing the blood and suffering every day.

Through my work in the administration office I got to meet a lot of visitors. One in particular changed the course of my future. David walked into the waiting room one day with his wife and two young children. I saw them from my window and knew they were Americans. Since I spoke English, I went out and asked if they needed any help. David told me that their youngest child had developed a rash all over his body and they needed to see a doctor. I went to the emergency room and arranged for a doctor to see them. While waiting for the doctor I got to know David and his wife, Shoshana.

David was an engineer working for Middle East Television. He lived in Israel but traveled to Lebanon daily to work. After they finished seeing the doctor, I invited them to my home for a cup of coffee, since I had just finished my shift. They accepted and drove me home. It was the beginning of a beautiful friendship with their family. Over the following months we became very close.

David told me one day that the Jerusalem office was looking for an Arabic-speaking news anchor for its Arabic news service. He suggested that I apply for the job. He said that the manager would be visiting Metulla the following Thursday with the new bureau chief from the United States. He invited me to stay overnight in their home in Israel and attend the evening meeting in the office in Metulla that they were having with the staff. I could meet the manager and ask for a job in Jerusalem.

At seven fifteen Thursday evening we parked in front of the office in Metulla. The whole office staff was there.

I met the bureau chief, Andrew, and Tim, the young supervisor accompanying him. I recognized Tim immediately because he was the current Arabic-language news anchor whose command of the language was not quite fluent. No wonder! He was an American, raised in the States by an American mother and a Lebanese father.

Tim was very warm and polite, not to mention tall and handsome. I told him that I watched him on TV, and that was the icebreaker. He smiled and started joking about his Arabic, which made me laugh. I said, "Since you brought the subject up, let me correct some of your more common mistakes."

The conversation went wonderfully. He asked me about myself, and I told him that I was a friend of Dave and Shoshana's, that I had heard there was a job possibility in Jerusalem, and that I wanted to meet him and see if I could work for the company. I told him about my situation with my parents. Tim answered me more like a friend than as a manager interviewing an employee. He told me that they were going to be expanding the office in Jerusalem and would be hiring some additional people soon. Tim gave me his phone number in the office in Jerusalem and told me to stay in touch. I promised him I would. I also promised him that I would watch him every night and call him to correct his mistakes in Arabic grammar. He laughed and said please do.

I spent the following few months watching Tim at night, taking notes on his grammatical mistakes, and calling him with my corrections. My only access to a phone line was the Israeli military phone in the emergency room. I would wait for a slow time in the emergency room when all the Lebanese doctors and nurses were out, and I would discreetly call Tim. I would tell him my observations and always end my conversation with the question, "When are you going to get me down to Jerusalem to work with you on the news?"

One Friday afternoon I called Tim with my usual commentary. After a pleasant conversation Tim asked me if I could go to Jerusalem on Sunday. He said he would have a taxi waiting for me at the Metulla office. I couldn't believe my ears. I was thrilled. I went to the Lebanese administration and asked for a week off. I had to explain to the nasty head sister what I was doing. After hurling insults at me for five minutes about how good girls didn't leave their parents' home to go live in Jerusalem alone, she granted me the vacation without pay and threatened that my job might not be waiting for me when I got back. I thanked her politely and left.

My parents were delighted but also saddened by the news. They knew that it was a great opportunity for a better job and better pay. But they worried about me living alone and far away from them. My mother played every guilt trip she knew, from heavy breathing to chest pains to talking about how I was going to miss warm meals and folded clean laundry.

The ride to Jerusalem Sunday afternoon was the first time in my life I ever rode in a car for three and a half hours. We started in the Golan Heights; drove down to Tiberias, passing by Capernaum; continued to the Jordan Valley; then went to Jericho; continued past the edge of the Dead Sea; and finally made our way up the desert hills until we reached Jerusalem. My first night was spent at the Hilton Hotel, which, compared to the bomb shelter, was the most magnificent palace I had ever seen.

I walked into Middle East Television's office on Monday, December 3, 1984. After a few meetings on Monday and working in the office on Tuesday and Wednesday, Tim handed me a contract on Thursday for a position as production assistant, news writer, and doing voiceovers in the news department. I went to Lebanon Friday and resigned from the hospital. It was the beginning of a new life.

7.

CLASH OF CIVILIZATIONS

Working and living in Jerusalem was the best gift anyone could have given me for Christmas that year. Jerusalem, Israel's capital, is one of the world's truly magical and exceptional cities. Established three thousand years ago by King David, Jerusalem is the pinnacle of East meets West. It is a combination of old and new, historical and modern, holy and secular. There is ancient beauty in the quiet solemnity of its stone walls and buildings, and a vibrant air of progress in its impressive modern architecture. It is the melting pot of the world's Jews, who brought their multitude of cultures with them from around the world. Jerusalem is a captivating experience of smells, sounds, and sights mixed into culture, diversity, and spiritual sanctity. It made quite an impression on a twenty-year-old girl who had never been away from home alone or taken more than a three-hour car ride.

Jerusalem is known as the City of Gold because of the magnificent golden hue that its limestone walls take on as the sun sets. It is sacred to the three main religions of Western civilization, Judaism, Christianity, and Islam. It is divided into three sections: the old city; the new city, where I worked and lived in West Jerusalem; and East Jerusalem, where the Arabs live. The old city is surrounded by the original wall built by the Ottoman sultan Suleiman the Magnificent between

1536 and 1541,[1] and is itself divided into four quarters: Muslim, Christian, Jewish, and Armenian.

It is in Jerusalem that you are able to see clearly the differences between Arabic and Jewish culture as represented by the two sides of the city. In the western side of the city you see order, structure, cleanliness, and beautiful flowers planted everywhere. I noticed this immediately having come from war-torn Lebanon. A little boy with a piece of paper trash made an effort to find a garbage can instead of throwing it on the ground. You see adults sitting benches reading books. You ride the bus in Jerusalem and hear twenty different languages.

If you walk one block into the eastern side of the city, the first thing you notice is uncleanliness. Garbage clutters the streets. A man eating a banana threw the peel on the ground instead of throwing it in the garbage can next to him. Walking down the sidewalk you catch the occasional smell of urine coming from some damp nook where two walls meet. People shove, yell, and hurl sexual gestures and language at females walking down the alleys. In my six years living in Jerusalem I never once saw an Arab man sitting with a book in his hand.

The difference between the two cultures has nothing to do with money, and everything to do with values. It is truly the clash of civilizations in its rawest form.

I worked in Benyanei Ha'Uma, "the Nations" building, a conference center and major stage theater in Jerusalem. It was also the home of Jerusalem Capital Studios, which provided production services supporting the Jerusalem bureaus of most American and international media, including ABC, NBC, CBS, Italian TV, German TV, Spanish TV, French TV, Worldwide Television News, and a few others.

I was eager and excited to learn the television business. Working for the Arabic newscast, I enjoyed the company of my new co-workers, especially a Lebanese girl named Paula, who was brought in from Beirut to be the news anchor for *World News*. Work didn't stop when the broadcast was over. Paula and I lived together and brought work home, brainstorming different stories. Paula trained me on voice-overs, reading, and camera presence. In less than four months I began training for the position of news director. I had new friends, a much higher-paying job, and no day-to-day fear of dying.

I worked in Israel Monday through Friday and took a taxi to Lebanon on Friday evening so I could take care of my parents during the weekend. My parents kept up our old family tradition of waiting for me on the balcony so I would not arrive to an empty-looking home. They stood out there even in the rain or snow. I usually arrived home around eleven o'clock Friday nights. I would rush into my father's shivering open arm, which hugged me as his other one held the cane balancing his wobbly body as we greeted. The stubble of his facial hairs would poke me as we kissed three times. I could tell they had been out on the balcony for some time by the chill my lips felt on my mother's soft cheeks. I adored my parents and lived every second of my life to love and honor them. Even though my living alone in Jerusalem worried them, they were proud I was working.

After five months as news anchor, Paula decided to go back to Lebanon and abruptly announced one day that she was quitting. Tim, the Arabic office supervisor, was scrambling to find a replacement and called me into his office after the newscast and informed me, "Starting tomorrow evening, you will be news anchor for *World News*." I was shocked at the sudden appointment, and its implications worried me. It was clear that by taking such a public job, with its high visibility, my life would change overnight. My travel between Israel and terrorist-infested Lebanon would make me an easy target for the Muslims and the PLO. While Paula was going back to live in the safety of Christian East Beirut, where Muslims couldn't reach her, I had to travel weekly to southern Lebanon to take care of my parents, and Muslims could easily get to me to kill me. After many assurances from Tim that security measures would be provided, I hesitantly accepted the job. Being a Lebanese Christian working for an Israeli-backed TV station was extremely dangerous in that part of the world, where Muslims looked upon killing both Christians and Jews as a sacred duty. To them I was not only a Christian but a traitor.

On May 5, 1985, I became evening news anchor for Middle East

Television's *World News* broadcast, seen throughout the Middle East. I covered world events and was exposed to world media where I could evaluate information that had not been distorted by the Arabic religious, cultural, and governmental propaganda influences that Arab viewers are oblivious of. As I saw the world in a broader context without this manipulative Arab media filter, I began to see the deceptive nature of Arabic culture for what it really was. My personal experience of meeting Israeli Jews from all over the world, talking with international journalists, and being exposed to the flood of information available in the free and open Western media showed me how deluded the Arab world was in its self-absorbed manipulative thinking. I began to realize that the Arab Muslim world, because of its religion and culture, is a natural threat to civilized people of the world, particularly Western civilization. As I began reading the Koran and the Hadith, I started learning that the basic commandment of Islam is intolerance to anything non-Muslim. Islamic teaching is filled with hate against Jews and infidels. The Koran is at odds with the Bible. While Christians and Jews learn to repair the world, love their enemy, forgive those who trespass against them, and turn the other cheek, Muslims are taught to fight the infidels, to consider them the enemies of Allah. The sad reality is that even today most Westerners have not read the Koran and Hadith and have no idea about what is to be found in Islamic teachings.

As a journalist I was immersed in the news and information business, so I got a closer look at the power the media had in forming the foundation for the thinking of most people. I realized how it had been and continued to be used to manipulate and foment Arab religious animosity into social and political hatred toward the Jews, and to carry on the hatred, which since World War II has been responsible for the mass exodus of nine hundred thousand Jewish refugees from Arab lands. The media are now the key to brainwashing a new generation of Arabs in preparing them to fight for the destruction of Israel. This theme of Arab hatred for Jews starts almost at birth. It's as if, as the Arabic expression goes, "They are fed hatred by their mother's milk." What they grow up watching on TV, reading in newspapers, and listening to on the radio reinforces what they hear at home, and vice versa. A cycle of hate and spiteful information and misinformation influences their views and opinions.

There are others who feel as I do. On December 21, 2001, the London Arabic-language daily *Al-Sharq al-Awsat* published a letter by Dr. Sahr Muhammad Hatem of Riyadh, Saudi Arabia, calling for a thorough self-examination in the Islamic world. "Our Culture of Demagogy Has Engendered bin Laden, al-Zawahiri, and Their Ilk," the letter said,

> *The mentality of each one of us was programmed upon entering school as a child, [to believe] that [Islam] is everything. Instilled in our small heads was the [notion that the Muslim] has a right—whatever the cause—and that he will triumph—even if he is armed with a stick of wood against a tank—because he [represents] the truth and the others represent falsehood. Instilled in our small heads was the [notion] that we have a monopoly on good values. . . . They have taught us that anyone who is not a Muslim is our enemy, and that the West means enfeeblement, licentiousness, lack of values, and even Jahiliya [i.e., ignorance—a term used to describe the pre-Islamic era] itself. Anyone who escapes this programming in school encounters it at the mosque, or through the media or from the preachers lurking in every corner.[2]*

Luckily for the good doctor, he and this Arabic paper share the freedoms the West has to offer.

Westerners need to understand that there is no free press in the Arab world. The press is used as a mouthpiece to reinforce and perpetuate a pan-Arab Islamic fundamentalist way of thinking. According to the pan-Arab party line, Jews are the problem in the Middle East. According to the relentless message of government-controlled media in the Arab world, all Arabs should be united against all things non-Arab and non-Muslim. The drumbeat of the Arab media is distinct with pedantic rhetoric. "Drive the Jews into the sea!" This form of "journalism" has as its base an unwritten vow to protect that which is Arab, rather than to be objective in any journalistic sense. "Jews are the devil!" Objectivity, which the Western press is so proud to claim adherence to, is held hostage by religious and governmental edicts. "Jews use the blood of Arab children to make Passover bread!" These Arab dictators and rulers are free to say whatever will sustain their continued dictatorial or religious hold on power or promote the pan-Arab cause against the Jews, the West, and America. Let me repeat again: There is no free press in the Arab world. "Kill the Jews!"

The biggest threat to freedom of the press was and still is fear. One Western journalist who was stationed in Jerusalem while I was anchoring Middle East Television's evening news had covered the Middle East for years and clearly understands the use of fear in suppressing objective and truthful reporting. In his 1989 book *From Beirut to Jerusalem,* Thomas Friedman wrote that "physical intimidation" was always in the back of a reporter's mind when covering a story out of Beirut, where news organizations were based in the Muslim-controlled western part of town.[3] Honesty and objectivity fell prey to the threats of ruling Muslim factions and the PLO. Honesty and objectivity could get a reporter's legs and arms broken, or get him killed outright. The most recent example of this prevailing intimidation of the press is the killing of four Lebanese journalists in 2005. One of them, Gibran Tueni, was a politician and publisher of the liberal newspaper *An Nahar.* Three others have narrowly avoided death, suffering serious injury.[4]

"There were . . . stories which were deliberately ignored out of fear," writes Friedman. "How many serious stories were written from Beirut about the well-known corruption in the PLO leadership . . . ? It would be hard to find any hint of them in Beirut reporting before the Israeli invasion."[5] Self-censorship by the Western and Middle Eastern press won out over revealing all and telling the truth about corruption or atrocities against the Christians. Newspaper and magazine readers and TV news audiences worldwide were unaware of how the foreign press was sucking up to Yasser Arafat. By providing only favorable coverage of the Palestinian suffering and underreporting the massacres, rapes, ravaging, and destruction the PLO inflicted on

Lebanon, newspeople gained access, received press credentials, and were able to stay alive. "The Western press coddled the PLO," Friedman contends. "For any Beirut-based correspondent, the name of the game was keeping on good terms with the PLO."

Unfortunately, the intimidation of journalists continues today, extending to the wider Arab and Western media. There are recent examples of the press's fearful cowering before intimidation in the Arab world. CNN's submissive coverage of Saddam Hussein in Iraq was revealed by senior CNN news executive Jordan Eason in a post–Iraq war op-ed column titled "The News We Kept to Ourselves."[6] Reporting honestly about Saddam's atrocious, murderous rule, he argues, "would have jeopardized the lives of Iraqis, particularly those on our Baghdad staff." After this revelation about what you, my reader, used to think was objective reporting, should you have relied on any information from any CNN stories about Saddam in forming your opinions? How much other press coverage of the Middle East have you taken at face value and let influence your thinking? Remember back during the Lebanese civil war when the Israelis entered Beirut and the world media reported it as an invasion of the country? No one mentioned how Israel and the Christians were working together to get rid of Islamo-fascist terrorists who had set up shop in Lebanon and turned it from the Paris of the Middle East into a terrorism center spinning out hijackers and terrorists throughout the world.

If the world had understood the goal of Islam to dominate the world back then and supported Israel and the Christians in their fight against Iran, Syria, and the jihadists infiltrating and fighting in Lebanon, Lebanon would not be a mini Afghanistan in the making today under the control of the fanatical Hezbollah, which is supported and financed by Iran and Syria. The Christian Lebanese were vilified for defending themselves and their country against the Islamists just as Israel was vilified by the world when it destroyed Saddam's nuclear reactor, and just as America is vilified today for protecting itself and trying to fight an enemy bent on killing its civilians. America is being portrayed as the aggressor attacking poor Muslim countries. Here we were minding our own business when we were attacked. If it weren't for the attacks of September 11, 2001, America would not be hunting down the killers of innocents across the globe.

What were your thoughts about Christian Lebanese and Israelis back then? Do you have a different attitude now that Islamists have attacked the World Trade Center and the Pentagon, and are waging a worldwide holy jihad? Our American administration is having to suffer accusation, scorn, second-guessing, and outright condemnation from these who still have their heads in the sand. Let me put nicely what a dear friend of mine says: "When you bury your head in the sand, all you do is make a big fat target out of your behind."

Anti-Western Arab factions use the media as a propaganda tool on Westerners and their own population just as the Nazis and the Communist Party used them to control and manipulate the millions they subjected to misinformation. As Islam moves to subjugate minds to the Koran, it will use the media to further its Islamo-fascist goals by creating anti-Israel and anti-U.S. sentiment, first in the Arab world and then in the West. It may already have played a hand in influencing your thoughts and opinions about the Arab-Israeli conflict and U.S. policy in the Middle East in a pro-Arab way. One glaring example is the film *Paradise Now,* which was nominated for a 2006 Academy award. *Paradise Now* attempts to explain away the actions behind mass murderers. In effect, it legitimizes this type of mass murder and portrays the murderers themselves as victims! Some Americans actually sympathize now with suicide bombers and blame their actions on desperation.

If you get nothing more out of reading this book, take this insight from someone who comes from the Middle East speaking to Western readers, and let the deception end here.

If you think I am politically incorrect in labeling the Islamo-fascists as radical, barbarian terrorists, try complaining to Egyptian professor Dr. Farag Fouda, who in 1992 was assassinated by a member of al Gamaat al Islamiya, an extremist Muslim organization. Dr. Fouda was an advocate of secularism whose assassin was motivated by a statement of the council of Azhar University Muslim scholars in Egypt calling Fouda "a follower of the nonreligious current and extremely hostile to anything Islamic." The murderer said he was fulfilling Islamic objectives. Fouda was an outspoken opponent of fundamentalism and was considered one of Egypt's leading secularists.[7] Fouda publicly challenged the haphazard jihadist war Islamo-fascists were waging. His murder took place in broad daylight, sending a clear message throughout the Middle East: Don't get in the way. Watch what you say about Islam, what you report, and how you report it.

Let me give you some background on why there is no free press in the Muslim-dominated world. The first reason is religious. Absolutely no questioning is allowed concerning Allah and his apostle Muhammad. Practitioners must adhere to, and disregard any irrationality within, Islamic teachings. The masses are taught to react violently toward anyone who questions or criticizes Allah, or Muhammad or his teachings.

A perfect example is the Muslim world's startling eruption of violence in reaction to the caricatures of Muhammad in the Dutch newspaper *Jyllands-Posten*. Muslim rage resulted in burning embassies, calls to butcher those who mock Islam, and warnings to be prepared for the real holocaust. The news pictures and video of these events represent a canvas of hate decorated by different nationalities who share one common ideology of bigotry and intolerance derived from one source: authentic Islam, an Islam that is awakening from centuries of slumber to reignite its wrath against the infidel and dominate the world, an Islam that has declared intifada on the West.

Some see Muhammad's life itself offering his followers graphic examples of his intolerance toward dissent, slight, or rebuke. Well-known and repeated stories of fact or lore discourage any interest in voicing dissent. There is the story of the murder of the poetess Asma bint Marwan, who paid with her life when she spoke out against Muhammad for having a man named Abu Afak murdered. In his displeasure toward her, Muhammad asked his followers to murder her as well. She was killed by a sword thrust to her abdomen while suckling her baby in bed.[8] Abu Afak was a Jew, and used to instigate the people against the apostle of Allah, and composed satirical verses about Muhammad. Whether these stories are fact or fiction, their effect is just as chilling to journalists in today's Arab world.

One of the most notable modern examples of the suppression of free speech is that of Salman Rushdie. For years since the publication of *The Satanic Verses,* fatwas calling for his death have been issued periodically by Muslim clerics and governments. It hardly registers concern from anyone in the press anymore. If a preacher in America put out a contract on some journalist who said derogatory things about Jesus, the press would be morally outraged. But Muslim clerics and governments can do it and they get a pass.

With the international and local Arabic press being influenced by the ground rules I've described, whose news coming out of the Arab Middle East are you going to believe? See how the influence of fear can go all the way around the world and end up on the front page of the paper on your breakfast table? The Islamo-fascists are trying to manipulate a mass audience to believe they are the victims, and the policies of the West in the Middle East make them the aggressor and oppressors. All the while they hate our democracy, they hate our freedoms, they hate who we are as people, and they are working toward one Islamic Caliphate throughout the world with Sharia rule as law. So far they are doing a pretty good job at it.

Their tactics are simple: use the Western media to wage psychological warfare—and it doesn't cost a dime. There are enough politically and philosophically motivated detractors who are also good-hearted and naïve in the U.S. media to rely on. Where the U.S. would want the press to present a picture of hope and success, the Islamo-fascists and our detractors use it to wear down our resolve, build up frustration, and create division within Western populations. Unable to defeat Western military superiority, our enemy depends on negative themes throughout the media to create disunity, opening schisms on the home front in our communities, on our campuses, and in our government.

General Bui Tin, who served on the general staff of North Vietnam's army, was asked why America was defeated in Vietnam. He said: "America lost because of its democracy; through dissent and protest it lost the ability to mobilize a will to win."[9] This answer should be sobering to all Americans in the fight against Islamo-fascism.

The irony that always amazes me when I see people up in arms about our war against Islamo-fascism is how they don't understand that the social freedoms they take for granted will be the first casualties of Islamic influence and control. The only social liberal thinkers in the Muslim Arab Islamo-fascist world are dead ones. Women's freedoms and their protection under the law, freedom of speech, separation of church and state, and other human rights will be the first to suffer. Oh yes, sorry, I forgot . . . there will always be the ACLU to depend on to keep the radical Muslims from taking these rights away. How foolish of me. Almost lost my head there.

One revealing phenomenon I discovered while covering the West Bank under Israeli rule was that the Palestinians living under the Israeli occupation had greater journalistic and religious freedom than they have under the Palestinian Authority today. When Israel was present in the West Bank, there were a larger number of varying viewpoints being expressed in the press. Most were anti-Israeli, but at least up to a certain point of vehemence they were freely expressed. Today under the Palestinian Authority and the newly elected Hamas, it is all anti-Israeli. Anything else could get you killed. Under Israeli rule, if you were a PLO collaborator and did an attack of some sort, you were given a trial and prison time. In Gaza or the West Bank today, if you are an Israeli collaborator, you get lynched and hung up on a telephone pole.

In the 1980s and 1990s Christians and Muslims got along together under Israeli control. I did a story in 1988 asking West Bank Christians what they thought would happen to them when the Israelis left. They were afraid to talk about it openly on camera. We had to obscure their faces and garble their voices to alleviate their fear of speaking out. They said that when the Israelis left they would be killed, persecuted, or subjugated under the heel of the Muslims, and today this is happening. Once predominantly Christian areas are being taken over by Muslims. It's just like what happened in Lebanon when the Muslims took control.

The freedom of the press in Israel completely shocked me. Here was a small country of 5 million Jews in the middle of a sea of 150 million Muslims who wanted them killed or pushed into the sea, yet Israel let the press say almost anything it wanted, good or bad, about the government, the military, and Israel's presence in the West Bank and Gaza. I could not believe how the Israelis let the press have so much access. Our news crew even had a government-issued beeper so it could be contacted by the Israeli government press office to inform it of press conferences and military confrontations with the Arabs in the territories. The Israelis did require us to take stories to the censors for review, but changes were hardly ever made.

Working as a news anchor for *World News* gave me a front-row seat at the international theater. With an Associated Press machine in my office, faxes coming in from Beirut, calls from reporters working on stories in Lebanon, and a daily satellite feed of worldwide stories, I was plugged in. With a show deadline every day, all this moved at high speed. But it didn't stop in the office or when the show was over. My friends were journalists and bureau chiefs who worked the odd hours with me and beyond. We would go out together in the evening for dinner, sit around the table, and talk about the news. Our life *was* the news.

While working in Jerusalem I met an American journalist who worked for the English department of Middle East Television. Together we traveled between Israel and Lebanon, changing the Israeli license plates on his car to French ones and making sure we had nothing on us to indicate we had been in Israel as we entered Lebanon. Time spent in Lebanon often involved dodging bombs and bullets. My journalist friend, probably the only American freely moving around in Lebanon at that time, called it the Wild West and traveled with his two friends, Smith & Wesson. Once while we were passing through a checkpoint in the Christian town of Jezzine, a car behind us sped through, passing us without stopping. The guards opened fire and we ducked as it sped by. Luckily the machine-gun position that fired on the car was higher than we were, so the shots went over our heads. Other times we ducked shells and looked out for roadside bombs. Needless to say, going through the war together was a bonding experience. We became best friends.

Back in Jerusalem doing the news show I soon realized there was a form of repetition developing with every broadcast I did. It was the same story but with different actors: hijackings, car bombs, and Muslims fighting non-Muslims was the news. The only differences were the locations, the vehicles used, and the names of the perpetrators and their victims. The names of the terrorists became all too familiar and similar. Muhammad, Ahmed, Hussein, Ali, were nothing but a repeat of Islamic names of Muslim youth who had been brainwashed with hatred and bigotry toward the infidels. They were always shouting "Allahu Akbar," the Muslim call to prayer, as their trademark celebratory cry for murder and glory as they slaughtered, killed, blew up, maimed, or beheaded non-Muslims. There were always new names for different groups springing up, which in the Middle East means nothing more than few Islamic militants with a cause. My friend the American journalist, ever aware of the fine line between his covering the news in Lebanon and the possibility of his being the news, would say, "Five guys with beards, AK-47s, and an American hostage make a movement around here."

The names of the targets or the kidnapped people were usually Western: Terry Anderson, Terry Waite, Lieutenant Colonel William Higgins, Pan Am or TWA flights, the *Achille Lauro*. The aggressors were always Muslims. The victims were always Christians or Jews. I began to see how the Middle East was dragging the world down into a war of ideologies based on religious hatred and bigotry. I began to understand that what I and the Christians were going through in Lebanon, which I had thought was just a regional conflict, was becoming a worldwide conflict with international implications. Time and time again, story after story, I was reporting the murderous, barbaric behavior of killers in different countries with Islam the reoccurring theme and "Allahu Akbar" always a part of the language used as they killed. America and the West found an excuse for every incident and boxed and labeled it under the context of the country in which it took place. They attributed Iran's conflict and the victory of Ayatollah Ruholla Khomeini to an inner conflict within Iran. They considered the Lebanese war a civil war among factions. They considered the overall Arab-Israeli conflict a Palestinian-versus-Israeli conflict over land. Yet in all these conflicts radical Islam was the driving force or lingered just under the surface. Here is a list of Islamic and Arabic aggression compiled by Abdullah al-Araby of the *Islam Review* reported in world media leading up to 9/11 while the West neglected to connect the dots.

1985

- June 14: TWA Flight 847 hijacking.
- October 7: October 10: *Achille Lauro* cruise ship hijacking by Palestinian Liberation Front, during which passenger Leon Klinghoffer is shot dead.
- November 23: EgyptAir flight 648 hijacked by Abu Nidal group, flown to Malta, where Egyptian commandos storm plane; sixty are killed by gunfire and explosions.
- December 27: Rome and Vienna airport attacks.

1986

- April 2: TWA flight 840 bombed on approach to Athens airport; four passengers (all of them American), including an infant, are killed.
- April 6: The La Belle discotheque in Berlin, a known hangout for U.S. soldiers, is bombed, killing three and injuring 230 people; Libya is held responsible. In retaliation, the U.S. bombs Libya in Operation El Dorado Canyon and tries to kill Colonel Muammar al-Gadhafi.

♦ September 5: Pan Am flight 73, an American civilian airliner, is hijacked; twenty-two people die when plane is stormed in Karachi, Pakistan.

1988

♦ December 21: Pan Am flight 103 bombing over Lockerbie, Scotland. The worst act of terrorism against the United States prior to September 11, 2001.

1989

♦ September 19: Suitcase bomb destroys UTA (Union des Transport, Aériens) flight UT-772 en route to Paris, killing all 171 passengers and crew. Libyan intelligence involved.

1993

♦ January 25: Mir Aimal Kansi, a Pakistani, fires an AK-47 assault rifle into cars waiting at a stoplight in front of the Central Intelligence Agency headquarters. Two die.

♦ February 26: World Trade Center bombing kills six and injures more than one thousand people.

♦ June: Failed New York City landmark bomb plot.

1994

♦ July 18: Bombing of Jewish center in Buenos Aires, Argentina, kills eighty-six and wounds three hundred. Generally attributed to Hezbollah acting on behalf of Iran.

♦ July 19: Alas Chiricanas flight 00901 is bombed, killing twenty-one. Generally attributed to Hezbollah.

♦ July 26: Israeli embassy is attacked in London, and a Jewish charity is car-bombed, wounding twenty. Attributed by Britain, Argentina, and Israel to Hezbollah.

♦ December 11: A small bomb explodes on board Philippine Airlines flight 434, killing a Japanese businessman. Authorities found out that Ramzi Yousef planted the bomb to test it for his planned terrorist attack.

- December 24: Air France flight 8969 is hijacked by Groupe Islamique Armé members who planned to crash the plane on.

1995

- January 6: Operation Bojinka is discovered on a laptop computer in a Manila, Philippines, apartment by authorities after a fire occurred in the apartment.
- July–October: Bombings in France by a GIA unit led by Khaled Kelkal kill seven and injure more than one hundred.
- November 13: Bombing of military compound in Riyadh, Saudi Arabia, kills seven.

1996

- June 25: Khobar Towers bombing. Dharan, Saudi Arabia. Nineteen servicemen lost their lives, hundreds of others wounded.

1997

- February 24: An armed man opens fire on tourists at an observation deck atop the Empire State Building in New York City, killing a Danish national and wounding visitors from the United States, Argentina, Switzerland, and France before turning the gun on himself. A handwritten note carried by the gunman claims this was a punishment attack against the "enemies of Palestine."
- November 17: Luxor massacre. Islamist gunmen attack tourists in Luxor, Egypt, killing sixty-two people, most of them European and Japanese vacationers.

1998

- August 7: U.S. embassy bombings in Dar es Salaam, Tanzania, and Nairobi, Kenya, killing 225 people and injuring more than 4,000.

1999

- December: Jordanian authorities foil a plot to bomb U.S. and Israeli tourists in Jordan and pick up twenty-eight suspects as part of the 2000 millennium attack plots.
- December 14: Ahmed Ressam is arrested on the United States–Canada border in Port Angeles, Washington; he confesses to planning to bomb the Los Angeles International Airport as part of the 2000 millennium attack plots.

2000

- The attacks against Israel in 2000 are too numerous to detail. Over thirty attacks of terrorism were committed, resulting in death. Forty-four civilians were killed and hundreds injured.
- The last of the 2000 millennium attack plots fails, as the boat meant to bomb the USS *The Sullivans* sinks.
- October 12: USS *Cole* bombing kills seventeen U.S. sailors.
- August 9: A suicide bomber in Jerusalem kills seven and wounds 130 in the Sbarro restaurant suicide bombing; Hamas and Islamic Jihad claim responsibility.

2001

- The attacks against Israel in 2001 are too numerous to detail. The death toll was 203 and hundreds of people were injured.
- 9/11: The attacks on September 11 kill almost three thousand in a series of hijacked airliner crashes into two U.S. landmarks: the World Trade Center in New York City, and the Pentagon in Arlington, Virginia. A fourth plane crashes in Somerset County, Pennsylvania.
- Paris embassy attack plot foiled.
- Richard Reid, attempting to destroy American Airlines flight 63, is subdued by passengers and flight attendants before he can detonate his shoe bomb.

The reason the West was unable to connect the dots had a lot to do with viewpoint.

As a native Lebanese journalist I observed the operations of the foreign press in Israel. They would fly in, all expenses paid; live the first-class lifestyle, with a nice hotel and expense account; report what was happening for a week or couple of months; and then leave. They blew in, blew around, and blew out. They came with their preconceived ideas, toed the network editorial policy line, and perpetuated what they unwittingly had been programmed with through subtle Arab and PLO propaganda, which had reached them wherever they came from. Scenes of wailing Palestinians they saw on the air in the States became the shot to look for. Usually their stories reflected badly on the Israeli occupation. They clamored for shots of kids throwing stones against border patrol soldiers firing tear gas and rubber bullets. Because I could speak the language and read the Arabic press and knew the nuances behind events, I sensed that reporters were being manipulated. You couldn't help but feel sorry for the Palestinians while watching the way they were living, and seeing young teenagers throwing rocks at Israeli soldiers, trying to expel them from the West Bank and Gaza. I wonder if many of the foreign press knew that the PLO was founded three years *before* the Israelis ever occupied Gaza and the West Bank, and that the PLO wanted Israel wiped off the map. But in a ninety-second story, who has time to remind viewers that when the PLO was founded, Gaza was illegally occupied by Egypt, and the West Bank by Jordan, but Yasser Arafat did not mind those occupations? Where were the voices of the Palestinians then for their independent state?

I wanted to think that the journalists stationed there, some of whom I knew, had better sense, but in order to protect their relationship and not offend Muslim or PLO sources they had to be careful about what they reported. It was from this perspective that I watched the West fall further under the spell of anti-West, anti-Israeli propaganda, just as it did during its coverage of Lebanon, which portrayed the Palestinians and Islamo-fascists as the victims instead of the aggressors. As Islamic aggression increased, the press slid more deeply into a submissive, easily manipulated relationship.

When I would visit my Christian Arab friends' houses in the West Bank and talk with the locals, they joked that the Muslims were playing the West like a violin. The Christians, whether in Lebanon or in Bethlehem in the West Bank, knew that the Islamic agenda was violently against anything non-Muslim. The West was ignorant and refused to learn and listen to what the Arabs and radical Muslims were openly saying to their people about what was in store: *"We will be victorious against the Jews. We will destroy Israel. We will conquer the Christians and claim the world for Islam. Islam will once again dominate the world."* The radical Muslims knew the West was completely ignorant as to what was coming their way. The West's biggest fault was continuing to judge the Middle East and trying to negotiate with it according to Western practices. The West didn't have a clue about their culture and what was important in understanding Arab Muslims. Because of fear, intimidation, or a special agenda, Arabs can say one thing but believe something entirely different. When being questioned in an interview, their response can vary depending on a range of influences: religion, gender, money, fear, society, and uncertainty. If they are Muslim they can lie and deceive if it is good for Islam. If the interviewed subject is a woman she may answer in the broadest of terms for fear of retribution from the males in the family. People's answers will be greatly influenced if they feel their financial or social position may be jeopardized. Usually they exercise herd mentality and voice the majority opinion. Uncertainty and fear concerning who is in power may leave them without an opinion or reiterating the talking points of the powers that be. Taking a position may bring retribution if power changes hands. Fear is the biggest enemy in getting the truth about something in the Middle East.

Because Middle East Television's *World News* was based in Israel, we were free to report the facts without corrupt Arab leaders dictating what we were allowed or not allowed to say. I read the news, reporting the facts without adding the lies and the propaganda required by Arab media to vilify Israel. The terrorists resented that. For that crime I had to fear for my life and alter my lifestyle to ensure my survival.

When I became an anchor, I knew that the freedom and security I had experienced for a few months living in Israel as an unknown production assistant would change. As my situation required me to travel back and forth between Lebanon and Israel to check on my parents, I knew every time I crossed into Lebanon or even traveled in the West Bank and parts of Israel that danger was always lurking in the air, threatening my life and security. As a survivor of the Lebanese war I now had to fear for my life again for being a Lebanese journalist working and living in Israel. This was a crime of betrayal to the Arab people and the Arab cause against Israel. They looked at me as a traitor because I was seen on a TV station backed by the Israelis, located in the Israeli security zone. A Lebanese living and working in Israel must be in bed with the Israeli enemy.

I went back to becoming a target. I learned to disguise my appearance. I had a collection of wigs. I also used the fictitious on-air name of Nour Saman. I was chased once for two hours on the highway between Tel Aviv and Haifa by two Palestinians driving a car with West Bank license plates. They recognized me at a traffic light and followed me to Haifa. I shook them by changing cars with people from our office who were traveling together with me. I was also chased between Tiberias and Metulla one Friday evening at ten o'clock as I was making my way up the mountains to Lebanon to see my parents. My car nearly flipped on a curve. My pursuers stopped after they saw me pull into the military base at the border and disappear inside.

During my years of broadcasting, Hezbollah became stronger and infiltrated the Israeli security zone, where my parents lived. Hezbollah activists took a photo of me on TV doing a broadcast and published it in their magazine, along with a picture of the Israeli news anchor for the Israeli evening news, linking me to Israel as a journalist collaborator. In early 1987 I was shot at in Lebanon from a car speeding by as I walked home from a store after shopping for my parents. I fell into a nearby ditch and lay there for a few minutes playing dead before crawling back home. It was like the snipers from my childhood all over again. That was the last time I walked in my hometown.

After two years of courtship, my relationship with my journalist friend became serious, and we decided to get married. I was twenty-two. Because my father was ill and unable to travel, we planned to have the wedding in Lebanon. Those plans were canceled because of death threats and security issues. The Israel commander at the Israel Defense Forces (IDF) headquarters in Marjayoun suggested that a wedding of an American journalist and the news anchor for a Christian-militia-protected, Israeli-backed, Jerusalem-based, U.S.-owned TV station might attract uninvited guests and anonymous wedding gifts. It was also 1987, and two weeks before our wedding day, the State Department issued an order for all Americans to leave Lebanon after the Muslims hanged American lieutenant colonel William Higgins after kidnapping him from his UN post. My future husband had no problem moving about in Lebanon as long as he stayed in the Israeli security zone. At the same time, he had recognized that the bad guys were playing by new rules. Being a hostage had moved beyond just being chained to a radiator. With the colonel's hanging, they were playing for keeps, so he began, as he puts it, "traveling with protection."

We had to quickly move the wedding to Jerusalem. My father's health prevented him from making the long trip, and my mother couldn't leave him alone, so neither could be there. I'll never forget the look of desolation on my mother's face as they stood in the driveway, slowly waving to us as we left for Jerusalem. She would not be there for her daughter, whose marriage she had waited twenty-two years to see. I stood in my white wedding dress in the church without my beloved parents as a few friends and co-workers attended our small ceremony.

My mother died a few weeks later. My father followed her nine months after. Their loss has been the biggest tragedy and pain I have faced in my life to date. I adored them with all my soul, and I live to honor them and their legacy. They are the drive behind everything I do.

After we got married, my husband was transferred back to America. The change opened a new chapter in our lives. Before we left Israel, I decided to make my final statement about how I felt about the Middle East and where my loyalty lay.

My father had been living with us after my mother passed away, and he died in Israel. I buried him in a Christian cemetery on Mount Zion on the southern slope of Jerusalem. Within a few days of my final departure from the Middle East, I went back to Marjayoun and took my mother out of her grave, and out of the coffin that had held her for a year and half. She was put in a coffin custom designed to fit the trunk of our car and made by the local cabinetmaker, who made the caskets for all the funerals in our town. I put my mother in my car and cried all the way to Jerusalem to reunite her with my father. It was a very sad and surreal experience.

We arrived in Jerusalem on Good Friday, April 1989. The bells of the Church of the Holy Sepulchre and other Christian churches were ringing as I reunited her with my father for eternity. There was no ceremony. The only people present were me, my husband, the gravediggers, and the wonderful Christian Palestinian lady who made the interment arrangements. My parents are buried in the same Mount Zion cemetery where the grave of a *ger tzaddik,* or righteous gentile, Oscar Shindler, would one day be. If you have ever visited Oskar Schindler's grave, you have walked right by theirs. They are the only couple buried with the word "LEBANON" on their gravestone. All during our seven years in the bomb shelter they never let me forget that they loved me higher than the sky, deeper than the ocean, and bigger than the whole wide world.

I believe actions speak louder than words. I wanted to ensure that my children would always be drawn to Israel and not the Arabic world, and that they would always know where my loyalty lay.

8.

TERRORISTS AMONG US

Muslims in the Arab world have a saying: "First comes Saturday, then comes Sunday." Every Muslim in the Middle East knows exactly what this means. This is their way of saying that first they'll get the Jews (who observe Sabbath on Saturday), and then they'll get the Christians (whose Sabbath is Sunday). In the modern Middle East, the Muslims reversed this—they got the Christians first. Lebanon used to be the only country in the Middle East with a Christian majority. It's not a coincidence that Lebanon was also the only democracy in the Arab world. Now Lebanon is dominated by Muslims, and the Christians who remain are a disrespected and irrelevant minority. They are oppressed and exploited by Syria and terrorized by Hezbollah. Through Hezbollah, Iran has sunk its radical Islamic fangs into Lebanon. Even if the Assad family dictatorship falls, the Syrians and their Iranian patron-paymasters will never leave voluntarily. Syria cannot leave, because most of the Syrian economy is based on plunder from Lebanon. Iran will not leave, because Lebanon serves as the perfect training ground and launching point for Hezbollah's international terrorist campaign.

Lebanon was the first country to fall to Islam in modern times. As commanded by the Koran, the Islamists have now put the rest of the world in their sights. The destruction of Lebanese democracy and subjugation of Lebanese Christians was not merely a strategic victory in Islam's jihad to rule the world. Along with the Iranian hostage crisis of 1979–80, it was an inspiration. The jihadists were encouraged by the West's ineffectual policies and pathetic responses to provocations and confrontations manufactured by the Islamists. During the Iranian hostage crisis, while Jimmy Carter alternately groveled and bungled, Ayatollah Khomeini exultingly proclaimed, "America cannot do a damn thing!" This became a slogan and a battle cry throughout the Middle East.[1]

When Iran's vicious puppet Hezbollah blew up the marines in Lebanon in 1983, America turned tail and ran, leaving the Christians to be slaughtered in town after town. It sent a strong, loud, and clear message to the Muslim radicals of the world, including Osama bin Laden: America is no longer the power it used to be.

After taking over Lebanon Arab Muslims turned their attention to countries outside of the Middle East. In their quest for world domination Muslims organized, grew stronger, and planned one attack after the other. As a result of the humiliation of America and the conquest of Lebanon, the flames of jihad now rage all over the world. Here are only a few examples.

Sudan

In April 1983, shortly after the United States fled from Beirut, the Arab Muslim government in Khartoum, Sudan, began a jihad to impose Islam on black African Christians and animists in the southern part of the country. The southerners' resistance to the imposition of Islam led to civil war, which the Khartoum government turned into a war of genocide and slavery.[2] Estimates of the death toll run as high as 2 million, one of the highest civilian death tolls since the Second World War. That's more people killed than in Rwanda, Liberia, the Ivory Coast, Kosovo, and Bosnia combined.[3] The Khartoum government used the profits from the slave trade to subsidize its war of genocide against the people of southern Sudan.[4] At the same time, Sudan became a haven for al Qaeda jihadists and a hub for international terrorist operations.[5] In addition, Since early 2003, the Khartoum government has been waging war against black African Muslims in the western Sudanese region of Darfur.[6] In its war against Darfur, systematic rape has joined starvation and mass murder in Sudan's repertoire of jihad terror tactics.[7] According to a United Nations estimate, more than 180,000 people died between October 2003 and March 2005; an average of 10,000 people have died per month,[8] and another 2 million have been driven from their homes.[9]

Unlike the world's apathetic response to more than twenty years of genocide in southern Sudan, the Darfur crisis has attracted worldwide media coverage and scrutiny by the United Nations Security Council. No doubt the sudden glare of publicity and Security Council scrutiny led to the realization in Khartoum that it could not wage two wars of genocide simultaneously, and this is why it agreed to a "peace deal" in the south, which was "finalized" in January 2005.[10] Kharoum's "restraint" in southern Sudan is nothing more than a *hudna,* a temporary cease-fire, which will last only as long as Sudan is under international pressure for its depredations in Darfur. The Arab League and Egypt have already announced their support for the Khartoum government, and have led efforts to prevent the imposition of sanctions.

Nigeria

In 1999, Muslim-dominated governments in twelve of Nigeria's thirty-six states began implementing Sharia, Islamic law, even though this violated the federal constitution of Nigeria. Under Nigerian Sharia, forbidden practices include building churches (or any other non-Muslim places of worship), playing music, women wearing pants, and riding in taxis with members of the opposite sex. Islamic punishments, such as flogging, stoning, and chopping off hands, are enforced by mobs of Muslim vigilantes.[11] In at least one state, all existing Christian churches were destroyed by government order.[12] In other states, hundreds of churches have been burned. At least ten thousand people have been killed in violence related to the imposition of Sharia.[13]

Indonesia

Most people are familiar with the more spectacular terror attacks that have been perpetrated in Indonesia, the world's most populous Muslim country. These include the October 12, 2002, nightclub bombings in Bali, which killed 202, mostly Australian tourists; the September 9, 2004, bombing of the Australian embassy in Jakarta, which killed 11; and the October 1, 2005, restaurant bombings, again in Bali, which killed 22.[14] In addition to attacking foreign tourists and targets inside the country, Islamists have been conducting a terror campaign against Indonesia's Christian minority, and have been seeking to impose Sharia law. Since 1999, over 19,000 have been killed in clashes between Muslims and Christians, and over 600,000 have been made homeless.[15] The Islamic terror campaign in Indonesia has included the trademark bombings, beheadings, and church burnings. On Christmas Eve, 2000, eleven churches across Indonesia were bombed simultaneously by an al Qaeda affiliate; 19 people were killed and approximately 100 were wounded.[16] On December 31, 2005, a bomb exploded in a Christian market in Palu, Sulawesi, as shoppers prepared for New Year's Eve. Eight were killed and 45 were wounded.[17]

South Asia: Pakistan, Bangladesh, India, and Thailand

Pakistan and Bangladesh have emerged as the major centers of Islamic terrorism in Asia. Jihadists trained in terrorist camps in both countries commit atrocities inside Pakistan and Bangladesh as well as in neighboring countries, particularly India and Thailand.[18] On August 17,

2005, there were five hundred synchronized terror bombings across Bangladesh.[19] Also in Bangladesh,

> *members of minority religions have suffered from ghastly violence, including collective terror. The Nation reports that some Buddhists and Christians were blinded, had fingers cut off or had hands amputated, while "others had iron rods nailed through their legs or abdomen." Women and children have "been gang-raped, often in front of their fathers or husbands." In addition, hundreds of temples were desecrated and statues destroyed; thousands of homes and businesses looted or burned. . . . As for Hindus, the human rights organization Freedom House reports they have been subject to "rape, torture and killing and the destruction of their cultural and religious identity at the hands of Muslims."[20]*

Since 2002, there have been at least seven terrorist bombing and shooting attacks inside Pakistan (not counting assassination attempts on government officials).[21] Pakistani schoolbooks state that Hindus are "backward, superstitious wife burners, and that they are inherently cruel and if given the chance would assert their power over the weak, especially Muslims, by depriving them of education and pouring molten lead into their ears."[22]

Muslims account for only 9 percent of the population of Thailand.[23] Between January 2004 and October 2005, at least 1,100 people have been killed in a series of Islamic terrorist attacks.[24] Muslim terrorist atrocities include bombings (including numerous simultaneous bombings), beheadings, and the burning of Buddhist monasteries.[25] India has also been the scene of numerous Islamic terror beheadings and bombings.[26]

In the last twenty-some years, while Americans were trying to understand how to reason with the Middle East, Islam has reinvigorated its export of fundamentalism. Our ignorance and complacency have been the radical islamists' ally. Their first major attack on America was the 1993 bombing of the World Trade Center. To show how far out in left field we were, the government handled it as a crime, not as an act of terrorism. Twenty years after a Hezbollah terrorist suicide bomber detonated a truck bomb at the marine barracks in Beirut, the perpetrators who drove the Ryder truck bomb under the World Trade Center were treated as regular everyday criminals. Later that year, in June, nine followers of Sheikh Omar Abdul Rahman of Egypt and the sheikh himself were arrested for planning a day of terror in New York City. They planned to bomb the United Nations headquarters, the Lincoln and Holland tunnels, the George Washington Bridge, and a federal office building.

After months of investigation by our government, days of reviewing documents, and many hours of court exhibits and interviews, we found out that the conspirators had come and worked together from five different terrorist groups, including the Egyptian al Gamaat al Islamiya (Sheikh Omar Abdul Rahman of Egypt); Sudan's National Islamic Front (members of the Sudanese mission in New York and five Sudanese were arrested for the second series of bomb plots in Manhattan); Hamas (Mohammed Saleh, owner of a Yonkers, New York, gas station, who was to supply the fuel for the second WTC-connected bombing plot and who was also a pivotal Hamas figure in arranging for Hamas military training in Sudan and for acquiring military equipment for Hamas forces in Jordan); Islamic Jihad; and al Fuqra (a militant black Pakistani organization with adherents in Colorado, New York, Canada, and Pakistan). This discovery showed the authorities a network of terrorist organizations woven into the fabric of American society.[27]

America never seems to learn the danger of letting your enemy think that you are weak, asleep, or careless. America sent message after message to the Islamists that while America possesses the most superior weapons of war, it does not possess the resolve or the will to follow through till victory. America proved it when it withdrew from Lebanon after the barracks were bombed and after it didn't finish the job in Iraq the first time around during the Gulf War. Ever since that signal was sent, the Islamists ratcheted up their attacks, and the

United States slept through every attack on its bases and interests overseas. They hijacked TWA flight 847 and the cruise ship *Achille Lauro* in 1985. They bombed another TWA flight and hijacked Pan Am flight 73 in 1986. They bombed Pan Am flight 103 in 1988. They bombed a military compound in Riyadh, Saudi Arabia, in 1995. The Khobar Towers, also in Saudi Arabia, were bombed 1996. They also bombed the USS *Cole* in Yemen in 2000. So what signal did the United States send to the Islamic terrorists during eight years of the Clinton administration? During those years the U.S. defense budget was depleted and the U.S. government was a social development center of political correctness, political corruption, and arrogance while the Chinese stole our military secrets. The United States was in the middle of a slumber party while the Islamists were organizing, training, recruiting, and infiltrating our country and counting on our blindness, carelessness, and ignorance. They knew that the leadership was busy lying and covering up sexual scandals instead of building our military, building our intelligence, increasing America's defense, and staying on the lookout for anyone wishing our country harm.

What was our response after the Muslim terrorists bombed the World Trade Center in February 1993, killing six people and injuring hundreds? Nothing. The outcome of our government's investigations should have rung like a morning alarm resonating in every government and military office in our country to wake up and fight against worldwide Islamic jihadist terrorism. Al Qaeda–trained Islamic fighters brought down two U.S. helicopters in October 1993 in Somalia, killing eighteen U.S. rangers. What did we do? Nothing.

What was our response when Muslims exploded a truck bomb in June 1996 in the air force's Khobar Towers housing complex in Dhahran, Saudi Arabia, injuring more than 500? Nothing. What was our response when Islamists exploded a truck bomb in August 1998, destroying the U.S. embassies in Nairobi, Kenya, and Dar es Salaam, Tanzania, leaving 234 dead, including 12 Americans, and injuring more than 5,000? Nothing.

What was our response when the same Islamic fanatics bombed the USS *Cole* in October 2000, blasting a hole in it as the ship took on fuel in Aden, Yemen, killing 17 sailors and wounding 39? Nothing.[28]

In a shameful effort to demonstrate strength, President Clinton launched some guided missiles onto a deserted terrorist camp in the desert, hoping that the headline would replace his sexual escapade with Monica Lewinsky in the front pages of America's newspapers.

Our antimilitary attitude as a nation and our cowardly responses to terrorists empowered our enemy to strengthen, grow, acquire weapons, recruit scientists, and place Islamic terrorists right here in our midst, learning flight lessons, to begin our destruction. Finally on September 11, 2001, they tried again and successfully attacked America. Do you have any doubt that if Osama bin Laden had had a nuclear bomb, he would have used it instead of airplanes?

Terrorist networks have set up shop in America. They took their time watching our reaction, learning our weaknesses, learning how to use our political system, and studying our immigration system and how it works. America has focused on al Qaeda only as the most threatening group du jour and America's number-one enemy. This is a grave mistake. Al Qaeda is nothing more than a melting pot of Islamists from different countries and various Islamic militant groups that share an ideology and a hatred for the West. Intelligence reports show evidence that Hamas, the terrorist organization that most Americans believe is Israel's problem, and Hezbollah, that most Americans believe is a Lebanese problem, have both established cells in the United States and networks with al Qaeda to perpetrate suicide bombings in American cities.[29] The Muslim Brotherhood is also active in the United States.[30]

America's problems with terrorist infiltration stem from its long, porous borders with Canada and Mexico. Our Canadian border stretches more than four thousand miles, while the Mexican one is about two thousand miles long. Almost half these borders are in unpopulated areas and are not patrolled. Thousands of terrorists can get in undetected. The Mexican border poses the most dangerous threat.

Non-Mexicans—called the politically correct OTMs (other than Mexicans) so that we do not call them for who they are, Muslim Arabs—are being sneaked into our country by the notorious Mexican MS 13 gang. It is estimated that thousands of sleeper agents have been smuggled into the country illegally through the Mexican border alone.[31] Many sources within the FBI believe that these terrorists are here in America raising funds and working on logistics, waiting for the opportunity to strike within the United States. Many of them have received training in Lebanon, Syria, Pakistan, and Afghanistan.

The majority of these terror cells are made up of Muslim immigrants from Pakistan, Saudi Arabia, and other Middle Eastern Muslim countries, people have families, relatives, or friends residing in the United States and came in the country legally. However, some of these cells include members who are U.S.-born American Muslim citizens. They are strongly established in Muslim communities, working and running small businesses under the radar, and having meetings, recruiting sympathizers, and offering videos, Arabic magazines, and other publications that encourage hatred of anything Western and glamorize *jihad fe samil el lah,* jihad for Allah. They are also able to raise funds for their cause under the cover of Islamic charities and foundations.[32]

Using our Laws, Bill of Rights, Constitution, and Fair-mindedness to Plot Our Destruction

International terrorist organizations of all sorts have set up shop in America,[33] and they are taking advantage of religious, civic, and charitable organizations, using our laws for their protection. They are fooling the American public by appearing to be charitable and human rights organizations. After September 11, 2001, the U.S. government shut down a few of these charities with links to terrorism, such as the Holy Land Foundation. Our politically correct law enforcement officials and especially naïve, ignorant leaders of religious or educational institutions, who want to believe the best about everyone and not judge anyone, are more than willing to encourage and sponsor groups such as the Council for American-Islamic Relations (CAIR) in the name of multiculturalism and diversity. We are facing total destruction at the hands of an enemy that is absolutely committed to killing *the Great Satan America.*

These American-based terrorists have been able to use such Islamic charities and front small businesses to send equipment to terrorist groups in the Middle East, to offer financial rewards to the families of suicide bombers, and to coordinate efforts with other terrorist networks around the world to attack American interests abroad while preparing for the right time to strike here in the homeland.

According to Philadelphia-based terrorism scholar Daniel Pipes writing in the *New York Post,* fifteen warrants were executed in March 2002. In Ann Arbor, Michigan, Rabih Haddad was accused of funneling money to terrorists via the Global Relief Foundation in December 2001 (he was later deported); in Justice, Illinois, Enaam Arnaout, executive director of the Benevolence International Foundation, was accused of funneling money to al Qaeda and other terrorist organizations (April 2002); in New York, Mohammed Yousry, Ahmed Abdel Sattar, and Yassir al-Sirri have been accused of passing messages between Sheikh Omar Abdul Rahman (serving a life sentence for his part in an attempt to blow up New York City landmarks) and his followers (April 2002); in Chicago, Jose Padilla was accused of being an al Qaeda member who was plotting to release a dirty bomb in a U.S. city in May 2002 (he pled guilty to a racketeering charge not involving al Qaeda); and in Sunrise, Florida, Adham Hassoun was suspected of organizing al Qaeda operatives in the United States (June 2002) . . . and the list goes on.[34]

The largest networks and most dangerous terrorist groups in the United States are Hamas, al Qaeda, and Islamic Jihad. Some of their members and supporters have entered the country illegally using visa fraud. For example, Abu Mezer, who was arrested by New York City police in 1997 for planning to bomb the city subway system, had been captured three different times by the INS within little more than a year prior to his arrest, each time for illegally entering the country from Canada.[35]

Terrorist Cells in the United States

Of all the Islamic terrorist groups in the United States, Hamas has developed the largest network of cells, spreading across the U.S. from sea to shining sea. According to intelligence information, it has cells in Boston; New York City; Laurel, Maryland; Potomac, Maryland; Washington, D.C; Herndon, Virginia; Springfield, Virginia; Raleigh, North Carolina; Boca Raton, Florida; Ft. Lauderdale, Florida; Philadelphia; Cleveland; Charlotte; Orlando; Tampa; Detroit; Houston; Columbia, Missouri; Plainfield, Illinois; Kansas City, Kansas; Chicago; Denver; Oklahoma City; Arlington, Texas; Dallas; Tucson; Seattle; San Francisco; Santa Clara; Los Angeles; and San Diego.[36]

Hamas is right in many of your towns and cities, right in your backyard. And it's our lazy and ignorant government officials and lax laws that have allowed them to come here to plan our destruction. Many are still blind in this country to the threat that we face. When are we going to wake up? Yes, we now have the Department of Homeland Security, but without all Americans, the public as well as all branches of government, supporting the war on terrorism, our success will be limited.

We need to know our enemy better. And I'm not talking just about al Qaeda. How many of you have read the Hamas charter published in August 1988? It is public information and will open your eyes as to why you need to become active and involved in protecting our country. For example, Article 22 states:

Our enemies have planned from time immemorial in order to reach the position they've obtained now. They strive to collect enormous material riches to be used in the realization of their dream. With money, they've gained control of the international media beginning with news agencies,

newspapers and publishing houses, broadcasting stations. They also used
this wealth to stir revolutions in different parts of the world in order to
fulfill their interests and reap their fruits. With their money they created
secret organizations that spread around the world in order to destroy so-
cieties and carry out Zionist interests. Such organizations are the
Freemasons, Rotary Clubs, Lions Clubs, B'nai B'rith and the like. All of
them are destructive espionage organizations. With their money they've
taken control of the imperialist states and pushed them to occupy many
countries in order to exploit the wealth of those countries and spread cor-
ruption there.[37]

Did any of you Rotary Club and Lions Club members know you are
mentioned in the charter of Hamas, the largest terrorist Islamic group
in the United States, and that you are considered the enemy to be destroyed?

We are now facing the distinct possibility of mass murder on a far
grander scale than the Holocaust. With al Qaeda threatening a nuclear attack on major U.S. cities,[38] with its desire to obtain weapons
of mass destruction including chemical weapons and radiological-
dispersion devices, and having some American Muslim citizens committed to our destruction in the name of jihad and in loyalty to Dar al
Islam (the house of Islam), we could be facing disaster.

Our willingness as a nation to support our intelligence community
and provide it with whatever laws that will enable it to track and infiltrate cells in America will determine our demise or survival. The
tragedy of September 11 could be the end of terrorism on American
soil or the beginning of the end of American civilization.

After driving most of the Christians out of the Middle East and
successfully infiltrating Europe, the Islamists have set their eyes on
fighting the infidels of the United States. They are using our laws, Bill
of Rights, Constitution, and fair-mindedness to plot our destruction.
When the news broke about federal officials checking U.S. mosques
for radiation levels, CAIR was in uproar. Ibrahim Hooper, CAIR's
spokesperson, stated: "This creates the appearance that Muslims are

targeted simply for being Muslims." A CAIR statement said that the monitoring "could lead to the perception that we are no longer a nation ruled by law, but instead one in which fear trumps constitutional rights. All Americans should be concerned about the apparent trend toward a two-tiered system of justice, with full rights for most citizens, and another diminished set of rights for Muslims."[39]

Here we have the head of an Islamic organization in America whose founders have been convicted of ties to terrorism with the audacity to use the Constitution against a genuine effort to protect our country from a catastrophic attack. If Mr. Hooper and CAIR invest their efforts in investigating the jihadists living among us, working with our authorities to turn them in, working with imams on preaching tolerance and American patriotism, maybe we wouldn't have to monitor mosques. Instead, all CAIR does is complain about every effort we put forth in trying to protect America. There is no constitutional right that will protect anyone or any institution that wants to harbor radioactive material to use in killing American citizens. We are in a time of war and must do whatever it takes to protect our citizens.

People and Organizations in the U.S. Who Are Aiding Our Enemies

Americans should be concerned when they hear the likes of CAIR up in arms condemning the surveillance of mosques and the monitoring of U.S. citizens' phone conversations when talking to terrorists in the Middle East or elsewhere in the world. Since September 11, 2001, there have been hundreds of arrests and convictions of Muslims inside the United States. These Muslims have been arrested for plotting terrorist attacks on American soil, for money laundering activities, for drug trafficking, for credit card fraud, and for car theft. Our U.S. authorities investigating and putting these people on trial have concluded that these activities have been linked to financing Islamic terrorist attacks against innocent civilians. According to a *Washington Times* article, criminal prosecutors and investigators, working with state and local authorities, have disrupted more than 150 terrorist cells and threats from Portland, Oregon, to Lackawanna, New York, incapacitating more than 3,000 known operatives. Law enforcement officials have also charged 375 persons in terrorism-related cases, 195 of whom have already pleaded guilty or been convicted, and have removed from the country more than 500 people linked to September 11. The targeted terrorists have included members of al Qaeda, Hezbollah, and Hamas as part of an effort to prevent and prosecute those who commit or intend to commit terrorist acts against the United States.[40]

As our federal agents and investigators have started digging deeper into the base of the Islamic American communities in their quest to discover and unveil terrorists living among us, they have implicated some of America's most politically active Muslim groups operating under the cover of human and civil rights organizations and charities. By August 2003 President Bush had named five Islamic charities and six senior Hamas officials as Special Designated Global Terrorist Entities (SDGTs). The assets of these organizations were frozen immediately.

One of the people named was Musa Abu Marzook, who founded the Islamic Association for Palestine (IAP) in Richardson, Texas, in 1981. Throughout the 1980s and 1990s the organization held annual conferences throughout the United States, inviting as keynote speakers radical Islamists and terrorists from Hamas and the Muslim Brotherhood who bragged about executing successful terror attacks on innocent civilians overseas, especially in Israel.

The IAP worked closely with another Richardson-based organization, the Holy Land Foundation for Relief and Development, whose assets the federal government froze on December 4, 2001. Then–treasury secretary Paul O'Neill accused the organization of masquerading as a charity while its primary function was raising funds for the terror group Hamas.

It is also out of IAP that the Council on American-Islamic Relations was formed by two IAP officials, Omar Ahmad and Nihad Awad.[41] Of all the Islamic organizations in America, CAIR has risen to the top as the most visible, most outspoken defender of Muslims in the United States. Masquerading as a civil rights organization, CAIR has had a hidden agenda to Islamize America from the start. Its cofounder and chairman, Omar Ahmad, a Palestinian American, told a Muslim audience in Fremont, California, in 1998: "Islam isn't in America to be equal to any other faith, but to become dominant. The Koran should be the highest authority in America, and Islam the only accepted religion on Earth." Ibrahim Hooper, CAIR's national spokesman, is on record stating: "I wouldn't want to create the impression that I wouldn't like the government of the United States to be Islamic." Three of CAIR's officials have already been convicted of terror-related crimes.[42] One even worked for Hooper. He's now in prison for conspiring to kill Americans.

Despite its links to terrorism or providing support to terrorists, CAIR grew to become a major player in Islamic American politics. The organization is lobbying in Washington, D.C., and working hard in fighting the United States government under the name of civil rights and civil liberty while complaining against every security measure our government is trying to take to fight terrorism at home.

CAIR has refused to come out and condemn terrorist organizations such as Hamas, Islamic Jihad, al Qaeda, al Gamaat al Islamiya, the Muslim Brotherhood, and Hezbollah by name. Any time CAIR speaks against terrorism, its verbiage is so vague and general, it's an insult to the intelligence of the American public to call the statements condemnations of terrorism. After the London bombing, CAIR issued a condemnation so meaningless it required explanation. CAIR's statement denounced "all acts of terrorism targeting civilians and innocent lives." Now that sounds satisfactory to the average American ears, doesn't it? CAIR counts on ignorance and the West's hunger to hear any condemnation coming from a Muslim organization. The fact is that Islamic jihadists do not consider innocent or civilian any American and most certainly any Jew. The Islamic jihadists consider any tax-paying American guilty of contributing and supporting the Great Satan with his or her money and allowing evil to spread via the American government elected by the American people. The Islamic jihadists consider every civilian Israeli a guilty soldier because at one time in their lives, all Israelis serve in the Israeli army, as mandated by the Israeli government. So every child is a future soldier and every grandmother is a former soldier. Their death is a gift to God, and martyrdom while killing them is the way to God and his blessings.

CAIR may talk a good and moderate talk, but its actions speak louder than words. The statement condemning terror was written by Taha Jaber al-Alwani, who himself happens to be an unindicted co-conspirator in the ongoing terror case against Sami al-Arian, the Florida professor linked to Hamas and the Palestinian Islamic Jihad in America.

What is also disturbing is that a Saudi foundation run by the crown prince of Dubai owns the deed to CAIR's headquarters, located practically in the White House's backyard. This terror-supporting foundation has raised millions using a TV telethon to support families of Palestinian suicide bombers and to glorify suicide bombers and martyrdom. During the televised event, Islamic clergymen made calls for the destruction of Israel and America. According to various reports, one Saudi offered his car so that it could be used "to blow up a military barracks and kill [Israeli] soldiers," and a six-year-old boy made a symbolic donation of fake plastic explosives.[43]

CAIR was also associated with and worked with the Global Relief Foundation and the Holy Land Foundation. After September 11 both organizations were closed down by the U.S. government on terrorism-related charges. According to a report by the Treasury Department, "the Global Relief Foundation has connections to, has provided support for, and has provided assistance to Usama Bin Ladin, the al-Qaeda Network, and other known terrorist groups."[44]

You would think that after that, CAIR would stay out of sight. Instead, CAIR came out vigorously defending these two groups. CAIR blamed the U.S. government for racial profiling in the closure of the Global Relief Foundation, calling it an organization that "had established a track record of effective relief work."[45] The great scholar of Islam Daniel Pipes sites:

CAIR is also on the wrong side in the war on terrorism. A few examples of many:

+ In October 1998, the group demanded the removal of a Los Angeles billboard describing Osama bin Laden as "the sworn enemy," claiming this depiction was "offensive to Muslims."

+ CAIR deemed the conviction of the perpetrators of the 1993 World Trade Center bombing "a travesty of justice."

+ CAIR called the conviction of Omar Abdul Rahman, the blind sheikh who planned to blow up New York City landmarks, a "hate crime."

+ When President Bush closed the Holy Land Foundation for collecting money he said was "used to support the Hamas terror organization," CAIR decried his action as "unjust" and "disturbing."

When evaluating anything CAIR says, readers should keep this organization's history—and demonstrated sympathies—in mind.[46]

In an article titled "Profile of Terror," Evan McCormick, a Research Associate at the Center for Security Policy in Washington, D.C., writes: Since September 11, 2001, no fewer than three CAIR officials—Randall Todd Royer, Ghassan Elashi, and Bassem Khafagi—have been found guilty on charges resulting from major counterterrorism investigations. Royer, who worked as a communications specialist with CAIR, was charged with providing material support to al Qaeda. Nihad Awad, one of CAIR founders, has stated, "I am in support of the Hamas movement." Communications director Ibrahim Hooper has defended Saudi financial aid given to families of suicide bombers.[47]

The sad reality is that CAIR and other Islamic groups speaking as representatives of mainstream Muslims in the United States and trying to influence U.S. antiterrorism policy are undeniably and clearly linked to the very terrorist network that U.S. officials are trying to thwart.

Another Islamic organization of concern in our war against terrorism is the Muslim American Society (MAS). The society was founded by extremists, and despite its efforts to clean up its public image, the core of its teaching remains hostile to non-Muslims. In 1993 American leaders of the extremist Muslim Brotherhood, an international Islamic fundamentalist group, decided to start calling themselves the Muslim American Society. Their founder, Hassan al-Banna, has endorsed violence as a means to spreading the rule of Islamic law throughout the world, according to the Brotherhood's goal.

Even though listening to Mahdi Bray, the society's executive director, speaking on Fox News, would give you the idea that MAS has moved away from its extremist foundation, its actions demonstrate that this couldn't be further from the truth. In an interview with Fox Bray said that MAS plan is to "inoculate our young people by making sure they're actively and constructively engaged in positive activities that reflect the main views of their faith tradition, as opposed to someone who would want to influence them into extremist points." This sounds wonderful. However, as you peel the layers off this rhetoric and look at MAS's policies, actions, and teachings, you will see that they are the exact opposite of his words.

MAS requires its members to read Hassan al-Banna's theological tome *Message of the Teachings*. In it, al-Banna clearly states that all governments must become Islamic, and he encourages his followers to "completely boycott non-Islamic courts and judicial systems" and to "dissociate yourself from organizations, newspapers, committees, schools and institutions which oppose your Islamic ideology." In addition to al-Banna's work, members of MAS are required to read Sayyid Qutb's book *Milestones,* in which Qutb states that a legitimate goal of jihad is "to establish God's authority on earth" or to "arrange human affairs according to the true guidance provided by God." Qutb is discussed at length in the 9/11 Commission Report because he is one of Osama bin Laden's theological inspirations.

Among the many books the society also recommends is *Methodology of Da'wah* by Shamim Siddiqui. According to counterterrorism consultant Daveed Gartenstein-Ross, the book argues for an Islamic takeover of America because Washington's "treacherous hands" allegedly intervened whenever Muslims were on the verge of establishing an Islamic state. Siddiqui states that society will polarize between Muslims and non-Muslims "in every walk of life" as Muslims gain power, but that if Muslims are careful, there will be a general "rush to Islam" that can make the faith dominant in the U.S.[48]

So let's look at Mahdi Bray, MAS's executive director. Here is an excerpt from testimony by Dr. J. Michael Waller, Annenberg Professor of International Communication the Institute of World Politics, regarding "Terrorist Recruitment and Infiltration in the United States: Prisons and Military as an Operational Base," before the Subcommittee on Terrorism, Technology and Homeland Security, on October 14, 2003:

Appendix 2: Key Organizations Involved in Muslim Prison Recruitment

National Islamic Prison Foundation (NIPF)—Contact: Mahdi Bray; 1212 New York Ave. NW, Suite 525, Washington, DC 20005. This is the same address as the American Muslim Council (AMC).

- *"Specifically organized to convert American inmates to Wahhabism."*

And at www.masboston.org, the Web site of the Boston chapter of the "Muslim American Society" there are quite a number of items of interest. The first is the listing of the "Trainers" of Muslim activists ("training" in how to talk to Infidels at Outreach Meetings or in the conduct of Da'wa [literally, "the call" to proselytize or preach Islam] or in dealing with inquisitive media). In fact only one "trainer" is listed: Mahdi Bray.[49]

So Mahdi Bray can fool some of the people some of the time with his peaceful talk. Luckily, Americans are becoming very informed about the double-talk of these so-called Muslim moderate organizations who are trying to clean up their images with their crafted words yet acting in a completely different matter when talking to their own.

Another organization that should be spotlighted in our investigation of Islamic organizations supporting our enemy in our country is the Muslim Public Affairs Council (MPAC). MPAC talks the sweet talk of interfaith dialogue and understanding. MPAC has defended Hezbollah, which until September 11, 2001, had been responsible for the deadliest attack on U.S. troops in decades. MPAC even lobbied against the United States designating the group, along with Hamas and Palestinian Islamic Jihad, which regularly commit and encourage suicide bombings, terrorists.

MPAC also encourages its Muslim members to send in their so-called grievances and report what they perceive as hate crimes, and actively discourages Muslim Americans from cooperating with U.S. authorities investigating terrorism-related issues.[50]

Because of the actions of these organizations, which supposedly represent mainstream Muslims in America, how can we as a country fight successfully this holy war declared on us by fanatics? When we are living with moles within our country, masquerading as a voice of understanding and using our laws to fight us under the banner of civil liberties and human rights, how can we expect to win this war? When those same Islamic organizations praise our enemies, using our freedom of speech, and not only refuse to condemn them, but state their agreement with them and lobby to stop our government from designating them as terrorists, how can we expect to win this war?

9.

THE TOXIC TSUNAMI
OF HATE

In order to become a citizen of the United States, I had to learn some basic facts about American history, which I was happy and proud to do. When I studied the American Revolutionary War, I learned about Patrick Henry, a great patriot and an icon in the history of freedom. Two hundred thirty years ago, Patrick Henry said, "Give me liberty or give me death." However, all he and the American revolutionaries had to worry about was taxation without representation and redcoat soldiers bivouacked in their parlors. The British weren't bombing their churches and beheading their families.

On September 11, 2001, nineteen Muslim terrorists gave us death. Citizens of the most powerful country on earth watched in horror as a handful of barbaric men used airplanes as missiles and flew them into skyscrapers and the Pentagon, our symbol of power. These men not only brought the Twin Towers down, they brought the United States of America to its knees. Wall Street froze, the stock market tumbled, and national air traffic ground to a halt.

Muslims have been sounding the call to war for the last thirty-some years, but until 9/11 America was not listening. Americans were not watching the evening news and were not interested in documentaries about world affairs, nor were they listening to radical Muslims proudly and repeatedly announcing their intention to destroy our civilization. On 9/11, and for days afterward, there was rejoicing all over the Arab world.[1] Arabs were dancing in the streets. They were dancing in the streets of Syria. They were dancing in the streets of Egypt, an ally to which we yearly give $2 billion of our hard-earned money. They were dancing in the streets of the Palestinian territories, for which our government brokered a peace deal with Yasser Arafat and the Israelis, and committed millions per year for their development. They were dancing in the streets of Lebanon and Jordan. They were dancing because the World Trade Center had collapsed and the Pentagon was burning. They were handing out candy and shouting "Allahu Akbar" because thousands of Americans had died.

Both the attacks themselves and their glorification in the name of God are incomprehensible to the vast majority of Americans. Americans asked why people would rejoice at the loss of innocent life. There is a three-word answer that is both simple and complex: because they hate. They hate our way of life. They hate our freedom. They hate our democracy. They hate the practice of every religion but their own. They don't just disagree. They *hate*. Not just Judaism. Not just Christianity. In various parts of the world today, Islamists are also waging terror war against Hindus, Buddhists, and all other "infidels." The imposition of Islam upon the entire world is not merely their goal. It is their religious duty. They are following the word of their holy book, the Koran, which is the guide to hatred of infidels, waging war, and victory through slaughter.

Don't take my word for it. Read it in their own words—and not just the words of Osama bin Laden, coming from some remote wasteland by way of Al Jazeera television. Read the words of the government of our so-called moderate ally Saudi Arabia, coming from Washington, D.C., by way of the Saudi embassy. A recent report by Freedom House/Center for Religious Freedom clearly reveals the toxic tsunami of religious hatred that Saudi Arabia has unleashed *here in the United States*.[2] The entire report can be found online at www .freedomhouse.org/religion.

In compiling the report, the center studied over two hundred books and publications collected from more than a dozen of the most prominent mosques and Islamic institutions in the United States, including those in Washington, D.C., New York, Chicago, Houston, Dallas, Los Angeles, and Oakland. All of these books and publications were financed and produced directly or indirectly by the Saudi government. Some of the books were texts from Islamic schools. Some were publications issued by the Saudi government specifically to provide guidance to Muslims living in or visiting the United States.

These Saudi books and publications repeatedly exhort Muslims, in their relations with *all non-Muslims,* to "hate them for their religion,"[3] to "hate . . . for Allah's sake,"[4] to "always oppose them in every way,"[5] to maintain a "wall of resentment" against them.[6] They say that democracy is "responsible for all of the horrible wars" of the twentieth century and that "attractive names like democracy, . . . justice, freedom, brotherhood and equality" cause all of the world's problems.[7]

They say that all religions but Islam are false, and that it is the religious duty of *every* Muslim to impose "functionally Islamic governments" on every country in the world. This religious duty is "binding in principle, in law, in self-defense, in community, and as a sacred obligation of jihad."[8] In order to fulfill this "sacred obligation of jihad," Muslims must "invade its western heartland, and struggle to overcome it until all the world shouts by the name of the Prophet [Muhammad] and the teachings of Islam spread throughout the world. Only then will Muslims achieve their *fundamental goal. . . .* [A]ll religion will be exclusively for Allah [emphasis added]."[9]

Are you outraged yet? These are supposedly our allies? With friends like these, who needs enemies? Where is our government, which is supposed to protect us? Have our politicians all been so corrupt and so paid to look the other way? Has Saudi money become far more important to our government and our institutions than the love of country? Our founding fathers are turning in their grave at our apathy. Keep on reading. It only gets better.

In addition to the hundreds of books and publications published by Saudi Arabia teaching arrogance, intolerance, and hate, the Islamic Affairs Department of the embassy of Saudi Arabia maintains a Web site entitled "The Religion of Islam" (http://www.iad.org/) which explains the principles and beliefs of Islam. This Web site contains such gems as:

> *Democracy and capitalism are two of "today's false idols, which dominate over the entire world."*[10]

> *"[A]ny form of worship that does not conform to Islam is not valid."*[11]

> *Under the presumptuous heading "Rights Granted by Nature," the official Saudi Web site states that in Islamic society, Christians and Jews "are not allowed to display any* abominable deed or gesture that could go into conflict with Islam, such as the cross or the bell *[emphasis added]."*[12]

This official Saudi Web site again explains the fundamental goal of Islam in simple, easy-to-understand English that even the most naïve reader will understand: "The Muslims are required to raise the banner of Jihad in order to make the Word of Allah supreme in this world."[13]

The material in the Saudi books and publications and on the embassy's official Web site clearly demonstrates that the hatred the Saudis teach and the jihad they preach extends not only to Christians and Jews, but to all non-Muslims, everywhere. Further, the poisonous hatred spewed into the United States by Saudi Arabia is gentle and benevolent compared to the curricula of applied terrorism taught at Saudi-funded madrassas in Pakistan, Indonesia, and other parts of the Muslim world. Young boys spend their mornings screaming verses from the Koran by rote (in Arabic that they do not necessarily understand), and they spend their afternoons learning how to slit throats, shoot assault rifles, and turn themselves into bombs. Between 1975 and 2002, the Saudis spent over $70 billion to spread their noxious brew of arrogant and intolerant Islam all over the world. In Pakistan alone, the Saudis spend approximately $350 million per year to operate madrassas. The Saudis have built 210 Islamic centers, 202 colleges, more than 1,500 mosques, and almost 2,000 schools to "educate" Muslims about their "sacred obligation of jihad" to make Islam "supreme in this world."[13] And we wonder where this hate is coming from? We wonder how fifteen out of nineteen hijackers on 9/11 were actually from an ally country?

This "sacred obligation" to impose Islam upon the entire world is not a distortion of Islam, nor is it the creation of a few extremists who have hijacked a peaceful and tolerant religion. It is mandated by the holy writings of Islam, as interpreted by a vast majority of the classical authorities. According to Islam, the Koran is the word of God (Allah), revealed to and through the prophet Muhammad. The Hadith, or "Traditions," are reports of the words and actions of Muhammad, "as witnessed by his followers and passed on through other reliable believers."[15] Sharia is Islamic law, as it developed under the Koran and Hadith. According the eminent scholar of Islamic history and culture Bernard Lewis, Cleveland E. Dodge Professor Emeritus of Near Eastern Studies at Princeton University,

> [i]n the Qur'an and still more in the Traditions, [the term jihad] . . . has usually been understood as meaning "to wage war." The great collections of hadith all contain a section devoted to jihad, in which the military meaning predominates. [Footnote omitted.] The same is true of the classical manuals of shari'a law. . . . The overwhelming majority of classical theologians, jurists, and traditionalists . . . understood the obligation of jihad in a military sense. . . . According to Muslim teaching, jihad is one of the basic commandments of the faith, an obligation imposed upon all Muslims by God, through revelation. . . . It must continue until the whole world has either accepted the Islamic faith or submitted to the power of the Islamic state.[16]

Throughout the Koran and the Hadith, harb ("war") and qital ("killing," "slaughter") are ordained by Allah as the unavoidable and immutable punishment for refusing to convert or submit to Islam. The most respected collection of Hadith, that of Muhammad bin Ismail bin al-Mughirah al-Bukhari (died A.D. 870), contains 199 references to *jihad,* and every one uses the term to mean warfare against infidels.[17]

People that tell you that Islam is a religion of peace are only announcing their ignorance and lack of understanding of a poisonous formula that has been developed for mass use on the whole world. This ignorance endangers the lives of millions who live in the West and enjoy a Western lifestyle. People who speak Arabic and can read the Koran in the language it was written in, not in any watered-down version or in selected verses fed to us by our enemy, know better.

"Moderate" Muslims, and apologists and propagandists for Islam, will attempt to deny or obscure the real meaning, nature, and intent of jihad. Some will say that jihad means only a Muslim's "inner struggle" to be a better person, and that jihad has no military meaning whatever. Others will acknowledge that Muslims have a religious duty to spread Islam throughout the world, but insist that it is to be spread only peacefully, through *dawah*—literally "the call"—meaning persuasion and reasoning. Finally, some will go so far as to admit that it can also mean warfare, but insist that in Islam, warfare is allowed only in self-defense or against oppression. However, all of these assertions are examples of a tactic that Islam encourages in waging jihad: *taqiyya* or *kithman*—"lying," "deception," "deceit." Muslims are encouraged to lie if, in the opinion of the liar, telling the lie will be "good" for Islam. This is a documented fact according to both ancient and modern scholars of Islam.[18] The renowned classical Islamic scholar and theologian Abu Hamid Muhammad al-Ghazali (1058–1111) instructs that "[s]peaking is a means to achieve objectives" and that "it is permissible to lie if attaining the goal is permissible."[19] More recently, Amir Taheri, author of numerous books on Islam and the Middle East, states that according to Islam, "Muslims have every right to lie and to deceive their adversaries, and a promise made to a non-Muslim can be broken whenever necessary."[20] According to Abdullah al-Araby,

> *within Islam there are certain provisions under which lying is not simply tolerated, but actually encouraged. The book* The Spirit of Islam, *by the Muslim scholar Afif A. Tabbarah, was written to promote Islam. On page 247, Tabbarah stated: "Lying is not always bad, to be sure; there are times when telling a lie is more profitable and better for the general welfare, and for the settlement of conciliation among people, than telling the truth. To this effect, the Prophet says: 'He is not a false person who [through lies] settles conciliation among people, supports good or says what is good.'* "[21]

Since the sacred goal of jihad is to make Islam "supreme in this world," every lie told to achieve that goal is not only permitted, but sanctified. Obviously it is "good" for Islam that the infidel should be kept ignorant of the true meaning of jihad. The Islamists' strategy is working perfectly on the gullible, good-hearted, fair-minded, make-love-not-war crowd, raised in the comfort of the West.

Taqiyya/kithman can take different forms. One form is blatant lying, asserting as fact something that is not true, such as claiming that jihad means only a Muslim's "inner struggle" to be a better person, and that jihad has no military meaning whatever. A more insidious form of *taqiyya/kithman* is dissembling, telling part of the truth, but intentionally concealing a more important truth in order to create a false impression. An example is acknowledging the Muslims' religious duty to spread Islam throughout the world, but insisting that it is to be spread peacefully, through *dawah,* persuasion and reasoning. This assertion is very reasonable and appealing to the Western mind. However, it is intended to deceive. While it is true that Muslims must *initially* use *dawah* to spread Islam, this *taqiyya* intentionally conceals the fact, based on numerous passages of the Koran and Islamic tradition, that when *dawah* fails, Muslims must *impose* Islam on the infidel through *harb* and *qital*—war, killing, slaughter.

A related example of *taqiyya* is acknowledging that Islam permits war, but asserting that it is permitted only for defensive purposes. This could be referred to as double *taqiyya*. First, according to the Koran and the Hadith, aggressive warfare for the purpose of imposing Islam on the world is the ultimate religious obligation of jihad.[22] Second, the history of the expansion of Islam clearly reveals its aggressive, offensive nature. In the seventh century, Islam did not emerge peacefully from the Arabian Peninsula floating harmlessly on the breeze. Islam was spread across the Middle East and North Africa at the edge of the sword. The only choice offered by the Muslim conquerors was conversion or submission to Islam, or death. The same choice was offered when Muslims subjugated Spain and Portugal in 711, and occupied all or part of the Iberian Peninsula until 1492, an occupation of almost eight centuries. Shortly after conquering Spain and Portugal, the Muslims invaded France, but they were repulsed in 732. Muslims also invaded, conquered, and occupied Sicily and large parts of Italy. In addition to invading Spain, France, Sicily, and Italy from North Africa, Muslim armies repeatedly invaded Europe from the east, until they were finally driven out for the last time in 1683. Islam was not waging "defensive" war when it conquered and occupied Spain, Sicily, and Italy or when it besieged Vienna three times.

We are seeing today an escalation of Islamic influence throughout the world as radical Muslims use their resources to finance terrorism and bring nation after nation to its knees. They are not robed Arabs waving swords and riding horses, charging at our borders. They are using their wealth, which the West has created for them with oil, to purchase Western corporations, establish schools, and buy and control media conglomerates to spread their radical message throughout the Arab and the Western worlds. They are buying plane tickets, arriving in our cities first-class, delivering their babies in our hospitals, and acquiring our citizenship legally and illegally using whatever resources they have to obtain it. They are coming in throngs and settling in our lands. They are outreproducing us almost seven to one.[23] Their invasion and declaration of war may be disguised under our Western lifestyle, but nevertheless it is an invasion. You just have to open your eyes and connect the dots to see the picture unfolding right before your eyes. They are so confident that they declare their message and intent from mosques, state it on television, and spin out suicide bombers throughout the globe. All we have to do is watch and listen. Just look at Europe (France, Denmark, Britain) and what is happening over there. The U.S. is not there yet, but we are not far behind before Islamic riots start breaking out on American streets.

Muslims deny that jihad has any military meaning, and assert that Islam permits only defensive warfare; Muslim apologists, propagandists, and so-called moderates will quote sura (chapter) and verse from the Koran to "prove" that Islam is a tolerant and peaceful religion. There are, indeed, verses in the Koran which call for patience and tolerance. This is the partial truth that is used to create a lie.

Taqiyya is created by concealing the fact that the Koran also contains verses, written *later* in Muhammad's preaching ministry, which call for unremitting war and violence against infidels until they submit to Islam. They conceal the fact that, under the Islamic doctrine of *naksh,* or "abrogation," when there is a contradiction between verses in the Koran, the later verse supersedes the earlier verse.[24] According to sura 2:106, a later verse "substitutes something better" in place of an earlier verse; according to sura 16:101, the later verse will "substitute one revelation for another." Chronologically, sura 9 was the second-to-last chapter written by Muhammad. Sura 9:5 commands Muslims to "fight the Pagans wherever ye find them, and seize them, beleaguer them, and lie in wait for them in every stratagem (of war)." Sura 5 was the very last chapter written by Muhammad. Sura 5:33 states that "[f]or those who do not submit to Allah their punishment is . . . execution or crucifixion, or the cutting off of hands and feet, from the opposite sides, or exile from the land." According to some scholars of Islam, verses 9:5 and 5:33, all by themselves, supersede and cancel at least 124 earlier verses in which Muhammad preached patience and tolerance.[25] For Muhammad and Islam, the revelations of violent jihad replaced the revelations of peace.

The hatred, treachery, and violence of the Koran and the Hadith are reflected in the relationships between the rival power centers of the Islamist movement. The religion of Islam has two main branches, the Sunni and the Shia, along with a number of smaller sects and denominations (e.g., the Alawis, the Ismailis, the Druze). A substantial majority of the Arab world is Sunni, but there are significant Shia minority populations in many Arab countries, and the Shia constitute a majority in Iraq and in non-Arab Iran.

The Wahhabi or Salafi school of Sunni Islam is practiced and propagated by "moderate" Saudi Arabia as well as by the Taliban and the al Qaeda terrorist network. All over the world, from Pakistan and Indonesia to the USA, this is the version of Islam that is preached at every institution built or supported by Saudi oil money.[26] According to Wahhabi Sunni religious doctrine, Shia Muslims are apostates from Islam, and therefore deserve death even more than Jews, Christians, and pagans.[27] The late Abu Musab al-Zarqawi, declared by Osama bin Laden to be the "emir of al Qaeda in Iraq,"[28] relied on this religious doctrine in declaring jihad in 2005 on Iraqi Shia Muslims.[29]

The Shia extremists, led by Iranian disciples of the Ayatollah Khomeini and exemplified by the terrorist organization Hezbollah, have demonstrated themselves to be just as hateful and just as murderous as the Wahhabi Sunnis. We must remember that it was the Shia of Hezbollah who pioneered the tactic of suicide bombing.

Furthermore, both the Sunni and Shia Islamists consider the nominally secular pan-Arab nationalist governments (such as Assad's Syria, Mubarak's Egypt, and the Iraq of Saddam Hussein) to be apostates deserving of death. On the occasions when Islamists have challenged the authority of these Arab nationalist dictatorships, the Islamists have been slaughtered, sometimes by the tens of thousands. In 1982, the Muslim Brotherhood, a Wahhabi paramilitary organization, sought to bring down the Syrian Baathist dictatorship of Hafez al-Assad. In response, Assad attacked and destroyed the city of Hama, which had been a stronghold of the Brotherhood. According to Amnesty International, between ten thousand and twenty-five thousand inhabitants of Hama were killed, most of them civilians.[30] More recently, the Muslim Brotherhood in Egypt was brutally suppressed after launching a terror campaign to destabilize the Mubarak government.

However, despite all of this intense mutual hatred and wholesale slaughter, Sunni and Shia Islamist terrorists will join forces with each other, and with secular Arab terrorist states, despite assumptions to the contrary by some "experts." They will do so whenever they believe it will serve their own tactical or strategic interests. For instance, secular Syria and Shia Iran have been close allies for over twenty years, since shortly after Saddam Hussein invaded Iran in 1981. The fundamentalist Shia Iranians had no theological problems in forming an alliance with Syria's Assad, a rigidly secular pan-Arab apostate who had killed thousands of Muslim fundamentalists. The terrorist alliance between Iran and Syria still exists today, even though the cast of characters has changed. In a truly remarkable display of Sunni-Shia-secular terrorist cooperation, Sunni terrorists from all over the Arab world are trained in Lebanon by Shia Hezbollah, under the protection of secular Arab nationalist Syria, paid for by Shia Iran. After their training is completed, these Sunni terrorists are transported through Syria and smuggled into Iraq, where they will commit terrorist atrocities, mostly against Shia Iraqis. There are numerous other examples of cooperation between some combination of Sunni, Shia, and secular Arab terrorists.[31]

If you want to understand the nature of the enemy we face, visualize a tapestry of snakes. They slither and they hiss, and they could eat each other alive, but they will unite in a hideous mass to achieve their common goal of imposing Islam on the world. This is the enemy we are fighting.

It is certain that there are genuinely moderate Muslims, perhaps a substantial number, who do not seek to impose Islam on this country and the world through violent jihad. However, they are conspicuous by their silence regarding the more problematic doctrines of Islam. To the extent that Muslim "leaders" and lobbying organizations in the United States even address the issue, they offer nothing more than vague, tepid condemnations of terrorist violence and heated denials that the behavior of Islamic terrorists has any connection with Islam.

Where is the Muslim outrage in this country over the supposed few who hijacked their religion? Where is the Million Muslim March on the Mall in Washington, D.C., sending a message to all Muslims in the Arabic world condemning the killing of human beings in the name of Allah? Where is the cry to raise the consciousness of the rest of the Muslim world about their hijacked religion? If something of yours had been stolen, wouldn't you scream to the world that someone had hijacked it?

Where are the voices of Western Muslims, particularly the American Muslim community, sending a clear message to the Arabic world that we are Americans, and when you attack one of us you attack all of us? We condemn and consider the enemy Hamas, Hezbollah, Islamic Jihad, al Gamaat al Islamiya, and the rest of the collection of barbaric Islamic thugs and murderers who have neither conscience nor humanity. Where is the outrage of the Muslim community? Why aren't the imams of every mosque holding press conferences, and inviting the media to tell the American public, "We are Americans first. Any enemy of America is our enemy. We will work to find, stop, arrest, turn in, and condemn anyone in our community who aspires to radicalize our religion and harm our country"?

You hear moderates giving excuses for the Muslims in America by saying that maybe they are afraid to speak because of retaliation. What a bogus excuse. What retaliation? This is America. If American Muslims feel free to burn an American flag on any street corner in the USA, they can voice their opinion freely and openly condemning our enemy, America's enemy. They live here in America, not in Iran or Saudi Arabia. I can understand why supposedly moderate Muslims in the Middle East are afraid to speak. They'd be lynched and have their bodies hung on electricity poles, as they do in the Palestinian territories, Iran, Iraq, and other Islamic countries, to send a message to silence other critics. They'd be hung in the public square for everyone to learn a lesson about speaking about their dictators. But Muslims living in America afraid to speak? Give me a break.

If American Muslims spoke forcefully to condemn terrorist

organizations by name rather than dispensing empty verbiage seeking to soothe American's pain, we in America could start buying their sincerity. Instead of all this talk about what a peaceful religion Islam is, why don't they show us that the majority of Muslims are truly against this barbaric killing being spread around the world in the name of Allah? When mullahs throughout the Arabic world and Europe get on their soapbox in their mosques calling for the killing of all infidel Jews and Christians and establishing Islamic rule, none of the recognized and respected Islamic authorities in America or the West find it necessary to correct them. What does that tell us? What does that tell you about moderate Muslims? Where is their voice? Are they really there? Or are they an invention by Jewish and Christian Westerners who cannot accept the fact that there are people that really, really hate by an order from God according to their religion?

You hear about Wahhabi Islam as the only extreme form of Islam. All the other Muslims are wonderful moderates. What about the suicide bombers who are Egyptians, Lebanese, Palestinians, Syrians, Iraqis, and Iranians? People of these nationalities were not raised in Saudi Arabia, but the common thread between them is written in the Koran. They are simply practicing Muslims. They are not the extreme, they are the mainstream.

Our leaders and politicians bend over backward to tell us how sweetly wonderful Islam is and that most Muslims are moderate, that a few radicals have hijacked this unbelievably sweet poetry called the Koran and are trying to twist it to do harm. Snap out of it, America. America and the West can no longer afford to stay in a state of ignorance. The consequences of this mental laziness are starting to attack the body of our country, and if the necessary medical steps aren't taken now to control it, death will be knocking soon.

The reality is, suicide bombers and mass murderers are produced, financed, and brainwashed from birth by a system, a community, that prepares them to strive to fight for the cause and to attain martyrdom. The Muslim community harbors these killers and arms them to go out into the world and wage jihad. Upon their death, the community celebrates them as heroes. Their funerals are like weddings and they become an ideal that every Muslim kid should strive toward. Terrorist organizations are like a business that is financed, managed, directed, and operated by employees and supporters. They have warehouses for, and purchasers and deliverers of, products such as visas, suicide belts, explosives, and communication devices, all paid for by many people, not just one rogue person. Those terrorists usually live and travel within Muslim communities throughout the world, protected by the Muslim *umma* ("nation").

Muslims are telling us exactly what their plan is. Muslims tell us straight out that their goal is to conquer us and establish Islamic law in Western lands. They are following through on every word they have said so far. It's the West that is refusing to believe what they are saying and even justifying their words by disregarding them as extremists who don't really reflect the views of the majority of moderate Muslims. That's exactly what the Christians thought in Lebanon. They thought that they shouldn't judge everybody, since the majority of Muslims were Lebanese first. Try asking that question to the Lebanese Christian refugees in the diaspora and let's hear what they say. And let us hear it from the moderate Muslims by their actions. When they demonstrate where they stand by their actions, not their empty words, then and only then can we put our guard down.

Moderate Muslims must directly confront the teachings in their religion which support jihad and the killing of infidels, instead of pretending that those teachings do not exist. Before they can be considered truly moderate, they must expressly repudiate the belief that Muslims have the divine right and duty to impose their religion and culture on the entire world. They must acknowledge and repudiate the doctrine of *taqiyya,* the divine right to lie to advance the cause of Islam. In the absence of a repudiation of the supposed right to lie, all promises remain worthless. On an individual and an institutional level, if Muslims are unwilling to relinquish the right to lie and kill in the name of Allah, how can they be considered moderate? It is Islam that declared perpetual war on the non-Muslim world. Unless Islam declares peace, Western civilization must defend itself, or disappear.

10.

THE IVY-COVERED FIFTH COLUMN:

Islamic Influence Alive and Well

on American Campuses

Since 9/11, experts, think tanks, and authors have published volumes about who our enemy is, what their modus operandi is, and what is in store for us in the future. Yet little attention is being paid to one of the least recognized attacks our adversary is making. Their tactic is a subtle flanking maneuver taking place right in the middle of our college and university campuses. The groundwork for this sneak attack was laid well before 9/11, as the United States was then and is still now being inundated with millions of Arab dollars being poured into academic organizations. The irony is that the enemy of our culture and values has successfully hijacked a program that was originally intended to protect us, and is now using it against us.

As the daunting reality of 9/11 set in, many Americans questioned why the United States intelligence community and the public were not better informed about Islamic terrorism and its vision to destroy America and its Western way of life. Discoveries of backlogs of Arabic-language intelligence intercepts, literature, and documents began to surface. Reports of low numbers of intelligence personnel who could read and speak Arabic were alarming. Where was the pool of Arabic-language and Middle Eastern experts in which the government had been investing since 1958?

In an effort to create a reliable resource of talent from which to recruit personnel for Middle Eastern intelligence and espionage, Washington looked to our colleges and universities as a training ground for people versed in the languages and cultures of the Middle East. It turned to a program developed in 1958 called Title VI of the National Defense Education Act (NDEA). The U.S. Department of Education describes the NDEA as a program "to ensure trained manpower of sufficient quality and quantity to meet the national defense needs of the United States." Title VI was the Language Development section of this act, focusing on uncommonly taught languages. Today, these language area centers, or National Resource Centers (NRCs), Foreign Language and Area Studies Fellowships (FLASF), and International Research and Studies (IRS) remain central programs in the Title VI array.[1] This program has not gone unnoticed by the benefactor of Islamic Wahhabism, the Saudis. They saw a good thing, subtly worked their way in, and hijacked Middle Eastern studies on college campuses to their own advantage.

While Saudi-supported Wahhabism fuels hatred within its own ranks in madrassas and mosques toward the West's religious tolerance, relatively liberal social agenda, and permissive lifestyle, it's on campuses across America that Arabs using their petrodollars are undermining our war on terror and softening the brains of Western college students toward radical Islamic fundamentalist dogma. These "lobbyists for Islam" are increasingly penetrating our prestigious centers of higher learning with enormous offerings of cash.[2] The Saudi royal family has spent close to $70 billion worldwide to further the teaching of Wahhabism through Islamic madrassas, and to spread anti-American and anti-Israel sentiment. Much of this money is spent deceptively on U.S. college campuses.[3] The millions they offer cash-strapped school administrations to supplement the NDEA concept and found Middle Eastern studies programs, complete with buildings, staff, and teachers, are hard to turn down. These schools and the majority of college-affiliated Muslim Students Associations (MSAs) in the United States are dominated by pro-Islamic and anti-American agendas, as are the majority of Islamic centers and schools funded by the Saudis worldwide.[4] It's their money, so they call the shots.

The *Middle East Quarterly* notes, "There is plenty of evidence for the MSA's strident advocacy of the Saudi-style Wahhabi interpretation of Islam." In "Wahhabism: A Critical Essay," Hamid Algar of the University of California, Berkeley writes,

> *Some Muslim student organizations have functioned at times as Saudi-supported channels for the propagation of Wahhabism abroad, especially in the United States. . . . Particularly in the 1960s and 1970s, no criticism of Saudi Arabia would be tolerated at the annual conventions of the MSA. The organization has, in fact, consistently advocated theological and political positions derived from radical Islamist organizations, including the Muslim Brotherhood and Jamaati Islam.[5]*

In addition to paying the salaries of the academics who are promoting the Saudi Wahhabi cause, money from Title VI supports Saudi "mercenaries" on campuses. These warriors are actually student activists that train overseas during the summer and return in the fall to put into action their newly learned skills. As a result, anti-American and anti-Jewish attacks are steadily increasing on college campuses.[6] So what return on investment has the government gotten? Not much, considering the poor numbers of Arabic speakers available in the intelligence agencies and State Department. With the Saudis muscling in with big bucks, the focus of these Middle Eastern studies departments that are 10 percent funded by Title VI has quietly changed to spread terrorist propaganda that turns students against our government instead of encouraging them to use their interest in the Middle East to help the government staff with Arabic translation and policy positions.[7]

Why should we be so concerned about what Saudi Wahhabism is up to? Let me have John L. Esposito, professor of religion and international affairs and of Islamic studies at Georgetown University, whom I consider an unabashed Islamic apologist, remind you in a revealingly candid appraisal in his book *Unholy War: Terror in the Name of Islam* what Wahhabi Islam is all about.

> *The Wahhabi religious vision or brand of Islam . . . is a strict, puritanical faith that emphasizes literal interpretation of the Quran and Sunmah (example) of the Prophet Muhammad and the absolute oneness of God. . . . Anything the Wahhabis perceived as un-Islamic behavior constituted unbelief (kufur) in their eyes, which must be countered by jihad. Thus jihad or holy war was not simply permissible: to fight the unbelievers and reestablish a true Islamic state was required.*

Clearly, we should be worrying.

I find the amount of money pouring into U.S. universities from the radical Wahhabi Saudis as revealing as it is distressing. As of this writing, the extent of influence peddling that has taken place is as follows: King Fahd has donated $20 million to set up a Middle Eastern studies program at the University of Arkansas; $5 million was donated to UC Berkeley's program by two Saudi sheikhs linked to al Qaeda.[8] Harvard has received $22.5 million, and $28.1 million has gone to Georgetown.

At Georgetown, a Catholic school started by Jesuits, the Muslim Students Association has initiated a segregated private living community on campus for Muslims and non-Muslims interested in being steeped in Islam. According to the community's promotional material, the "Muslim Interest Living Community (MILC) [was] designed to create a strong support group for Muslims and non-Muslims who want to be steadfast in prayer and in their commitment to campus building and cooperation." I thought the era of segregation proved that *desegregation* was the key to "campus building and cooperation" on a social level. Europe is finding out how dead set Muslims are about not wanting to integrate into heathen, idolatrous communities. They want all the social welfare benefits but to have their own, separate community life. When you read the rest of the MILC's material you get a better idea of what its intent is: "[t]o establish an Islamic living environment for those who wish to increase and strengthen their faith." Georgetown sounds like a very respectable place for a mini madrassa. I hope and pray that this is all in the spirit of what Georgetown's president, John DeGioia, says in his Internet welcome letter describing the university as a place where "students and faculty examine the modern world in its infinite complexity" (http://reslife.georgetown .edu/llc.html). I hope "modern" wins out over cloistered thinking and a return to the days of Muhammad envisioned by the Islamo-fascists. As someone who comes from the Middle East, I recognize the places and conditions that Muslims use to incubate their line of thinking and then inject it into young minds.

And now back to the list of Saudi funding: $11 million to Cornell; $5 million to MIT; $1.5 million to Texas A&M; $1 million to Princeton. Rutgers received a $5 million chair endowment, as did Columbia, which tried to conceal the source of funds.[9] Other recipients of Saudi-tainted monies include UC Santa Barbara, Johns Hopkins University, Rice University, American University, the University of Chicago, USC, UCLA, Duke University, Syracuse University, Howard University, and countless others.[10] We pump the gas; they pump their way into the hearts and minds of young freshmen.

These endowed chairs give the Saudis ultimate power to influence the curriculum taught to vulnerable American students. This curriculum is typically anti-Western, anti-Christian, and anti-Semitic. What better way to combat the war on radical Islam and pave the way for its takeover of a culture than fifth column psychological warfare. It's a great opportunity to openly fund some *dawah* (persuasion and reason) accomplished by *taqiyya* (lying and deception) protected by the right to academic free speech and endorsed by the boards of directors of U.S. colleges!

I ask you, how far will the perverse use of funding to American universities by the Saudis continue before Americans realize that they have helped and even encouraged the brainwashing of our future generations to hate America, resent our foreign policy, work with our enemy against us, and indirectly sabotage everything we are doing to fight this war on Islamo-facism?

After receiving a $2 million grant from a Saudi sheikh, Khalid al-Turki, Harvard chose Zayed Yasin, a graduating senior, as its commencement speaker for its 2002 graduation ceremony, seven months after 9/11. In his speech—originally titled "My American Jihad" but changed after criticism arose to "Of Faith and Citizenship: My American Jihad," though listed on the program as "Of Faith and Citizenship"—he attempted to mollify his audience with a pacifistic explanation of jihad. In other statements he has praised Hamas and supported the efforts of suicide bombers, arguing that their families must be paid. Yasin also raised money for the Holy Land Foundation, a charity that was linked to al Qaeda before it was shut down by the Bush administration.[11]

According to Martin Kramer, a historian whose subject is the Middle East, Columbia University has become a breeding ground for terrorists.[12] When a chair is endowed by Saudi money, it is usually filled by a Palestinian activist who presents not only a one-sided view of the Arab-Israeli conflict, but anti-American sentiment as well. One such professor is Joseph Massad, a relentless antagonist of the United States and Israel. He preaches hatred and intolerance for America to students, constantly alluding to America's history of slavery and accusing America of mass murder during World War II, using nuclear weapons to end the war.[13] Ironically, Massad forgets to mention the genocide (2 million) and enslavement (2 million) of black Christians in the Sudan by Muslims.[14] Terrorist propaganda in the classrooms abounds at Columbia. Lisa Anderson, head of the International Studies Program, has publicly stated that Middle Eastern studies programs at Columbia and at other universities across the country are unbalanced.[15]

The Web site Campuswatch.org, which reviews and critiques Middle Eastern studies programs on North American campuses, observes examples of abuses of power over students. Middle East scholars impose their views on students and sometimes expect students to embrace their own politics, punishing those who do not with lower grades or weaker recommendations.[16]

A student in a class on contemporary civilization taught by Massad wonders why he must listen to "an apoplectic rant about U.S. foreign policy" when the subject matter at hand has nothing to do with current events.[17] In a UC Berkeley course called "The Politics and Poetics of Palestinian Resistance" conservative students were informed that they should seek other sections:

> *This class takes as its starting point the right of Palestinians to fight for their own self-determination. Conservative thinkers are encouraged to seek other sections.*

A student who took the course found "anti-Semitism tolerated" by the instructor.[18] At the University of Chicago, a doctoral student in the Middle Eastern studies program was discouraged by faculty from studying militant Islamic ideologies, told that this topic was created by a "sensationalist media" and promoted "Zionist" interests.[19]

I have spoken on college campuses across America, including Columbia, Duke, and Carnegie Mellon, and have seen the far-reaching hand of Saudi petrodollars coming back to haunt us. The sentiment of all the Saudi-supported schools is the same; anti-American and anti-Israeli sentiments reign supreme. Pro-American, pro-Israeli, and anti–radical Islamist conservative speakers like me who do not accept any excuse for murdering innocent civilians in the name of resistance are met with blatant harassment by school administrations and student Arab communities. I was one of the speakers at a Duke University "Antiterrorism rally" in October 2004 on the eve of the Palestinian Solidarity Conference, which was practically a hatefest of anti-Semitism and anti-Americanism. When I started condemning the justification of suicide bombing in Israel and around the world, Arab students started hurling insults at me. As I walked off the stage, many of them were shouting in Arabic, "How dare your betray the Arabic cause?" and "You are an insult to the name Arab" and "You are a traitor" and "You deserve to be dead." Many pro-American and pro-Israeli speakers like me have to have security while speaking on any campus in the U.S. and Canada. While security officers surrounded me on one side of the Duke University campus, Daniel Pipes, who was speaking in another hall, had metal detectors for people to go through before entering his lecture. It is a sad state of affairs when any speaker on any American university campus has to fear for his or her safety when giving a speech. America is the country where free speech was invented, and it is protected under the Constitution.

The University of Idaho, Washington State University, Ohio State University, Arizona State University, the University of Michigan, UC Irvine, UC Berkeley, UCLA, the University of South Florida, Georgetown, Columbia, Harvard, and numerous other schools have been linked to terrorist ties funded by Saudi money.[20] In fact, UC Berkeley, Harvard, and Georgetown have each been given large sums of money by Saudi benefactors who are currently being sued by the families of the victims of 9/11 as having financed the brutal and cowardly attack on American citizens.[21]

I would like to point out one alarming parallel in history. Adolf Hitler exploited the minds of university students and professors by using anti-Semitic sentiment and Nazi propaganda. Hatred for the Jewish people became so prevalent that in 1938 the Nazi Party decreed that Jews were forbidden to attend any and all universities.[22] Academic administrations across Germany quietly complied. Ironically, the grand mufti of Jerusalem, Haj Amin al-Husseini, Yasser Arafat's kinsman, role model and predecessor of the Palestinian Arabs, directly helped Hitler to carry out his plan to eliminate millions of Jewish people.[23] Al-Husseini played a pivotal behind-the-scenes role in urging Nazis and pro-Nazi governments in Europe to transport Jews to death camps, in training pro-Nazi Bosnian brigades, and in funneling Nazi loot into postwar Arab countries.[24]

I believe it was in Hitler's plan to use the degradation of the Jewish people to distract Germans from his plan of mass elimination of any individual who did not fit the description of a member of the "Aryan race." My background as a Middle Easterner and as a journalist makes me very aware of how people's minds are manipulated. On 9/11 America cried and the civilized world cried with it. Three years later you have people on college campuses across America saying that

America asked for the attack by its behavior in the world. We even have Professor Ward Churchill stating that the Americans who died on September 11 deserved to die.[25] How did we get from the sympathy of 9/11 to the resentment of America today? It's Muslim dollars and the PR machine at work on our college campuses, nurturing young, impressionable minds and shaping them into whatever they want them to believe.

As a Maronite growing up in once predominantly Christian Lebanon, I witnessed the genocide of my people by the Palestinians and the rest of the Muslim community, who came from all over the Muslim world to fight the Christians. They too distracted the rest of the world with anti-Semitic sentiment while quietly slaughtering and scaring off the Christian population of Lebanon. Yet all the world remembers about the Lebanese war is the Israeli invasion and the Palestinian-Israeli conflict that took place on our soil. Islamic radical Hezbollah rules with an iron fist in Lebanon today and has won its way into the Lebanese parliament. The radical Islamic movement has the same plans for America and the rest of the world.

While the Muslim groups on college campuses are distracting the college communities with their anti-Semitic and anti-American attitude, they are paving the way for an easy and forgiving public opinion of barbaric terrorists, who are excused for being driven to commit such acts. "It's not their fault," these groups say. "Let's look at what we have done to have them hate us so much." Can you imagine us analyzing and trying to understand the Japanese after attacking Pearl Harbor and wondering what we did to deserve their hatred? It would have been unthinkable. America's protection was the number-one factor that all Americans united on. This is not so today. We have young Americans who hate our country so much they would rather see us fall than be the "aggressor." Our universities have become the battleground where we must fight to win back the opinion and allegiance of our American youth.

I can say from experience that these Middle Eastern studies departments, professors, and groups that spew hatred and violence for

Israel and the U.S. in American universities are sympathizers of the enemy that uses airplanes as missiles and flies them into skyscrapers. I have argued with professors and faculty members who attended my lectures at the University of Pittsburgh and at SUNY Purchase who were justifying and defending the actions of the terrorists who attacked us and pointing out that it is our fault that we were attacked. They are sympathizers with beheaders of Western hostages, with suicide bombers, and with terrorists—in their opinion, freedom fighters—around the world who kill in the name of resistance. We are dealing with monsters, and these monsters are infiltrating our universities and using our children to engage in their criminal activities and to spread their violent propaganda. They may be more Westernized in their view of their faith and not as radical or vicious, or perhaps they are naïve and being manipulated, but they are still working toward the same goals.

Incredibly, the Nazi card is still being played against America today. In February 2005, Malik Shabazz, a Black Muslim who is Louis Farrakhan's right-hand man, was invited to speak at Carnegie Mellon. Immediately after he walked in, he asked the students seated to "raise your hand if you're a Jew! Now! Raise your hand if you're a Zionist." His entourage, dressed in brown shirts and jackboots to simulate Nazis, pointed to those students whose hands were raised and shouted, "We're watching you! We're watching you!" Amazingly, Michael Murphy, dean of student affairs, was in the audience and sat in his seat doing nothing, even as the students' cries filled the room.[26] (I wonder whether Shabazz or Farrakhan know that in Muslim culture, the word "black"—*abeed* in Arabic—means "filth" or "slave.")[27]

Why was there nothing done on the part of the university and the part of the parents to protect the civil liberties of the students? Why didn't the media report this incident? Apathy. No one wants to make waves. Apathy played a huge part in the demise of the millions of people who were exterminated under Hitler's regime, Jews and Christians. And what school administration wants to upset the fat cat Arabs with the big checkbooks? Apathy and money are allowing our social conscience to be whittled away.

So we now have innocent parents slaving night and day to send their children to college only to find the purveyors of Islam brainwashing them, and using their wealth in the name of charity to poison the minds of our academic community with anti-American and anti-Israeli propaganda. When is it going to stop?

We, as parents and as citizens of the greatest country in the world, the United States of America, must become involved in combating the emerging Islamic indoctrination of our nation's youth on college campuses. As parents, when do we say enough is enough? When do we demand that universities not accept blood money from terrorist-linked organizations and individuals, using treason as our rationale? When do we demand that Congress take a long hard look at what has happened to the programs that Title VI helps finance? When do we demand that anti-American and anti-Jewish sentiment not be allowed as part of a college course, endorsed or deliberately overlooked by a university, using incitement to hate as underlying principal? When do we demand that the media step in and accurately inform us of terrorist activities? When do we start to feel rage at the subtle and not so subtle terrorist behavior that is increasingly infiltrating our universities and poisoning our children's minds? When do we know when the time is right to act? Now is the time! Before it's too late.

11.

BULL'S-EYE OF THE
MIDDLE EAST

The main objective in the radical Islamists' strategy to dominate the world is the destruction of the United States. They know that if America, the keystone, falls, then the arch of Western civilization will collapse. A parallel strategic objective, of perhaps greater symbolic importance, is the destruction of the state of Israel. The Arab world has been pursuing this goal with bloody single-mindedness since 1948.

Some Americans still believe that the terror war against Israel and the terror war against the United States are somehow unrelated. Others believe that radical Islam is waging a terrorist war against the U.S. because of America's support for Israel. Americans who subscribe to either of these theories need to remember that through Islamo-fascist eyes, Israel is merely "the Little Satan." The United States is "the Great Satan." Even if Israel were to disappear, the destruction of America and the subjugation of non-Muslim civilization would continue to be the strategic objective of radical Islam.[1]

Lies, Ugly Lies, and Crazy Lies

When it comes to concocting *taqiyya,* there is no lie about America, Israel, or the Jewish people that is too ugly or too crazy to be spread and believed in the Arab and Muslim world and Iran. These lies are not confined to "extremists" on the fringes of Arab and Muslim society. They are told and retold by religious leaders, high government officials, and teachers—in schools, in mosques, on radio and television stations, in books and newspapers, all rigidly directed and controlled by Arab governments. With repetition they become the topics of everyday conversation. "Hey, Ahmed, did you hear this one about those murderous filthy Jews? Did you hear what the American butchers did in Iraq? I read about it in the paper and heard it on the radio, so it must be true!" And on and on until they take on a life of their own, with further embellishments as they spread.

Many of the fabrications about Israel allege insidious plots to murder non-Jewish children. Again, looking further into the Arab mind, here are a few truly repulsive examples of the lies about Jews and Israel spread and believed in the Arab Muslim and even Arab Christian world:

- For ritual religious purposes, Jews use the blood of Muslim (and Christian) children in Passover matzoh and Purim pastries. Jews and Israelis are literally "vampires" and "bloodsuckers."[2]
- Israel is sending AIDS-infected prostitutes to spread the disease by seducing and infecting innocent young Muslim boys.[3]
- According to Palestinian Authority officials, Israel brought two hundred tons of strawberry-flavored chewing gum intentionally spiked with sex hormones into the West Bank and Gaza Strip. This allegedly sexed-up Israeli chewing gum "was sold 'only at the gates of primary schools or kindergartens' because Israelis 'want to destroy [the Palestinians'] genetic system' by giving sex hormones to children before their bodies can cope with them."[4] Samples provided by Palestinian "health officials" were analyzed in tests commissioned by the *Washington Post*. According to the scientific analysis, the gum contained no contaminants whatever.[5]
- "The Jews" build "ovens" to "bake" Palestinians.[6]

Sometimes the *same* crazy, ugly lies are told about both Israel and the United States. For instance, on December 13, 2004, the Iranian Sahar 1 TV station began broadcasting a series entitled *Zhara's Blue Eyes*. This series asserts that Israelis steal the organs of Palestinian children for transplant into Israeli medical patients. In the first episode, the beautiful eyes of the title character, a little Palestinian girl, are stolen for transplant into the son of an Israeli army officer.[7] In the second episode, (first broadcast on December 20, 2004), the audience is informed that the president of Israel "is being kept alive by organs stolen from Palestinian children."[8] In an interview, the producer of the series stated that "Zionists" kidnap "children only one or two years old" raise them to teenagers on "a white ship sailing the oceans . . . under constant physical monitoring and supervision" so that they (the Israelis) can steal "the heart, the kidneys, and their other organs. . . . This story is a collection of facts. As I mentioned, we conducted research and reached conclusions, and we have turned them into this film to make the world aware of what the Zionists are doing to the Palestinians."[9] Did this fellow get a peek at the screenplay for the movie *The Island,* in which people are raised for spare body parts, or did he just catch a preview of coming attractions? As Goebbels said: "If you repeat a lie long enough it becomes truth." That's *taqiyya* at its best. Or worst, depending on your moral compass.

Less than a week after the broadcast of the first episode of *Zhara's Blue Eyes,* Saudi Arabia produced a variation on this ugly lie and applied it to the United States. On December 18, 2004, the Saudi Arabian government daily newspaper *Al Watan* published an article which accused the United States of stealing eyes and other organs from dead and wounded Iraqis. According to this official Saudi newspaper, "[a] secret team of American physicians follows the troops during their attacks . . . to ensure quick operations for extracting some organs and transferring them to private operations rooms before they are transported to America for sale. . . . These teams offer $40 for every usable kidney and $25 for an eye."[10] This story was immediately picked up and repeated in government-controlled newspapers in Iran and Syria.[11]

Now for some real award-winning *taqiyya*. This is about both Israel's and the United States' responsibility for the 9/11 terror attacks.
According to numerous Arab government officials and "journalists,"
the 9/11 attacks were orchestrated and perpetrated by Israel, the
Mossad, the Jews, the international Zionist conspiracy, the United
States military, the CIA, the FBI, conservative Christians, a conspiracy
headed by President George W. Bush and then–secretary of state
Colin Powell,[12] and/or the "World Council of Churches, which was
enacting the Vatican's plan to eradicate Islam and Christianize the
world."[13] Choose your own cast of conspirators. This insanity is repeated at the highest levels of Arab governments[14] more than four
years after 9/11, even after Osama bin Laden acknowledged that al
Qaeda was responsible for the 9/11 attacks.[15]

Why would anyone spread and believe such crazy, ugly lies? Because they want to be America's friends? Because they are willing to
live in peace with Israel (if only Israel would withdraw to the 1967
border)? No, they spread and believe these atrocious lies in order to
perpetuate hate and to justify the real terrorist atrocities that they
themselves commit in their jihad against America and Israel. Israel has
been on the front line of the war against international terrorists since
before the Arab-Israeli conflict became one of the fronts in the worldwide jihad of radical Islam. In order to understand more clearly the direct connection between the terror war against Israel and the terror
war against the United States, it is necessary to understand how the
Arab-Israeli conflict began, and how it evolved.

Many scholars believe the Arab-Israeli conflict did not start out as a
war between religions, but as a territorial dispute between two competing groups—Jews and Arabs—with *nationalist* claims and aspirations,
and that religion was one of the characteristics that identified the competing nationalist groups. I will agree that that is what it might look like
on the surface. But for these two particular groups whose religion, at
least for the Muslims, is a significant daily part of their lives, it is hard
to believe that religious beliefs do not influence their thinking and

aspirations. All you have to do is read a few scriptures from the Koran about the Jews and hear the holy book recited weekly in every mosque and you'll begin to understand where this resentment is coming from, regardless of what country this hate verbiage is coming out of. The major difference between the religions is that Judaism does not aspire to convert the world as Islam does. Jews can live within the context of a different society without seeking converts. Jews do not go to temple every Friday and read that God's will is victory over all Muslims. They do not read that all Muslims are apes and pigs because they are cursed by Allah, which is what Muslims teach about Jews in their mosques. Muslims are out to convert everyone. Once they have the upper hand, they want to run the whole show and subject everyone to their own rules.

Growing up in the Middle East, I came to find out that Arab children are taught hatred of the Jews from their mother's milk. From a young age, Arab children are constantly bombarded with stories and information presenting Jews as barbaric, conniving, manipulative, warmongering people. Meanwhile, Jews teach their children patience, humility, service, tolerance, understanding of others, and charity to all. They call it *tikkun olam,* "to repair the world."

The Arab-Israeli conflict has remained intractable because the Arab world refuses to accept the right of a Jewish state to exist autonomously in the middle of the Muslim Middle East. At first this refusal was based on what appeared to be pan-Arab nationalism, and then on Palestinian nationalism. There is a lot of bluster, pride, and honor among Arabs, which supports the nationalism angle. But as a Lebanese Christian looking at it from ground level and willing to blow the whistle on the hatred that Arabs harbor and teach their children against Jews, I can tell you that religious hatred, humiliation, and resentment are the driving factor behind the Israeli-Arab conflict. As a Christian who was raised in a country where people were shot at checkpoints because their ID card said "Christian," I see it differently. I think that with the Iranian Revolution of 1979, and especially after the rise of the Palestinian Islamic Resistance Movement (Hamas) during the 1987 intifada, the world is seeing the true reason for the Arab world's refusal to recognize Israel's right to exist: radical Islamic supremacism. It has come to the surface, overshadowing the nationalist rationale and moving on, seeking bigger game in the West.

Israel has become one of the most innovative and technologically advanced countries, contributing to the world's improvement in fields from medicine to communications. It is a successful, modern, educated, Western-thinking society in the midst of a sea of Arabic failure, corruption, backwardness, and ignorance. Israel's success in turning a desolate desert land into an oasis blossoming with Western culture and wealth irks its failing neighbors. It is in contrast to everything they are not and cannot be because of their culture, values, and religion, which suffocate the individual and drown out human rights.

Israel has the highest ratio of university degrees per capita in the world, while most of the Arabic world still wallows in ignorance. About one-third of Arab men and half of Arab women are illiterate.[16] This simple fact about Israel is a reflection of the society and its hunger for education and growth and has nothing to do with America's financial support. Money doesn't buy brains or a desire to learn and be informed. Israel has the highest average living standard in the Middle East. Its $100 billion economy is larger than all of its immediate neighbors combined despite the fact that it is in a constant state of war trying to defend itself and doesn't have a drop of crude oil to sell.

Israel has more than three thousand high-tech companies and start-ups, giving it the highest concentration of high-tech companies in the world apart from Silicon Valley. Voice-mail technology, the first PC antivirus software, and the cell phone were developed by Motorola, which has its largest development center in Israel. Four young Israelis developed the technology for AOL Instant Messenger.

What have the Arabs contributed to the world other than suicide bombing and terrorism? Where is their contribution to science, medicine, technology? If Israel did not exist, the Arabs would have to invent something like it to blame their failures on. It is their fundamental ways of thinking and own culture that hold them back, not the Jews.

In a region that shuns outsiders and other religions, Israel stands out like America, a free society, a melting pot of people who came from all around the world and brought their rich cultures with them. Israel is one of the most multiracial and multicultural countries in the world. More than a hundred different countries are represented in its population of 6 million. Consider how the Israeli government spent tens of millions of dollars airlifting more than forty thousand black Ethiopian Jews to Israel in 1984 and 1991. Since 2001 Israel has reached out to help others, taking in non-Jewish refugees from Lebanon, the Ivory Coast, Sierra Leone, Vietnam, Liberia, and Congo, and even Bosnian Muslims. How many such refugees have the twenty-two states in the Arab League taken in? The Arab world won't even give Palestinian refugees citizenship in their host countries. Remember, Jews can't live in the neighboring Hashemite Kingdom of Jordan or in the Kingdom of Saudi Arabia. But Arabs are living as citizens in Israel. What does that tell you about their respect for other cultures?

Over 1 million Arabs are full Israeli citizens. An Arab sits on the Supreme Court of Israel. There are Arab political parties expressing views inimical to the State of Israel sitting in the Knesset, Israel's parliament. Women are equal partners in Israel and have complete human rights, as do gays and minorities. Show me an Arab nation with a Jew in its government. Show me an Arab country with half as many Jewish citizens as Israel has Arab citizens. Show me freedom of speech, freedom of religion, freedom of the press, and human rights in any Arabic country in the Middle East the way they exist and are practiced in Israel. It is those same freedoms that the Muslims resent as a threat to Islam and that they are fighting against, be it in Israel, Europe, or the United States.

Regardless of their hatred and disapproval of Israel's existence in the Middle East and their desire to seek its destruction, Israel has a historical, legal, and moral right to exist as a Jewish state. Let me crunch a lot of history, laws, and deal making by world powers into a few paragraphs.

According to the Arab-Palestinian-Muslim narrative, Israel is an alien colony, recently planted in the Arab world by American and European imperialism. This narrative recognizes no history prior to the arrival of the first Zionist pioneers in the 1880s, and emphatically denies any ancient historical connection of the Jewish people to the land of Israel. This is the central lie, the mega-*taqiyya,* offered to justify uncompromising opposition to Jewish national rights. It's almost as if they honestly expect people to think the word "Israel" was invented in modern times. The alarming truth is that their seemingly successful revision of history has taken hold in some minds.

The truth is carved in Egyptian stone. According to a well-known hieroglyphic inscription, the tribes of Israel were a significant, established presence in Canaan no later than 1212 BC.[17] There is a vast body of archaeological evidence that demonstrates the ancient Israelite/Jewish presence in Israel/Judea as far back as 925 BC.[18] This historical presence is verified in the ancient records of the Egyptian, Assyrian, Babylonian, Persian, Greek, Roman, Byzantine, and Muslim empires. The Arab conquest did not occur until AD 638. An exercise in elementary arithmetic reveals that the Jewish people were there *eighteen and one-half centuries* before the arrival of the Arabs. Despite being conquered many times, the Jewish people have had a constant, uninterrupted presence in the land of Israel for over thirty centuries.[19] The Arabs and Islam have been there less than fourteen centuries.[20] It has conveniently been forgotten that the Jews and Christians were there first.

Furthermore, in the thirty centuries preceding the establishment of the State of Israel in 1948, there have been only two periods when there was an independent, internationally recognized state in the area that now comprises Israel. Both of them were Jewish states.[21] Even when this land was part of the Arab empire (AD 638 through AD 1099), there was never an independent Arab state in "Palestine," by that name or any other.[22] No wonder the Arabs are donating millions of dollars to U.S. colleges for Middle Eastern schools of study. They have a lot of hard historical evidence to rewrite in the young minds of students.

Finally, the Jewish people have a distinct national identity. Religion is only one of the unique characteristics that define this national identity. (A large majority of Israeli Jews, 70–80 percent, do not practice the Jewish religion as a belief but more as tradition, although they are still Jewish.) In addition to a unique religion, the Jewish people have a separate and distinct language, culture, and customs, with a documented history of development over the past three thousand years. The Jewish people have created a vast body of art and literature, both secular and religious, which reflects the connection of the Jewish people to the land of Israel. The Dead Sea Scrolls, written when the descendants of the Maccabees ruled an independent Judea, demonstrate that the Jewish people, both in the Holy Land and in exile all over the world, have been reading and writing secular and sectarian literature in the same distinct language for over two thousand years. In contrast, the Arabic language and culture and the Muslim religion of the Palestinians are essentially indistinguishable from those of the wider Arab world. Prior to the mid 1800s there is no trace *whatever* of uniquely "Palestinian" art, literature, music, or any other manifestation of a distinct culture. If you find this hard to believe try to think of one "Palestinian" book, or author, or artist, from the year 1300 through the year 1800. That's a period of five hundred years. There must be one book written by a "Palestinian" Arab author. There must be one painting by a "Palestinian" Arab artist.

Guess what? *There are none.* If you still don't believe it, ask a Palestinian nationalist or a Columbia University professor of Middle Eastern history to name one. The most honest response you will get is silence. The most likely response you will get is *taqiyya*.

In terms of historical presence and sovereignty in the land of Israel, and distinct characteristics of national identity, the Jewish claim of national rights in the land of Israel is at the minimum equal to the Palestinian claim. Any objective observer would conclude from the facts that the claim of the Jewish people to national identity and sovereignty in the land of Israel is much stronger than that of the Palestinians in every respect. However, Israel does not deny Palestinian national rights. On the contrary, the State of Israel, and the Zionist movement that preceded it, have accepted in good faith or initiated every proposal for a genuine "two-state solution" that has ever been put forward. In contrast, the Arab world, Palestinian nationalists, and radical Islamists have consistently denied Israel's right to exist, and they have responded to every settlement proposal with extreme violence. The missed opportunities for peace include the 1937 Peel Commission proposal,[23] the 1947 United Nations Partition Plan,[24] UN Security Council Resolution 242 in 1967,[25] and the proposals made by Israel at Camp David in 2000.

Even after the death of Yasser Arafat, the Palestinian nationalist movement and the wider Arab Muslim world *still* do not accept Israel's right to exist as a Jewish state. This has not changed with the ascension of Mahmoud Abbas to president of the Palestinian Authority, despite the mantle of "moderate" conferred upon him.

Abbas was Arafat's devoted acolyte and loyal henchman for four decades. Abbas is sometimes referred to as "Doctor," perhaps to conjure up the image of a kindly family physician making a house call. In fact, he received a Ph.D. from Moscow's Oriental University in the early 1980s. The title of his doctoral thesis is typical of Arab reasoning; "The Secret Relationship Between Zionism and Nazism." In addition to parroting conventional Holocaust-denial formulations (there were no gas chambers, less than a million Jews were killed, and so forth), Abbas's tract contained one original and imaginative assertion: that Zionists provoked the Nazis into perpetrating the Holocaust in order to spur Jewish immigration to what was then called Palestine. Doctoral candidate Abbas wrote, "The Zionist movement led a broad campaign of incitement against the Jews living under Nazi rule, in order to arouse the government's hatred of them, to fuel vengeance against them, and to expand the mass extermination." I wonder where he stands on who brought down the World Trade Center. Abbas's doctoral dissertation also asserts that Hitler did not decide to exterminate European Jewry until he was provoked by David Ben-Gurion's declaration of war on the Nazis in 1942. "Doctor" Abbas has never retracted the assertions upon which his doctoral thesis is based (see http://en.wikipedia.org/wiki/israeli-palestinian_history_denial).

As prime minister of the PA in 2003, Abbas was touted as "independent" and "moderate" because he frequently clashed with Arafat and eventually resigned in frustration. However, the clashes and resignation occurred because Arafat refused to relinquish any real power to Abbas, not because of any strategic difference between the two. Abbas began calling for a halt to terrorist bombings against Israeli civilians not because the intentional targeting and murdering of civilians is wrong, but because it had been tactically ineffective and had a negative public relations impact on the Palestinian cause. As both a candidate for president of the PA and as its president, Abbas has *never* questioned the morality of terrorist bombings and murders. His *sole* criticism (and the occasional criticism of his PA cronies) has been limited to asserting that suicide bombings, terrorist shootings, and rocket and mortar attacks against Israeli civilians "harmed Palestinian national interests."[26] This is tantamount to intentionally running your car into a crosswalk full of schoolchildren, and then saying it was a bad thing to do because it dents your fender.

As one who speaks both English and Arabic, I have seen how the Arabs are the best at taking advantage of the language barrier between them and the West. While they mechanically issue tepid, self-pitying "condemnations" to Western news agencies *in English,*[27] the PA-controlled media, mosques, and schools continue to glorify the terrorist murderers in Arabic, and incite others to commit terrorist acts. Neighborhoods, streets, schools, and even a children's soccer tournament are named after *shahids,* "martyrs." Financial incentives are still paid to the families of terrorist murderers.[28] Further, Abbas has repeatedly stated that he will *not* disarm and dismantle the terrorist organizations, as required by step one of the "road map." Instead, he has incorporated Hamas and Islamic Jihad into the Palestinian security services, putting their gunmen and bombers on the Palestinian Authority payroll.[29] In explaining to the terrorist organizations that his opposition to violence was only tactical, he stated that negotiation with Israel is "a phase,"[30] and that, therefore, "[t]his is not the time" to launch terrorist attacks into Israel.[31] So, are we to wait for a better time, Commander Abbas?

Most important, although Abbas purports to accept the "two-state solution"—two independent and democratic states, Israel and Palestine, living side by side—such acceptance is specifically conditioned on an unlimited "right of return" for Palestinian "refugees." Abbas has insisted many times, as prime minister of the PA and as its president, that the Palestinian "right of return" is nonnegotiable. According to this "right of return," some 5 million Palestinian refugees would have the right to live within Israel's pre-1967 borders, relegating Israeli Jews to minority status in their own country almost overnight. This is the strategy by which Abbas and the "moderate" Palestinians seek to destroy Israel by demographic rather than military means. This "moderate" strategy has very little support in the Palestinian "street." In a June 2003 Pew Research poll, "80 percent of Palestinians said their 'rights and needs' cannot be met as long as Israel exists."[32] The vast majority of Palestinians don't even pretend to accept Israel's right to exist.

If the Arab Muslim world had chosen to accept Israel's right to exist, in 1947, or 1967, or 1993, or 2000, or at any time in the past half century, by now Israel would have helped them make their deserts bloom. Instead, the Arab world has chosen to fertilize the land with the blood of Israeli children. Could anything be more barbaric and depraved? Yes. In response to Ehud Barak's offer at Camp David in July 2000, the Palestinians chose to sacrifice the blood of their own children to satisfy their hatred of Israel. The more Israel has tried to defend itself, the further into the forefront the Palestinians have pushed their children. First the Palestinians gave their children stones to throw. Now they wrap their children in dynamite and nails and send them to blow themselves up in Israeli restaurants and religious observances.[33] Now Palestinians rejoice at the death of not only Israeli children, but their own.

In an attempt to mitigate or explain away this barbaric depravity, the Palestinian nationalist movement and its apologists cite the "desperation" that Palestinians experience because of the Israeli "occupation" of the West Bank and Gaza. However, Israel's presence in the West Bank and Gaza began in June 1967. The first major terror bombing committed by Arabs against the Jewish state occurred more than nineteen years *before* the Israeli presence in the West Bank and Gaza. In fact, it occurred ten weeks before Israel became an independent state. On Sunday morning, February 22, 1948, *in anticipation of* Israel's independence, a triple truck bomb was detonated by Arab terrorists on Ben Yehuda Street in what was then the Jewish section of Jerusalem. Fifty-four people were killed and hundreds were wounded.[34] Thus, it is obvious that Arab terrorism is caused not by the "desperation" of "occupation," but by the *very thought* of a Jewish state.[35]

Further, and even more significantly, throughout history there have been populations that have lived in desperation, and none of them have resorted to the intentional targeting and murder of children as an officially practiced and widely praised mode of achieving political ends. When extremist elements of otherwise legitimate liberation movements such as the Republican Sinn Fein have committed such atrocities, their actions have been unconditionally condemned by the civilized world, and their political objectives have been discredited by their vile crimes. This is not so with the Palestinians. Once upon a time there was a special place in the lowest depths of hell for anyone who would intentionally murder a child. Now that place is in the pantheon of Palestinian heroes. Now that behavior is legitimized as "armed struggle" against Israeli "occupation" by, among others, the United Nations General Assembly, the UN Human Rights Commission, and the European Union.

Since the Iranian Revolution of 1979 and the rise of Hamas in 1987, the campaign to destroy Israel has taken on an ugly, fanatic religious tone. Holy obligation reinforces (and is replacing) Palestinian nationalism as the motivation for committing terrorist murder. As we have seen the secular, "moderate" factions of the Palestinian nationalist movement (such as Abbas's Fatah Party) will shrink into insignificance, and is replaced by terrorist Islamic factions such as Hamas and Islamic Jihad. Hamas receives financial and material support from the same sources as al Qaeda, and from al Qaeda directly. Islamic Jihad receives financial and material support from Iran, directly and through Hezbollah. These are the same international criminal entities that wage religion-based terror war against the United States. They do it for the same reason and by the same means: to make Islam supreme in the world, by the sword or the suicide bomb.

Hamas' sweeping victory in the Palestinian election was a loud declaration by the Palestinian people to elect a radical Islamic movement dedicated to wiping Israel off the map.

The august international organizations charged with preserving peace and human dignity in the world—the UN, the EU, among others—would have preferred that terrorist atrocities be limited to Israel. However, once the intentional mass murder of innocent civilians was legitimized against Israel, it was legitimized *everywhere*, constrained by nothing more than the strongly held beliefs of those who would become the mass murderers. Because the Palestinians were encouraged by most of the world to believe that the murder of innocent Israeli civilians is a legitimate tactic to advance the Palestinian nationalist cause, the Islamists believe that they may commit mass murder anywhere in the world to advance their holy cause. As a result, we suffer from a plague of Islamic terrorism, from Moscow to Madrid, from Bali to Beslan, from Nairobi to New York, authored and perfected by the Palestinians. Israel and the United States are not separate targets of Islamic terrorism. The whole world is its target. Israel and the United States share the bull's-eye.

12.

SOCIETIES ARE
NOT CREATED EQUAL

From birth, people are born with physical differences and into different political, social, religious, and economic situations. Some have
higher IQs than others. Some have greater physical challenges than
others. Some are born deaf, blind, crippled, or mentally challenged.
Some are blessed with health throughout their lives, and some suffer
from aches and pains and develop diseases at a young age. Some live
to be a hundred and some die of a heart attack at forty-five. Some of
the situations we face are drawbacks which are permanent and impossible to change or overcome. Others require a frank recognition of the
problem, finding a solution, then implementing the solution and moving on. What sets individuals, nations, and cultures apart is how they
overcome their physical or social and cultural challenges and develop
into productive people making the world a safer, happier, and better
place to live.

When someone is born with a physical or emotional problem, the
malady or handicap becomes apparent right away because there are
plenty of examples of what the norm is as seen in other people. On
the larger scale of societies and cultures, it is more difficult to recognize problems within. Since societies and cultures are made up of the
very people who are born into and raised with the community's traditions and standards, it is hard for those same people to recognize

problems within, as they often have no point of reference to anything better. Any attempt to become countercultural and improve the situation or correct problems is often discouraged or outright forbidden, with dire consequences. What's a rebel going to do?

When I first saw a dollar bill in the Middle East, I looked it over to see what it had to say or show me about this country that had captured my imagination. It gave me a couple of surprises. First, there was an Egyptian-style pyramid on the Great Seal, and second, there were the words "E PLURIBUS UNUM," which I had never seen or heard while watching *The Love Boat* or *Dynasty*. It wasn't till I was studying for my U.S. citizenship that I learned the words meant "Out of many, one." It introduced me to the fact that this country was originally made up of people who recognized the problems and drawbacks their societies and cultures had, and wanted better. I also learned about the Washington whose picture was on that bill. I found out that he and others risked their lives as they spent their time and resources fighting for the ideals they knew would be the foundation for a better country. They worked to establish rights for the individual, rights that did not exist under other forms of government at that time. Their wisdom made this country a powerful and great nation, and there are people who will do anything to leave their societies and cultures and come here.

To borrow from the army recruiting slogan, you can be all you can be here in America. I recall visiting a chamber of commerce when my husband and I were starting our business and seeing a large display of informational pamphlets put out by the government to help small businesses prosper. Appreciating the wealth of information being freely offered, I said to him, "If you can't make it in America, you can't make it anywhere." Your only limitations are the barriers created in your own mind. In Lebanon, the place I am most familiar with, to start a business you have to budget especially for bribery just to get the necessary legal documents you need to begin operations. Government employees and agencies not only are of no help but are actually a part of the problem. If you need special information about anything, you don't even know where to start to get it.

America is a place of opportunity. It's people-friendly! Very much so, compared to the Muslim countries in the world. People looking for better lives flock to America because we as a society do not mutilate young girls' genitals, do not cut off people's hands for stealing. We do not stone people to death for committing adultery. We do not rape women and men for speaking up against our government. We do not forbid people to go to school and to learn because of their gender. We assume people are innocent until proven guilty. We give people the freedom to criticize our government and even burn our flag as an expression of speech. This is but a partial list of why America is superior in culture and values to many other countries in the world. This type of culture also thrives in Israel, the only Western-style nation in the Middle East, one that Arabs despise, feel threatened by, and vow to destroy.

Raised within the Judeo-Christian value system, we are taught from childhood "Do not judge others lest you be judged," "Do unto others what you want others to do unto you," and "Hear no evil, see no evil, speak no evil." We in America have taken this a little further and have become deaf to evil, blind to evil, and incapable of speaking out against evil because as long as it does not affect us, it is none of our business. The Declaration of Independence says that "all men are created equal; that they are endowed by their Creator with certain unalienable rights; that among these are life, liberty, and the pursuit of happiness." We the people are entitled to equal rights under the law and should have the same opportunity to pursue our dreams, whatever those dreams may be; but it is not said anywhere that we as people are created equal in the material or societal and cultural sense by our creator. Societies and cultures are not created and do not develop equally. This harsh judgment may make you wince. It is not politically correct to say that our Western societies are better than the Muslim Arab societies, but we are, we have been, and we always will be, not because of our wealth but because of the way we think and live, and the values we hold dear and pass on to our future generations.

It infuriates me to hear self-loathing Americans, who have never experienced life in an oppressive culture or under an oppressive leadership such as is found in the Middle East, badmouth and put down our culture, government, and country in general. They find all sorts of things wrong with America and think it is insulting to non-Americans to acknowledge that our Western culture is in any way better than others. They are so concerned about hurting "feelings," and nobody wants to be accused of being a holier-than-thou type. They should get out and see the world and how Arab Muslim leaders are really messing up other people's lives and getting away with it. Just as it's time to hold people accountable for their actions, it's time to hold societies and cultures accountable for theirs also. It is by not judging others that you end up with evil people like bin Laden, Saddam Hussein, and suicide bombers driven by the ideology that you are worthless infidels who should be killed as Allah ordered. When you don't stop evil in its tracks when you first recognize it, you will end up with a monster force that will spread its tentacles and affect the lives of millions. Because we did not want to judge evildoers such as the Palestinians bombing innocent Israelis, the Taliban taking over Afghanistan, and Saddam Hussein gassing his own people, we have helped create the monsters we are dealing with today.

Don't be afraid to stand up and lift your head and be proud of what America and Western culture stand for. America did not pull itself out of the grip of tyranny and feudalism for nothing. America as a Western culture and as a nation is a tribute to men and women and God's creation at its best. What other country offers a farmer's son the opportunity to become president; lets an immigrant become a governor; allows a poor individual to attain the highest levels of education free of charge; and permits all to practice their religion openly, and respectfully, and to pursue the accumulation of wealth no matter their race, gender, or social status?

Lack of Education and Human Development

While many countries in the world are advancing, Arab countries are not only not moving forward, they are sliding backward. As the populations get poorer and poorer, their corrupt leaders become richer and richer. The UN recently published a report by "distinguished Arab intellectuals" about human development in Arab countries. Figures show that despite their oil wealth, the gross domestic product of all twenty-two Arab countries combined at the end of the twentieth century was little more than that of Spain and less than half that of Italy.[1] Italy has 53 million people while Arabs number 300 million! And the Arab population is expected to increase to between 410 million and 459 million by 2020.[2] The way things are going those Muslim Arab societies don't have to create anything, just destroy what others have done, terrorize them into submission, and walk in and take it over for Allah.

The illiteracy rate in the Arab world is not only higher than the world average; it is higher than the average in developing countries.[3] For instance, the illiteracy rate in the Arab world is more than three times higher than in Latin America and the Caribbean,[4] and illiteracy in the Arab world is increasing.[5] About one-third of Arab men and half of Arab women were illiterate in 2002. The scientific research and technological development produced by all of the Arab countries combined is less than 1 percent of the world's total.[6] In the Arab world, approximately 330 books are translated into Arabic each year. By contrast, each year Greece translates over 1,500 books into Greek, and Spain translates approximately 100,000 books into Spanish.[7]

Does that give you an idea about the lack of education and the lack of development in human resources, and in creating a productive, informed, viable population in these countries? In 1998, a grand total of three technology patents were granted to the entire Arab world. The Republic of Korea alone received 779 technology patents in the same time period.[8] Also, between 1980 and 2000, the combined patents created by the Arab world totaled 370. South Korea alone created more than 16,000 patents in the same time period.[9] What has created such an impediment to what was a flourishing area in ancient times?

If you take their oil away, oil that the West discovered and developed, what have the Arab countries exported to the world other than grief, suicide bombers, and terrorism? Their list of exports in the last century and this one has provided us with severed heads, mutilated bodies, the murder of innocent children, the spilling of infidel blood, and celebrations of the death of Americans and Jews. While the Western world focuses on space exploration, developing scientific cures for deadly diseases, rescuing tsunami and earthquake victims, and creating beautiful art for the world to enjoy, Arab Muslims are creating museums, such as the Palestinian Museum at al-Najah University in Nablus, that display pictures of savagely mutilated bodies and heads floating in a pool of blood, and show videos that glamorize booby traps, blood spilling, and martyrs enjoying the bliss of heaven. When they could be giving money to alleviate human suffering, filthy-rich Saudi sheikhs are spending millions on self-aggrandizing monuments such as mosques, Islamic schools, and higher-education centers to promote a radical ideology that has caused and threatens to cause untold death and destruction in the Western world. Relatively feeble attempts to appear humanitarian, such as when Saudi prince Al-Waleed bin Talal tried to donate $10 million to New York City after 9/11, are rejected. Ten million dollars spent to rid Islam of its radical, dangerous, and intolerant element within would be better spent. Ten million dollars spent on books and schools teaching tolerance and respect for other faiths would make the world a better place. Ten million dollars goes a long way in a country where people make on average twelve thousand dollars a year.

The Middle East is lagging behind not because Arab Muslims are not created equal as human beings in the eyes of the creator. It is lagging behind because of social and religious values. As a result of these values, they have an ingrained corruption than runs throughout their societies. They respect craftiness and deceit over honesty and virtue. They are consumed with hate for one another. They do not allow human beings to be free and to express themselves. They control their population by subjugating 51 percent of the population—that's what most Arab and Muslim societies do to their women. I personally suffered. Women are not given a voice or rights and are treated as property owned by the male who is in charge of them, be it her father, husband, or brother. If the women in Libya were as educated and articulate (and as opinionated) as I am, do you think Gadhafi would stay in power? Do you think the royal family in Saudi Arabia would keep living the high life in power? If half of the Libyan population were freed and allowed access to education, free thinking, and self-determination, do you think the situation would remain as it is?

I believe the degraded state of Arab societies is caused by Islam. It kills self-expression, self-improvement, and empowerment because the religion demands that Islam be the center of one's life and existence, and it dictates how you should be, how you should live. Unless you live under Sharia law, according to Islam you are considered less of a human being and should be killed. It has spawned generations of people who celebrate death over life, who glorify mass murderers, who exhibit a lack of forgiveness and instead have the drive for revenge as taught by the Koran. It is their lack of open culture, their lack of advancement, and their continuous disrespect for infidels and anything non-Muslim that is the poison killing them from within.

The reason Arabs in the Middle East will never be able to recognize or address the real issues that are holding them back is because of *taqiyya.* From the moment they are born they are programmed to blame Israel and the United States for their ills. Instead of practicing self-examination to discover why a third of their men and half of their women are illiterate, why they are not free under their governments, why creativity in science and technology is nonexistent, why they have economic sclerosis despite having the world's oil wealth under their feet, they turn their eyes and look for a scapegoat. It is much easier and more bearable to put the blame somewhere else instead of facing the truth. This tactic is freely being employed by their fundamentalist mullahs and corrupt leaders to mask the detrimental effects of corrupt values and lack of freedom.

Above and beyond what you may have gathered from my personal experiences in the opening chapters of this book characterizing Islamic-dominated cultures, I give you Saudi king Abdullah at the December 2005 meeting of the Organization of the Islamic Conference in Mecca. He recognized that "a vast majority of Muslim countries today face political, economic and social underdevelopment that has evolved into a major crisis,"[10] and said this situation had led to a "diminishing position of Muslims in the international arena." If you don't want to take my word because I am Christian Arab, take his; he's a Muslim. Luckily, we found a hint of an ally in him when he tried to galvanize the assembled Islamic leaders in fighting terrorism when he lashed out at al Qaeda terrorists for "unleashing evil and corruption on Earth."[11] To some extent that is the pot calling the kettle black, but I applaud him for being unusually candid with his economic and human development assessment of the Arab world. Hopefully his objectiveness is an inspirational start down the road toward joining the twenty-first century for the Muslim world.

Corrupt, Oppressive Leaders

Also affecting the Muslim and Arab nations' ability to become a positive contributing member to the world are their forms of government. Most countries in the Middle East have been ruled for generations by dictators. You can identify each country with one man, one family, or Islam. Libya: Gadhafi; Syria: Assad; Jordan: King Abdullah; Saudi Arabia: the royal family of Sand; Kuwait: the royal family. In Iraq it used to be Saddam Hussein. Iran: Muslim fundamentalists. Even in Jordan, home of Western-educated King Abdullah and Westernized queen Rania, where relatively free elections occur, the ultimate power is controlled and maintained by an unelected king. The only opposition these dictators have comes from extremist Muslims, whom they have managed to suppress up until recently. In the global community of developing democratic societies, this concentration of autocratic and royal purveyors of power seems absolutely medieval. Israel is the only truly democratic, secular country in the Middle East, right in the middle of all of them.

In line with the medieval thinking, Arab rulers know how to control their populations: keep them ignorant. That's how you rule people, keep them ignorant and control the content and flow of information into society. You brainwash them into believing whatever you want them to believe, using the government-controlled newspapers, radio, and TV. Then let human nature, pumped with hatred, anger, rage, pain, and suffering and spiced with Islamic holy deception, take its course.

Another method these one-man or religion-based regimes use to stay in power is to create a sideshow to distract the population from problems at home. That's why the Arab world has done nothing to help the Palestinian refugees they created when they attacked Israel in 1948. It's called the "Palestinian refugee problem." This is one of the best tricks that the Arabs have played on the world, and they have used it to their great advantage when fighting Israel in the forum of public opinion. This lie was pulled off masterfully, and everyone has been falling for it ever since. First you tell people to leave their homes and villages because you are going to come in and kick out the Jews the day after the UN grants Israel its nationhood. You fail in your military objective, the Jews are still alive and have more land now than before, and you have thousands of upset, displaced refugees living in your country because they believed in you. So you and the UN build refugee camps that are designed to last only five years and crowd the people in, instead of integrating them into your society and giving them citizenship. After a few years of overcrowding and deteriorating living conditions, you get the media to visit and publish a lot of pictures of these poor people living in the hopeless, wretched squalor you have left them in. In 1967 you get all your cronies together with their guns and tanks and planes and start beating the war drums. Again the same old story: you really are going to kill all the Jews this time or drive them into the sea, and everyone will be able to go back home, take over what the Jews have developed, and live in a Jew-free Middle East. Again you fail and now there are even more refugees living in your countries, and Israel is even larger, with Jerusalem as its capital. Time for more pictures of more camps and suffering children. What is to be done about these poor refugees (that not even the Arabs want)? Then start Middle Eastern student organizations on U.S. college campuses and find some young, idealistic American college kids who have no idea of what has been described here so far, and have them take up the cause. Now enter some power-hungry type like Yasser Arafat who begins to blackmail you and your Arab friends, who created the mess, for guns and bombs and money to fight the Israelis. Then Arafat creates hell for the world starting in the 1970s with his terrorism, and the "Palestinian refugee problem" becomes a worldwide issue and galvanizes all your citizens and the world against Israel. Along come the suicide bombers, so to keep the pot boiling you finance the show by paying every bomber's family twenty-five thousand dollars. This encourages more crazies to go blow themselves up, killing civilians and children riding buses to school. Saudi Arabia held telethons to raise thousands of dollars to the families of suicide bombers. What a perfect way to turn years of military failure into a public-opinion-campaign success.

The perpetuation of lies and uncritical thinking, combined with repetitious anti-Jewish and anti-American diatribes, has produced a generation of Arab youth incapable of thinking in a civilized manner. This government-nurtured rage toward the West and the infidels continues today, perpetuating their economic failure and deflecting frustration away from the dictators and regimes that oppress them. This refusal by the Arab regimes to take an honest look at themselves has created a culture of scapegoating that blames western civilization for misery and failure in every aspect of Arab life. So far it seems that Arab leaders don't mind their people lagging behind, save for King Abdullah's recent evidence of concern. (The depth of his sincerity remains to be seen.)

Arab Countries: Tribes with Flags

To get a better understanding of the societies that introduced mass killing by suicide bombers we must understand how the culture operates. Arab countries are tribes with flags. As Arab tribes in the Middle East were divided by the British and the French and given land that both these powers controlled, new countries emerged that are now considered a part of the international community. However, these tribes kept to themselves because of their religion, culture, and way of life. The lack of transition, education, and business development in these countries ensures that most people stay trapped within their societies and cultures, ruled by centuries-old tribal customs, traditions, and ways of thinking that are still revered and followed as they were hundreds of years ago.

Tribal and spiritual leaders are the real power brokers in Arab societies in the Middle East. They are honored, respected, and obeyed by the rest of the community. Every word they utter is considered a word of wisdom not to be questioned. Children are raised with the idea of obeying and respecting as ultimate authority the family patriarch, the elders of the community, and the religious leaders; in almost all areas of life the religious leader, known as sheikh or mullah, is the one with the utmost authority. In most cases those religious leaders lack proper education, which is irrelevant as long as they know the Koran and live according to its law. The West has now come to see the power mullahs have in their communities and on political issues. A shoe bomber, the World Trade Center truck bombing, hundreds of suicide bombings, and of course 9/11—all inspired by religious leaders preaching the vision of jihad and martyrdom—speak of this mesmerizing power and influence. More recently, when riots in France erupted, the French government turned to the mullahs to calm down the crowds and maintain control after all police efforts failed. A few words from the Muslim mullahs quieted the streets of Paris and the surrounding areas.

Honor Killing

These tribal countries are maintaining an aspect of their culture I hold just as accountable as their religion for the death and mayhem that are commonplace: the rituals of tribal life based on honor (*ard*). The concept of honor in the Arab world is the driving force behind wars, killing, and international conflict. Any perceived injury to the honor of one member of the clan by an outsider is considered an injury to all members of the Arab world. Any dishonorable action by one member of the tribe reflects on the whole community. Therefore the drive for revenge to cleanse the honor justifies the killing of innocents, who have to pay the price to wipe away the shame. Positions of power are given to unqualified individuals simply to honor them as a favor for past deeds or for killing individuals for dishonoring or betraying the tribe, or allying themselves with an enemy tribe.

The family's respect and position in the community in an Arab or Islamic country is directly linked to and dependent on the family's honor. That honor is the sole responsibility of the women of the family, who are taught from childhood the consequences of their behavior. The male members' honor lies between their women's legs. The woman is the property of the man, be it her father, husband, or brother, a whole network of male members who ensure that the family's honor is guarded at all times. The word *aib* ("shame") is used frequently and associated with everything a woman does, from her dress code, to her social behavior, to her language, to her makeup, down to a hair that has escaped her headscarf. A married woman cannot leave home without the permission of a male member of her family. When the father is absent, the son must give permission to his mother to leave. An unmarried woman must remain a virgin with her hymen intact until marriage. In most Islamic countries a woman has to produce a proof of her virginity to her family-in-law on her wedding night. If she fails to bleed, it means she is not a virgin in their eyes, and then her death becomes the obligation of her immediate family members, her father and brothers.

It is shameful for an Arab woman to be seen with a male who is not a relative or a family member. Merely creating the suspicion of being touched by another man can cost her her life. Hundreds of women and young girls are savagely butchered in the Middle East every year. Human rights organizations can't even come close to counting the number of murders because of the close guarding of such shame by families. Even if a young girl is raped, she still has to die because she soiled the family's reputation and honor. Only her sacrificed blood will be able to cleanse the family's name.

Even in Jordan, under British-educated King Abdullah and his wife, Rania, Article 341 of Jordanian law justifies murder when honor is in question. It states that if the act of killing another or harming another was committed as an act in defense of his life, or his honor, or somebody else's life or honor, then it was justified. In many cases the murderers of girls who are killed in the name of honor are innocent of any crime. My doctor, who is an Iraqi and now resides and practices in America, tells me stories about the many girls she saw during her practice in the Middle East. Butchered and beaten girls were brought to her to examine, and after examination were found still to be virgins. Most of the girls were either dead when they got to her or were unsavable.

Women have no rights in Islamic societies. Women are not permitted to get an education. They are not allowed to leave the house or work without a male guardian's written approval. The Koran gives the husband the right to beat his wife. Sura 4:34 in the Koran says, "Men are the managers of the affairs of women. Those you fear may be rebellious admonish and banish them to their couches and beat them."

I have seen Arabic TV talk shows where men who have beaten their wives black and blue calmly defend their actions with the confidence and assurance learned from their culture and the stamp of approval from their religion. Watching Muslim imams and other clerics on TV describe their support for the practice and even clarify it with verses from the Koran is equally disgusting.

In Islam a wife has no right to divorce. That right belongs only to the husband, who can at a whim utter the words "You are divorced" three times in a row, and she is divorced. Then after being divorced she is looked upon as used goods by men, who will not stoop to marry her. They want a virgin, of course!

A highly circulated story of an honor killing, distributed by Knight Ridder/Tribune Information Services, was that of Rofayda Qaoud, a Palestinian teenager who was raped by her two brothers, who shared her bedroom, and became pregnant. Her mother bought her a razor and asked her to commit suicide by slitting her wrists. The young girl refused. So, says her mother, Amira Abu Hanhan Qaoud, she did what she believed any good Palestinian parent would: restored her family's "honor" through murder. Armed with a plastic bag, a razor, and a wooden stick, Qaoud entered her sleeping daughter's room. "Tonight you die, Rofayda," she told the girl, before wrapping the bag tightly around her head. Next, Qaoud sliced Rofayda's wrists, ignoring her muffled pleas of "No, Mother, no!" After her daughter went limp, Qaoud struck her in the head with the stick. It took her mother twenty minutes to finish the job.[12]

A girl born in the Middle East is doomed to a life of misery, especially if she is a Muslim. Many girls commit suicide as the only way out of a miserable situation, be it a forced marriage, soiled honor because of rape, or just rumored sexual promiscuity. The world did not pay attention to this phenomenon until it started seeing female suicide bombers, which made the Western world start questioning what drives a woman to become a suicide bomber. This seventh-century Middle Eastern Islamic tribal practice of degrading women is now a threat to the civilized world, a source for willing recruits who strap on bombs to kill innocent people. In the West it is completely beyond our imagination why women could be willing to kill other women and children. We know that in Islam the man is rewarded with seventy-two virgins in heaven, but what is a female martyr's reward in the afterlife? Her real reason for becoming a suicide bomber is to cleanse her honor. A few examples will dispel any misconception that these women suicide bombers exemplify the heightened frustration of people and societies so oppressed that they resort to suicide bombing as their last hope of achieving freedom. That's what the Islamic terrorists and Palestinians want the uninformed Western minds to think.

In January 2004, Reem al-Reyashi, a Palestinian from Gaza, became the first female Hamas bomber. She faked a medical condition at the Erez crossing and killed four people, leaving her two young children motherless. According to numerous reports, al-Reyashi had committed adultery and was given the terrible choice of dying at the hands of her family or attaining an "honorable" death by becoming a suicide bomber. Her lover, a member of Hamas, gave her the explosives and instructions for conducting the deadly mission, and her husband drove her to the Erez crossing to commit the heinous act.[13]

In April 2004, Israel prevented two young women recruited by the terror group Tanzim from executing attacks to "clear their names." The first woman, Tehani Zaki Ali Halil, was persuaded to carry out a suicide attack in Tel Aviv after being accused of infidelity. The other, a nineteen-year-old girl named Ramah Abed el-Majid Hasan Habaib, was recruited after accusations of premarital sexual relations.[14]

Women in Muslim societies are especially vulnerable to such coercion due to their subordination, which is enforced both legally and socially. The truth is, terror organizations frequently recruit women with problematic social statuses, such as suspected adulteresses and rape victims. In fact, one of the most despicable methods used by Yasser Arafat's own terror organization, Fatah, is to seduce young women or to arrange for their rapes and subsequently to pressure them into rehabilitating their social status by becoming "martyrs." Such a deal! Such a culture! Such lack of moral outrage!

Wafa Idris, who on January 27, 2002, became the first female suicide bomber, was married off at a very young age and could not have children. In that society a barren wife is considered worthless. Her husband divorced Wafa, married someone else, and had children with her. Wafa stood on the street at his wedding passing out candy. Her humiliation and dim future as a barren woman ensured that she would never marry again, and would be sentenced to a life as a servant to earn a living and be mistreated and abused. She had three options: (1) live a humiliated, depressed life; (2) commit suicide; or (3) become a suicide bomber and an instant hero admired the world over by Muslim Arabs.

Immediately after her death, Wafa Idris became a hero. Huge parties were thrown in her honor. Her funeral was like a wedding celebration. The Palestinian Authority undertook a very public campaign of indoctrination of its women to see themselves as potential suicide bombers. The PA immediately turned Idris's murder into an act to be emulated. According to the Palestinian newspaper *Al-Ayyam* in its issue of February 1, 2002, the PA held a demonstration in her honor with young girls carrying posters with Idris's picture, and the words "The Fatah Movement . . . eulogizes with great pride the heroic Martyr Wafa Idris."[15]

Observing a society's worship of heroes offers insight into its nature and values. In the West we honor people who have done great things for mankind, accomplished amazing feats of exploration, knowledge, or athletics. In the Middle East women martyrs, just like men who conduct suicide attacks, are widely revered, with their pictures hung on walls, buildings and streets named after them, and songs sung commemorating their deeds. Hundreds of Palestinians show up at their funerals to pay their respects. When they were alive, the women who committed these actions were dishonored, disrespected, and discarded. However, from the moment they killed infidels, they died as martyrs, achieving redemption. The only way to become a respected citizen is to become a *shahida,* to die for Allah. The only way a Muslim woman can achieve equality with a man is in death.

These deplorable tactics to recruit women suicide bombers are not often publicized, but pose a major threat to Muslim women and Western civilization. The ones who are vulnerable are the ones targeted. Just as terror groups use sermons at mosques to incite anger and hate in Muslim men, they exploit women's discontent with their so-called inferior status by working actively to portray suicide bombings as a way to achieve equality. Underlying all of this is the disturbing notion that in life women are *only* women, but they can rise to the status of "martyrs" in their death.[16]

13.

IS ISLAM
A PEACEFUL RELIGION?

America and the West are truly in a different world when trying to understand Islam and its influence on the devoted. This gap in understanding between East and West boils down to differing viewpoints, mentality, logic, culture, morals, and ethics. Without a point of reference on the Middle Eastern mind frame, Westerners become lost in their idealism and conceptions when trying to fathom the mentality and backwardness of the Arab and Islamic world. It's ironic, but to our own detriment, we just happen to be a society that cannot relate to fathers and mothers butchering their daughters; educated, wealthy men as suicide bombers; and mothers willingly blowing themselves up to kill other women and children. We fall prey to our innately Western, rational thinking and so believe these are mentally disturbed individuals who represent neither Islam and its teachings nor the majority view of peace-loving Muslims. We then go into deep self-examination, beat our heads, and wonder what we did wrong to cause them to hate us so much. Not only are we deceiving ourselves by our delusions, but we are becoming more vulnerable to falling prey to them. Before that becomes our fate, let's look at some facts.

Most of the barbaric and vicious acts of terror committed against innocent civilians around the world in the last thirty years have been done by Muslims. They have even carried out more bombings than the less-publicized Hindu Tamil Tiger separatists, who have committed more than two hundred suicide attacks in Sri Lanka. It is a fact that the nineteen terrorists who highjacked airplanes and flew them into the World Trade Center and the Pentagon, were Muslims who practiced the teachings of the Koran and sought mental fortitude in its verses as their planes crashed. It is a fact that it was in the name of Allah, not Jesus or Buddha, that they destroyed the lives of thousands and obliterated an American landmark and a symbol of progress and democracy at its best. They destroyed in several hours what took years and thousands of workers to build. These were killers of the worst kind. Yet they were heroes in the eyes of Jordanians, Palestinians, Lebanese, Syrians, and Iranians who danced in the streets in celebration of the mass murder of thousands of Americans in New York, at the Pentagon, and in Pennsylvania. Who could forget the images of Osama bin Laden gloating and grinning with joy as he said: "We were overjoyed when the first planes hit the building. So I said to them be patient. More is coming."[1] It was sickening to watch his followers follow every phrase he uttered about the attack with the chant of "Praise Allah."

The literal translation of the word *Islam* in Arabic is "submission." The word *Istislam* means "to surrender after a fight." The Koran says those who do not submit (*yastaslimoun*) to Islam should be killed. That means death to Christians and death to Jews, and to all other non-Muslims.

Islam Not Only Condones Violence but Commands It Against Infidels

Sura 8:59 in the Koran says, "The infidels should not think that they can get away from us. Prepare against them whatever arms and weaponry you can muster so that you may terrorize them." Does that sound peaceful to the politically correct types, or to the moderate,

202 ◆ BECAUSE THEY HATE

Western-raised Muslim? (That is, to the ones who say, "I did not know the full implications of what I signed up for.")

The Islamo-fascists have been quite faithful in carrying out this Koranic exhortation. Just look at Islam's history of 1,400 years of violence and bloodshed around the world. The Muslims did expand throughout the Mediterranean basin before faster-advancing civilizations and technology pushed them back. Today they are using the petrodollars and technology these civilizations provided to give it another try on a worldwide scale. Sura 9, verse 5, of the Koran says: "Fight and slay the pagans wherever you find them, and see them, belittle them and lie and wait for them in every strategy of war." (The pagans are you, dear readers, Christians, Jews, other non-Muslims, and moderate Muslims whom the Islamo-fascists feel are not faithful enough.) For the people who resist Islam, the Koran instructs in sura 5, verse 33: "Their punishment is execution or crucifixion or cutting off of hands and feet from the opposite sides or to be exiled from the land." Islam commands that. Is that what tolerant, progressive, and politically correct people consider peaceful? In America we don't even cut off body parts of serial rapists or child molesters.

The prophet Muhammad, founder of Islam, was a warrior who preached violence and the slaughter of thousands in establishing and spreading Islam. He participated in seventy-eight battles and approved the beheading of prisoners taken in battle. He ordered the assassination of those who offended him, be it women such as the poetess Asma bint Marwan, or a ninety-year-old man. He said to his Muslim followers: "Whoever relinquishes his faith. Kill him." He also said: "I have been ordered by Allah to fight with people till they testify that there is no God but Allah and Mohammed is his messenger."[2] His behavior inspired Iran's Ayatollah Khomeini to say: "The purest joy in Islam is to kill and to be killed for Allah."[3] Is that individual fanaticism? Or is it simply being faithful to the Islamic teachings found in the Koran? With the Koran commanding the faithful to kill the infidels, the question must be asked, were the nineteen Muslims who flew their hijacked planes into the World Trade Center, the Pentagon, and a Pennsylvania field fanatics, or just followers of the Islamic faith? Were the people who blew up passenger trains in Spain fanatics or just followers of the Islamic faith? Were the people holding children hostage and massacring them in Beslan fanatics or just followers of the Islamic faith? Were the people blowing up busses and pizzerias in Israel fanatics or just followers of the Islamic faith? Muslims consider the Koran the word of God and Muhammad the perfect model. The prophet Mohammed, a successful military leader who led his Muslim army against non-Muslims, is an inspiration to almost a billion people around the world. Considering the rise of Islamists around the world today, this fact should be of the utmost concern to "infidels" worldwide. If you listen to Friday sermons in mosques across the Middle East you hear hate and violence being preached from the pulpit by the mullahs. Go to www.memritv.org and download a cross-section of weekly sermons translated into English. The Middle East Media Research Institute (MEMRI) explores the Middle East through the region's media. MEMRI bridges the language gap which exists between the West and the Middle East, providing timely translations of Arabic, Farsi, and Hebrew media, as well as original analyses of political, ideological, intellectual, social, cultural, and religious trends in the Middle East.

What you will see is an eye-opener. It should send chills down the spine of moderate Muslims here in America who have no clue as to what is waiting in store for them when Islamo-fascism begins to take hold in their mosque or community. Their obedience to their faith is going to be put to a test that could require them to make a decision to either kill or be killed as a martyr for Allah.

The Palestinian Authority, according to the judgment of the media, has a secular leadership and is waging a nationalistic fight for territory. There is some basis for that assumption, but it's also through religious rabble-rousing that the leaders sway and motivate the masses. Here is a sample of the hundreds of quotes being spewed on a weekly basis to incite and motivate a jihadist movement not only against Israel but also against all infidels:[4]

- ❖ Suleiman Satari, PA TV, November 18, 2005
  "Destroy the Infidels and the Polytheists! Your [i.e., Allah's] ene-mies are the enemies of the religion . . . ! Count them and kill them to the last one, and don't leave even one."
- ❖ Yusuf Abu Sneina, Voice of Palestine, September 2, 2005
  "The Infidel countries—first and foremost, the USA—have suc-ceeded greatly in tearing our Islamic world apart."
- ❖ Ibrahim Mudayris, PA TV, February 28, 2003
  "The United Nations, to our regret, has become Dar al-Nadwa [literally "House of Assembly," the term for the pre-Islamic meet-ing place in Mecca], because that is where the Infidels meet."

This enmity is neither time nor event dependent, but is presented as part of Allah's plan. According to a report by Palestinian Media Watch, the call for genocide against all infidels on PA TV has become a regular occurrence. The ultimate victory of Islam over the Christian West is said to be predetermined: "The Palestinian nation is the strongest on earth. . . . We [Muslims] have ruled the world and a day will come, by Allah, and we shall rule the world [again]. The day will come and we shall rule America. The day will come and we shall rule Britain."[5]

The Palestinian Authority, like many Arab political leaderships, is careful to exclude this religious hate ideology from its English-language presentations to the foreign press. But what the PA's leaders say in Arabic to their own population feeds extreme, underlying Is-lamic tenets. To the utter frustration of world leaders who for years have been trying to negotiate an Israeli-Arab peace agreement, Arab and Muslim religious leaders have been preaching about and praying for the destruction of Israel and Western countries. In Egypt, Syria, Iran, Saudi Arabia, Jordan, Lebanon, and the Palestinian territories, they are presenting the destruction of the Christian-Jewish West as a

part of Allah's plan, a plan that is not falling on deaf ears. Islamic terrorists the world over, whom we characterize as fanatics, are really just
very devout followers of Muhammad. They are following his example
and doing exactly what the Koran teaches and their mullahs exhort
them to do with a daily diet of righteous jihad. American and Western
leaders and their citizens are deluding themselves and endangering
their very existence because of their refusal to acknowledge, read
about, and become informed about the violent history behind Islam
and to understand what it is today. These radical Islamists do not hide
what they want to do. Just as the Muslim Arabs beat the war drums
and rattled their sabers before every war with Israel and did the same
against the Christians in Lebanon, so they are doing now on radio and
TV, in mosques and every terrorist audio- or videotape that Al Jazeera
plays. We must listen and take action to stop them from doing what
they are clearly saying they will do. Listen and act accordingly if you
don't want your daughters to have to choose which type of head cover
they will wear in the future.

Can We Trust Our Muslim Neighbors?

It is a sad state of affairs when we as Americans, as people who came
from all around the world to build a life in the land of the free and the
home of the brave, have to look at some of our neighbors, colleagues,
and business associates and wonder if we can trust them; have to wonder if they are loyal to our country or to our enemy; have to wonder
how much their religion plays a role in their lives, and if someday they
may want to kill us in the name of God because supposedly we are
cursed by Allah for adopting polytheism. Whether or not you accept
this new reality, this is where Americans are today.

I voice what many in America are thinking but are afraid to
say out loud, for fear of being labeled a racist, a bigot, Islamophobic,
or intolerant. When I gave a speech at Duke University in 2004
condemning suicide bombers and the culture that nurtures them,

saying, "The difference between the Arab world and Israel is a difference in values and character. It's barbarism versus civilization. It's dictatorship versus democracy. It's evil versus goodness," I was criticized and condemned. Duke's Freeman Center for Jewish Life apologized for my comment to the same Arabs who supported the killing of innocent civilians and were unwilling to criticize and condemn terrorism.

We have gotten to a point in this country where we have to whisper and watch what we say about protecting America because we don't want to offend anyone. We have an enemy living among us, yet we are afraid to admit it, afraid to point it out. Nineteen Muslim men perpetrated September 11, yet we insist on taking the shoes off little old blue-haired ladies from Iowa boarding a plane with their grandchildren en route to Walt Disney World. Have we gone mad?

We have Muslim organizations that refuse to condemn our diehard enemies by name, yet we are afraid to challenge and confront them for fear of offending them. Do you think that if George Washington were alive today he would keep his mouth shut about the obvious decay in our society by American Muslim citizens who have been granted the blessing of citizenship by our country, yet their loyalty lies somewhere else? The Muslim community in this nation has lost our trust, lost our respect, lost our understanding and our compassion for whatever problems it has. Muslims' actions, or better still, their lack of actions, speak volumes. Where is the Muslims' voice in America speaking up in defense of America to our enemy? Why have they remained relatively silent?

The deeper we dig in trying to uncover terrorist cells, the more we find American Muslims stabbing America in the back right in the heartland, aiding our enemy while using our resources, freedoms, and laws against us. They are using the same laws and freedoms that are nonexistent in their home countries, those same countries that they left so they could come here to enjoy the blessings and richness of America. We must ask ourselves: Are the majority of Muslims living in America today who practice Islam loyal to the United States or loyal to

its enemy? Here is a little politically incorrect survey taken and published by *USA Today* in February of 1991.[6]

The survey queried Arab Americans regarding the Gulf War. This
is when America actually went into the Gulf region to protect Kuwait,
a Muslim nation, from Saddam Hussein's aggressive invasion. The
survey found that two-thirds of Arab Americans supported the United
States in attacking Saddam Hussein. But the degree of support hinged
on whether they practiced Christianity or Islam. Of the 501 Arab
Americans polled, 70 percent were Christian and 30 percent were
Muslim; seven in ten Arab Americans are Christians, mainly from
families who emigrated to the United States to escape the Islamic influence of the Middle East and who quickly assimilated. Seventy-seven
percent of the Christians supported the war; only 36 percent of the
Muslims did. Similarly, Christian approval for the way Bush was han-
dling his job closely resembled that of the U.S. population as a whole,
at 70 percent; however, Muslim approval was only 38 percent. Pollster
John Zogby of the Arab American Institute said, "You have two distinct world views. . . . The Muslims . . . have a tendency to be more
Arab in their world view."

Other results are probably going to shock you. The survey asked:
"Are you willing to have your son or daughter fight for the United
States in this war against Saddam Hussein?" Eighty-two percent of
Muslim Americans said no; they would not have their children fight
for the United States of America against a dictator who had invaded
another Muslim country. Only 18 percent of the Muslim Americans
surveyed said they were willing to back America in a war against
Iraq.

What does that tell us when 82 percent of a certain group living in
America, benefiting from America, protected by America, enjoying
our laws in America, is not willing to fight with America, to defend
America or the principles America stands for? It tells us that the ma-
jority of American Muslims would not support the United States of
America in any war against any Arab nation for any reason, period.

When you bring up the sensitive issue of Muslim loyalty to the

United States and the possibility of terrorists living among us, you are immediately countered by people who say these were a few trained terrorists, and they did not represent the views and beliefs of the majority of Muslims. This brings to mind the interview I watched on TV of one 9/11 hijacker's landlord in Florida who stated: "They were such nice gentlemen. They kept to themselves, never caused a problem, always paid their rent on time." If you had just tuned into the story you would think he was talking about two blue-eyed, American-as-apple-pie, Baptist guys from Tulsa.

These murderers were just your average nice neighbors who spent time in the United States cultivating a few friendships, going to school, getting together with occasional friends over dinner and coffee. You could have sat next to them in a movie theater, walked past them in the mall, or smiled at them at a traffic light. These were not some crazy criminals who just sneaked in through our borders only to quickly commit their terrorist act. Instead, they spent time blending into America's fabric while preparing and planning for the right time to strike and die.

Let's look at your average American Muslim, someone like Siraj Wahaj, the recipient of the American Muslim community's highest honors. Mr. Wahaj had the privilege in June of 1991 of becoming the first Muslim to deliver a daily prayer before the U.S. House of Representatives. In his prayer he recited from the Koran and appealed to almighty God to guide America's leaders "and grant them righteousness and wisdom."

The same Wahaj spoke to a Muslim audience a year later in New Jersey. This time Wahaj was singing a different tune to a different audience, and his words were far from his moderate ones in front of the U.S. House of Representatives. "If only Muslims were more clever politically," he told his New Jersey listeners, "they could take over the United States and replace its constitutional government with a caliphate. If we were united and strong, we'd elect our own emir [leader] and give allegiance to him. . . . [T]ake my word, if 6–8 million Muslims unite in America, the country will come to us."[7]

If Wahaj is the example of the American Muslim community and the receiver of its highest honors, who needs enemies? If this is whom our government calls a "moderate" and invites to deliver a prayer before the House of Representatives, we have ignorant elected officials sitting in our capital running our country. Do you feel safer now knowing that not all Muslims are plane-flying, bomb-wearing, or car-driving terrorists? Talking about overthrowing our government and replacing it with an Islamic caliphate is terrorism of a different kind, but it is still terrorism. This is the more dangerous kind, the kind that circles you slowly, so that by the time you realize you are about to be killed, it's already too late to do anything about it. Where is the outrage? Have we lost our sense of patriotism and loyalty to America? Do you consider this "moderation"? A highly respected, award-winning Muslim from the Islamic American community calling to overthrow the United States government?

Hold on to your seats, it gets better. This same man served in 1995 during the World Trade Center bombing trial as a character witness for Sheikh Omar Abdul Rahman. No wonder he has such ideas. Wahaj was also listed by the U.S. attorney for New York as one of the "unindicted persons who may be alleged as co-conspirators" in the Abdul Rahman trial.[8] And that is not the only scary part. What's more frightening is that, after all this, our mindless, ignorant, oh so politically correct elected leaders still insist that Islam is a religion of peace and the majority of Muslims are moderate.

If you listen to what Muslims articulate, you'll find Islam is exactly the opposite of what our leaders are saying. The visible Muslim leaders in this country who are appointed to positions of influence within Islamic communities tell us exactly what their intentions, desires, and aspirations are. Zaid Shakir is a former Muslim chaplain at Yale University. He argues that Muslims cannot accept the legitimacy of the existing American order, since it "is against the orders and ordainments of Allah. . . . [T]he orientation of the Koran," he adds, "pushes us in the exact opposite direction."[9] This guy is a chaplain at Yale University; this is the type of poison young American Muslims are exposed to. I have yet to hear anyone from the Muslim community condemn people like Shakir or set them straight, calling them liars who do not represent the voice of the Muslim majority in America. Their silence is not golden, it's revealing.

When Steven Emerson produced his documentary *Jihad in America* in 1994, viewers could not believe what they were seeing. Emerson infiltrated Islamic cells across America with a video camera and documented young Muslims being recruited for holy war in Oklahoma and Kansas in America's heartland. American Muslim leader Fayaz Azzam in Brooklyn was documented giving a speech and stating, "Blood must flow, there must be widows, orphans, hands and limbs must be severed and limbs and blood must be spread everywhere in order that Allah's religion can stand on its feet."[10] What Emerson documented was so shocking you would have thought our government would have declared a state of war and locked our borders immediately. But our inability to accept that these people were serious kept us from connecting the dots. Some people point to the 9/11 Commission's report stating we lacked imagination. Maybe we lacked imagination for the attackers' modus operandi and the way they pulled it off. However, we knew the Islamists intended to attack America. I call it a bad case of political correctness when we can't bring ourselves to examine critically what people say instead of comfortably shrugging it off and feeling good that it was just people exercising their freedom of speech here in wonderful America. If we keep this up much longer it won't be so wonderful anymore; a few million of us will be dead. Emerson should be applauded for shedding light on a darkness that is spreading; *Jihad in America* should be required viewing for every citizen registered to vote.

When we have Muslim Americans advocating the overthrow of the U.S. government, when they are preaching in their mosques that Islam's way is superior to America, when millions of Muslim Americans do not take to the streets to condemn such statements and to demonstrate against the very Islamic radical organizations that call for murder in the name of Islam, then Muslim Americans are guilty, and we need to take a stand.

With millions of lives at stake in our major cities, we can no longer afford to continue to give Islam the benefit of the doubt. We can no longer turn a blind eye to a supposed few "extremists" in our midst. We can no longer listen to our elected officials speak nonsense about an imaginary war called the war on terrorism. It should be a war on radical Islam. How long can we carry on this charade of stupidity and political correctness?

Muslims in this country need to prove their loyalty to America by their actions, and I am not talking about writing letters to America's newspaper editors complaining about discrimination and being searched at airports. If they take the time to write about profiling, they can take the time to condemn what is causing them to be profiled and what is being done in the name of their supposedly hijacked religion. I have no doubt that moderate Muslims do exist. I actually know a couple. One of the most visible Muslim moderates in America today is Kamal Nawash, founder and president of the Free Muslim Coalition Against Terrorism. Nawash repeatedly voices his concern to the press and colleagues, and he told me personally, "We're going to have to clean our own house first. We're trying to convince Muslims that we have a problem. We have a problem with extremism. Unless we address it, we can't solve any other problem we have. The only way we are going to fight extremism is explore a modern and secular interpretation of Islam. An Islam that is democratic and peaceful and is compatible and respectful of other faiths and beliefs."

Nawash tried to organize a rally in Washington, D.C., for moderate Muslims to condemn terrorism and radical Islam. Nawash reached out not only to Muslim groups but also to Jews and Christians, including my organization, the American Congress for Truth, to help him put the rally together, and to attend to support him. I made it clear to him that while I was more than delighted to help him in any way I could to make the rally possible, including distributing posters to every local mosque and Islamic institution in my area, the demonstrators must be Muslims from the Muslim community. Americans did not need to see a rally of a thousand participants and only fifty of them being Muslims.

While over eighty Christian and Jewish organizations and sponsors lined up to help and participate, leaders of well-known and established Muslim groups in this country shunned the rally. The Council on American-Islamic Relations, the Muslim Public Affairs Council, and the Muslim American Society declined to stand with him against extremism, radical Islam, and terrorism. They not only refused to participate, but were both irritated and defensive and began attacking Nawash. Moderate Muslims need to take a closer look at who and what groups they are supporting. CAIR forwarded all calls to Hussein Ibish, the former Communications Director at the Arab Anti-Discrimination Committee (ADC). In two rambling smear jobs posted on Muslim WakeUp.com, Ibish labeled Nawash's Free Muslim Coalition Against Terrorism as "the ugly" among leading Muslim groups, and called Nawash's invitation for other Muslim leaders to denounce radicalism a "crude ploy."[11]

The denial and disbelief that I sense in the politically correct crowd, particularly those who come from New York, where there is a big hole in the ground in lower Manhattan, sometimes makes me feel that they think a Muslim extremist is a mythical invention of Jews and Christians. We are fighting an enemy that doesn't wear a uniform, an enemy that lives in our midst, an enemy that strives to die just to kill us. We are fighting an army in disguise. This army doesn't work independently but is supported and protected by a community and a neighborhood. It is suicidal to label any Islamic community moderate, because it is this same community that protected, supported, and shielded the extremists and made their suicide operation possible. I know the Middle East, Middle Eastern culture, and how Middle Eastern communities are connected. The Muslim Arab community is not an American community on American soil. It is a minority community that just changed geography yet still practices Middle Eastern customs. Nothing can go on in a vacuum, because there is no vacuum. Everyone knows everything about everyone. Walk into any city in the USA and go straight to the Arab grocery store and ask about anyone in the Arab community, and he or she will know the person you are asking about and know details about them that will shock any American. The Islamic community in the United States knows a lot and has a lot of information to give to authorities about the numerous terrorist cells that exist inside our country. I challenge the Muslim American "moderates" to stand up and be counted. Prove me wrong, and take back and redeem your heritage as it was before Islam sidetracked Muslim countries from becoming one of the great civilizations of the world and became instead one of the most backward, barbaric, unproductive, and uneducated parts of the world. If we don't wake up and challenge our Muslim community to take action against the terrorists within it, if we don't believe in ourselves as Americans and in the standards we should hold every patriotic American to, we are going to pay a price for our shortsightedness.

We have been seeing and reading stories from around the world about Muslims who do not have loyalty to whatever country they have emigrated to. In France, Britain, Denmark, and here in the United States, Islamic extremists are declaring their loyalty foremost to Islam, not to their host nations. Just listen to world news on any network and hear about Muslims from different Western countries on different continents who have been arrested and convicted for having ties to jihadists and for supporting terrorist organizations and ideologies.

Let's look at three recent examples, Denmark, Britain, and the U.S.

In Denmark a Muslim imam and Danish citizen, Imam Ahmad Abu Laban of the Islamic Belief Society, started a letter-writing campaign, went to Egypt and Syria, and riled up Muslim nations about the controversial Muhammad cartoons published in the Danish newspaper *Jyllands-Posten*. He even invented some phony over-the-top cartoons and passed them off as the product of the same newspaper. The result was an inflamed Islamic world, the burning of Danish embassies in Muslim countries, protests and deaths in the hundreds, a boycott by Iran and several members of the Arab League of Danish products, and suppression of free speech via intimidation that reached all the way to the U.S. And this from a Danish citizen who enjoyed the free speech and social welfare benefits given him as a citizen by that generous country.[12]

In London, Egyptian-born British citizen Imam Abu Masri al-Masri was at the center of the infamous Finsbury Park Mosque; undercover video led to his conviction by a British court on February 9, 2006, for inciting hate and murder against Christians and Jews, while urging suicide terrorism on British Muslim citizens. The Finsbury Park Mosque—described by antiterrorist police chief Peter Clarke as a "honeypot for extremists"—was attended by both September 11 plotter Zacarias Moussaoui and failed "shoe bomber" Richard Reid and has been linked to several other suspected terrorists.[13]

Ahmed Abu Ali, a twenty-three-year-old U.S. citizen and honors grad from a local high school in suburban Fairfax, Virginia, was caught in Saudi Arabia, where he was in terrorist training, and deported to the U.S. and tried for his part in a purported al Qaeda plot to kill President Bush. He has been sentenced to thirty years in U.S. Federal Court.[14]

Or take the case of the Islamic Thinkers Society in Jackson Heights, New York. Demonstrating on a street corner in exercise of their "protected" speech rights, society members stomped on and tore the U.S. flag. Using bullhorns, they publicly laughed at Americans for being dummies while they used and abused our free speech rights to argue that our Constitution should be replaced with Sharia law overseen by a new caliphate. The Islamic Thinkers Society is considered an offshoot of Al-Muhajiroun, which has ties to al Qaeda.[15]

The ball is in the Muslims' court right now. They must control and turn in to the authorities the "extremists" in their midst, the scholars, the imams, the operatives who meet in the coffeehouses to sway recruits. It is not our duty to show how tolerant, open-minded, and loving we are toward a community that harbors people who want to kill us. The responsibility is theirs. Until we can be convinced that they have shaped up, we should watch them like a hawk. Every mosque, every imam, every Islamic charity that gives money or receives it from suspected terrorists, every madrassa in America funded by the Saudis, every Muslim working in every section of our government, even the janitor—all should be suspects. The louder CAIR shrieks, the more we should investigate. If they don't like our scrutiny, they can stop being part of the problem and start becoming part of the solution.

14.

POLITICAL CORRECTNESS
GONE MAD

The term "political correctness" has evolved out of the Marxist and Freudian philosophies of the 1930s to become a tool for multiculturalism, multisexualism, multitheism, and multi-anythingism. It was created to discourage bias and prejudiced thinking that discriminates against an individual or group. It has become society's way of not offending anyone, whether it is an individual, a group, or a nation. In many instances, however, it is a simple, disarming way of ignoring or deflecting the truth about a situation. Today, the use of political correctness has become so abused that anyone who voices his or her opinion contrary to "politically correct think" is immediately tagged with some form of disparaging label, such as racist and bigot. This exploitation has gotten so out of control that this name-calling accusation is used as a simple and mindless means to manipulate academic, social, or political discussion. The result is a social paranoia which discourages free thought and expression. It's like living in a totalitarian state in which you are afraid to say what you think. Now who wants to suffer that? So people keep quiet. Their opinions are held captive to fear. How handy for the Islamo-fascists, the American-hating, Jew-killing, Israel-destroying, women-abusing, multireligious-intolerant Muslims. Oh! Excuse me. Did I say something not quite PC?

This social paranoia is similar to the attitude that developed in the late 1980s and 1990s, when people became so concerned about children's self-esteem that failure could not be acknowledged or misbehavior corrected. "Now, let's not hurt their feelings" was the standard approach. This degree of concern led to teachers giving passing grades for poor performance and youth sport activities where no one kept score. And what has been the fallout of all that psychobabble? High school kids who can't read their diploma or make change for a dollar, internationally embarrassing scholastic performance scores, and young adults ill equipped to face the competitive lifestyle the world has to offer. They are left watching the television show *The Apprentice,* not competing to be an apprentice. America got itself into a mess by not upholding the high standards and expectations it once had, instead giving in to mediocrity; and we're getting into a mess now with political correctness.

The radical Islamic movement has availed itself of the PC mentality to convince good-hearted people around the world that the Jews, Israel, and the "fascist government of the United States of America" are responsible for the ills of the Muslim people, and that their daily suffering is because of them. The PC crowds label anyone who disagrees with this notion a bigot. Human rights groups such as Amnesty International and the like have picked up on this phenomenon. Their adversarial attacks against America and Western powers have become scary and foolish. They have gone so far out of their way to protect the "rights of the underdog" that they are actually promoting dangerous radical Islamic views that may indirectly put you in peril. Anyone who disagrees with radical Islamic propaganda is being attacked in the media, on college campuses, and at rallies countering events that promote the Islamic cause.

The West is not failing the expectations of terrorists worldwide. The constant apologizing, the appeasement, the sensitivity training, and our destructive ignorance from not studying and evaluating our enemy are masking the threat we face and hastening our defeat. Every public instance of political correctness is dragged through the Arab world media as an example of just how wrong America is and how right the terrorists are. The terrorists have been watching and learning from our reactions over the last thirty years, and they have learned that they have a better chance of defeating us in Washington, D.C., and through the media than on the battlefield. Meanwhile, our politicians have forgotten the World War II lesson that appeasement never works, and the principle of warfare, Know your enemy.

Former deputy homeland security secretary Admiral James Loy testified before the Senate Select Committee on Intelligence that recent information showed that al Qaeda has calculated plans to infiltrate the Southwest border of the United States.[1] It's open. It's easy. The Mexican government and pro-immigrant organizations even give out maps. And if you get caught, it's no problem. Come back later. Just like what the UN forces did in Lebanon to the terrorists trying to infiltrate into Israel. Catch them, let them go, and they can try again. A notorious Latino street gang, which refers to itself as MS-13, is being recruited by al Qaeda for help. This gang is based in Mexico and Los Angeles and is helping the terrorist group penetrate our borders.[2] There are more than three thousand MS-13 gang members in Washington, D.C., alone.[3] It is comforting to know that there are so many potential terrorists residing in our nation's capital ready to work for a payoff. A growing number of people categorized as "other than Mexicans" (OTMs) are citizens from other countries that are aggressive to the United States: Iran, Egypt, Iraq, Lebanon, and Afghanistan.[4] Calling these infiltrators OTMs make it sound as if they are some miscellaneous group of the "other" category, when in fact most of them are terrorists looking for a way into our country.

Think about the Roman Empire, the greatest civilization of its time. What brought down the Roman Empire? It was decay from within. What brought down the Greek Empire? Decay from within. You are seeing the beginning of the demise of the greatest nation in the world, the United States of America, because of a cancer that eats and devours from within. Neither the Islamo-fascists nor any nation can ever defeat us militarily; we are the one and only superpower. But if we allow them continued, unabated access, they can definitely wound us with terror tactics and strategically placed weapons of mass destruction. We are giving them the tools and allowing them to let us commit suicide. They are watching as divisions among us in the press, across the nation, and in the government on policy and the war on terror are destroying us from within.

While elements on the extreme left, both private and elected, are attacking our troops' morale and constricting our intelligence agencies, our media are demonizing and destroying America's image throughout the world. Al Jazeera loves what is being handed them on a silver platter. The radical Muslims laugh watching our government bend over backward, trying to appease the critics by constantly defending itself for protecting us from those who wish to do us harm. They love the press in America unwittingly doing such a good job doing their bidding digging up classified information such as our prisons in Europe that the Arab press can sling around.

They smirk because the stupid Americans have demonstrated how weak and spineless they are by caving in to stories about maltreatment of Guantánamo detainees or who hurt whose feelings at Abu Ghraib. They are watching our critics in this country and counting on them to embolden the radical Islamic cause and weaken our resolve. The more we stumble over ourselves questioning our goals and tactics, the more they think we are weak and easy to defeat.

Americans bashing America has become so fashionable that some people are wearing their anti-Americanism on their arms as a badge of honor. Politicians and Hollywood stars speaking against our government here and abroad have become the norm. Every critical word they utter is immediately transmitted via satellite and the Internet throughout the world. It will air on Al Jazeera before most Americans have seen it themselves. When Democratic senator Dick Durbin criticized America for its policy at Gitmo, for example, the story spread around the world like lightning. It was the most downloaded story on Al Jazeera within hours of his statements. Title 18 of the U.S. Code defines "treason" as follows: "Whoever, owing allegiance to the United States, levies war against them or adheres to their enemies, giving them aid and comfort within the United States or elsewhere, is guilty of treason and shall suffer death." Someone agreeing with and providing words that encourage and support the goals of our enemy is a traitor in my book. Under the legal definition of treason there are grounds to indict virtually the entire Democratic leadership of the United States of America and most of the allegedly "free press." I would apply it immediately to media outlets that reveal secret programs we are using to protect our country such as the NSA spying program.

Now, we can sit around making diversity quilts, singing love songs, and painting beautiful pieces of art about harmony and peace all we want, but it is not going to change reality. The pseudorealists of the West, pushing their touchy-feely, goody-two-shoes, righteous-indignation attitude and view of the world and how they think it should be, are chasing a concoction of idealistic imaginings like little children chasing butterflies. There is a big hornet's nest ahead and they're going to run headlong into it. Our lives are on the line. Our civilization is on the line. If the Islamo-fascists take over, the only art you are going to see is huge painting of mullahs and dictators along the highways. The only sounds you are going to hear are the moaning and groaning of someone's hands being cut off, or the cries of a daughter being killed by her father in the name of honor, and the Islamic call to prayer "Allahu Akbar" resonating across town from the Islamic mosques five times a day. When was the last time you visited any country in the Middle East controlled by the Muslims? The last time I visited Beirut I was greeted as soon as I drove out of the airport by a huge picture of an Iranian ayatollah. This is Beirut, once known as the Paris of the Middle East. And you think it can't happen here? Wake up. We didn't believe it either when the war started in Lebanon.

We cannot play Russian roulette with our safety, the security of our children, and the future of Western civilization. We cannot base our survival strategy on some exaggerated theory of moderate Muslims who pick and choose verses trying to downplay the savagery behind Islam while refusing to see evil, refusing to hear about evil, and condemning the people who warn you about the evil coming your way. This is a flat-out suicidal strategy. The stakes are too high for the wrong assumptions. People tell me they don't know whom to believe anymore; they are confused. I tell them to believe the people who preach in their mosques and say on TV that they want to kill them. They usually follow through.

I think the biggest disservice the American media did to the American public was not airing the videos of the beheadings of Daniel Pearl, Nick Berg, and the rest of the innocent victims of Islamic horror. They got lots of airplay in the Middle East. Why not here? The American public needs to see what is at stake and what type of enemy we are dealing with. I have such respect for Sean Hannity for having the spine to play the audiotape of the beheading of Nick Berg. As painful as that was to hear, it shakes you to the core. I remember that precise moment I heard the audio. I had just finished shopping at the mall and having lunch with a friend. I got in my car, started driving down the street, and turned on the radio. I didn't realize in the beginning what I was hearing. By the time my brain made the connection and heard Hannity explaining, I felt weak and nauseated. I had to pull to the side of the road, where I shakingly parked my car and then sat for twenty minutes staring at the road. It was a tremendous flashback to the violence, fear, and terror of those many years in Lebanon. It took me by surprise that I would react this way, as I was here in this wonderful country, where I have been enjoying freedom and security. At the same time it reinforced what I realized while watching the events of 9/11: what happened in Lebanon has come to America. We need to get active, get involved, and fight. We are at war.

The president and Congress need to declare war against radical Islam and Islamic countries harboring and financially supporting terrorist organizations. Stop pussyfooting around with political correctness, negotiations, and diplomacy and declare war. These radical Islamists are already acquiring nuclear suitcase bombs and trying to smuggle them into our country to detonate them in an American city or many cities simultaneously, as Osama bin Laden already stated.[5] We are not talking about the death of a few thousand only. We are dealing with their goal of killing millions. The have already told us they want to kill at least 4 million Americans. Why aren't we listening? We must declare war and set our eyes on victory, and only victory, as an end result. Partial victory, as was the case with the first Gulf War in the 1990s, is not victory. It's a *hudna,* a trucelike period where our enemy gets more organized and strengthened and we get lulled into a feeling of accomplishment and success. It's a lie. Victory is where you kill your enemy and eliminate its threat. Unless we act decisively and eliminate our enemy effectively, it is not victory. Now, as radicals seek to get their hands on nuclear bombs, I wonder if by the end of the day there will be anyone left alive to admit how wrong they were in their misjudgment. I wonder who will be calling for a special investigation and who will be around to hold congressional hearings?

I want to take this opportunity to humbly salute the men and women of the United States military who are fighting every day on the front lines away from their families and the comfort of America to protect our freedoms. As a survivor of war, I thank you humbly from the bottom of my heart for preparing a country where I can live and prosper because of your contribution to our laws, freedoms, safety, and country. Without your sacrifice America would not be what it is today. Without your dedication to what America stands for, people like me would not be able to be here writing this book and exercising my freedom of speech, freedom of religion, and freedom to live in peace. You are not only my heroes and the heroes of America, but you are the heroes of millions around the world who wish they had a dedicated army like you to protect them, to fight for them, and to save them. Even though you may never hear it from those millions, allow me to speak for those under the tyranny of Islamic regimes. Even during the years in my bomb shelter I always knew that America's military was a beacon of light to the world. My father would say that we needed America's army to come liberate us like they liberated Europe in World War II. They were the true freedom fighters and protectors of human rights and dignity. I didn't realize what shackles the U.S. Army had around its feet until I got to America and learned about our self-defeating, self-destructing groups such as the ACLU, who do not realize the value of our great military and the importance of supporting it in every way. Citizens from all around the world look up to you as the defenders of freedom. They may not be able to verbalize it in their oppressive society, but they know it deep down inside their hearts. On their behalf I salute you one and all. God bless and protect you.

What Must Be Done to Protect Our Country?

Our government needs to take stronger action not only against those persons who seek to destroy us, but also against those individuals who impede our fight on the war on terrorism, well intended or not. Tougher laws must be implemented that protect our right to life and liberty, and if that means a declaration of war putting other rights on hold for a while, so be it! As I have learned from my own life's experiences, nothing in life is free, especially freedom. Here are several initiatives that I believe will protect us in the homeland.

Close Our Borders

We can arrest and expel all we want, but if the terrorists are sneaking right back in through our borders, we are wasting our time, financial resources, and efforts. We need to build fences that divide us from Mexico and Canada and install the latest technological equipment to monitor them and ensure that no one is crossing. People argue that it would be a major undertaking which would cost billions of dollars. We can take the billions of dollars annually that illegal immigrants are costing our nation in social services and crime (paid for by with our tax dollars),[6] and use it for our protection instead. That money could be invested in a fence and employees monitoring surveillance cameras at our borders, stopping our enemy from entering the U.S. At this point the cost to security is not the poor Mexicans who want to come here to work for minimum wage or less. It is al Qaeda sneaking in a suitcase bomb to detonate in a major American city. The cost of a nuclear attack on New York City would be immeasurable. We already have legal ways available for anyone wishing to enter our country legally.

Reform the Immigration and Naturalization Process in America

The immigration and naturalization process needs to be whipped into shape. Even after the transfer of INS immigration enforcement responsibilities into the DHS and forming the new Bureau of Immigration and Customs Enforcement (ICE) we still have problems. ICE needs to be more diligent with its lists of aliens who have applied for a visa or green card. But at least it is a step better than what we had with the INS. The INS approved Mohamed Atta's student visa six months after he died while blowing up the World Trade Center on September 11, 2001. How could someone actually look at Mohamad Atta's application and stamp it approved? The INS should never have approved even his tourist visa, since he was considered an "intending immigrant," one who was likely to seek permanent status. Atta overstayed his visa and should have been deported.[7] There is only one ICE agent assigned to thousands of immigrants. The ICE cannot adequately achieve its goal of monitoring and keeping track of visitors without a system that monitors visa expirations and a method to track the location of foreign tourists.[8] There are some four hundred thousand aliens still living and working within our nation's borders even though they have been ordered deported. Some eighty thousand of these aliens have serious criminal histories. How can we expect so few agents to effectively deal with so vast a problem?[9]

America has an immigration lottery system available to people in every nation across the globe. Those who want to come here legally we welcome with open arms. They bring energy and excitement to our nation. They are the first-generation immigrants who come here and are willing to work and improve their lives and are a great asset to our nation. Those we gladly welcome.

Increase Human Intelligence

Spying is essential to fighting the war on terrorism. We have satellites in space to obtain information about other countries, but there is nothing like good old human contact to acquire indispensable facts. How can you establish the trust of the locals who are essential for supplying information on the individual you're spying on if you are a satellite traveling in space? It takes years for humans to gain the trust and confidence of different groups. We need to have our human intelligence embedded in every country around the world.

President Bush signed a secret order in 2002 sanctioning the National Security Agency to eavesdrop on Americans and foreigners, despite a current ban on domestic spying.[10] Bush received a huge amount of criticism from the liberals on this matter. Why? Because we are spying on people talking with al Qaeda? Those Americans who actually have things to discuss with terrorist groups whose goal is to attack our country need to be watched and investigated. Do you think I have anything to hide from the FBI or CIA? They can listen to my conversations all they want. (They might get a few laughs.) If the FBI or CIA want to show up to search my home, I say: Be my guest. I have nothing to hide. The goal of the program is to quickly monitor phone calls and other modes of communication of individuals believed to be associated with al Qaeda. If the idealists get their way and keep blowing the cover on all our efforts to stop terrorism in the U.S., then the terrorists will get their way also.

Profile, Profile, and Profile

When we experience another 9/11, and it's only a matter of time, the same people who accuse the administration of tampering with their right to privacy will complain that the government wasn't doing enough to stop potential terrorist attacks. But will there be anyone or any place to hold hearings as to who dropped the ball on security after the radiation levels drop in Washington, D.C.?

We are at war, and in times of war some freedoms may have to be infringed upon until the fight is over. We need to start implementing steps to find terrorists here, in America. That includes profiling. Almost every terrorist attack in the past three decades has been perpetrated by Muslim men between the ages of sixteen and forty. To keep in line with the usual newspaper reports about crime, where detailed eyewitness descriptions are given in the hopes that readers can help locate the perpetrators, let's add more descriptive language: men with Middle Eastern features, some with beards, between the ages of sixteen and forty. If the press thinks it's doing a good deed by telling us whom to look out for after a crime, why do editorial writers get so bent out of shape when authorities want to describe to the cops and airport screeners whom to look out for before there is an attack?

What we call profiling and security searches in America is a joke. I know what profiling is about. When I worked in Israel and traveled to Lebanon every weekend to check on my parents, I had to go through an intensive search every time I came back into Israel. And this was every week. Even though I was well known as a news anchor, that did not make any difference. Every Sunday afternoon when I entered Israel, a female soldier took me into a room and asked me to take my outer clothes off. I was then asked to empty my bag. The lady squeezed my toothpaste out, turned my hair dryer on, opened the wrapping of every tampon I had, and patted my half-naked body, including my breasts and between my legs. That's what I call security. I gladly submitted to it every time. I knew the threats the Israelis faced and that they were protecting my security and well-being just as much as theirs. I was willing to give up five minutes of inconvenience and a somewhat uncomfortable procedure in exchange for safety and peace of mind. That's what you do when you are really serious about protecting your fellow citizens.

There is nothing wrong with profiling and identifying suspicious behavior. Most Arab Americans, who happen to be Christians, have no problem being profiled, me included.[11] I would much rather be inconvenienced for few minutes than risk losing my life and the lives of my loved ones because some fanatic is dying to kill.

Control Education of Foreign Students of Hostile Countries

With the infiltration of radical extremists in our universities, it is fool-ish to allow Muslims to take any type of science courses, especially any of them that deal with chemistry or nuclear physics. We are actually supplying them with the knowledge for destroying a democratic soci-ety without really trying. We make it so easy! A lot of these students come here on a scholarship by their government to study. I know from personal experience with Lebanese friends that the Hariri Founda-tion, headed by the late billionaire Rafik Hariri, made it possible for Lebanese students to come study here in the U.S. on the condition that they would return to Lebanon. I wonder how many of these stu-dents studied chemistry and physics and are now applying their knowl-edge to Hezbollah terrorist operations.

Develop Alternative Energy Sources

Another way that our government can eradicate terrorism among the radical Islamists is to stop their cash flow. Saudi Arabia is the largest oil supplier to the United States and Europe[12] and the main provider of funds to promote Islamic terrorism throughout the world. Lack of rev-enue from oil profits would stop terrorism cold in its tracks. The de-velopment of American natural gas and oil reserves along with conservation projects are essential to curbing terrorism. Incentives are being offered right now by the government to businesses to create so-lar, wind, and nuclear energy. The elimination of energy dependency and Arab petrodollars will go a long way in the elimination of Islamic terror.

Silence Any Teaching of Hate and Intolerance Against Our Country

In addition to regulating Muslim classes at the universities, the govern-ment needs to ban all Islamic books and literature inciting hate in any mosque and madrassa in the United States. The material distributed in

228 ❖ BECAUSE THEY HATE

these institutions by the Saudis is inflammatory and an incitement to murder non-Muslims. Any members of mosques or madrassas who spew and preach hatred and are not American citizens, should immediately be sent back to their own country. We need to send a clear message that this type of hate education is not and will not be tolerated or accepted in our great country. In addition, the government should monitor Islamic Web sites.

What We Can Do to Make a Difference

Everyone can make a difference. I hope my personal experiences and the information in these pages will serve as a catalyst to motivate and compel readers into an activist's role. None of us can fight terrorism alone. But if everyone commits to just one idea that I will discuss in this chapter, then we will win the war on radical Islamic terrorism! Here are several suggestions for how individuals and groups can make a difference. Remember, while you are reading this book, terrorist cells around the country are planning your death. The very people who devastated my homeland of Lebanon and massacred its Christian citizens are here in America and hope to carry out a similar plan in the name of their merciful and compassionate God, Allah.

Contact Your Elected Officials

Politicians are here to serve the people. If they want to be reelected, they will aim to please. Voting for candidates who are taking an objective and informed approach to our security makes a colossal difference. Your elected official can submit proposals and/or vote on legislature that has an impact on curbing terrorist activities. Get out there and be a participant in controlling the spread of radical Islam by making an appointment with your congressmen for you and a group of friends (groups wield more power). Let your politicians know that you take your grievances seriously. Discuss issues that you are concerned with and bring documented information in case your officials are uninformed regarding your subject matter. Let them know that you want to get involved in order to make a difference. Make sure not to leave their office until they have agreed to look into the matter and get back to you with suggestions on how they plan to initiate change for the better. Follow up with a note expressing gratitude for their time. Have friends and relatives write letters to your politicians to express their concern or satisfaction with a politician's position, action, or legislation. Initiate legislation or sign petitions to change laws that hinder security, and start or sign petitions to promote legislation that strengthens security and makes a difference in slowing down terrorism. Who knows, this could be the beginning of your political career for a stronger, united America! Pressure your congressional representatives to:

- Pass laws that will publicly disclose which countries sponsor terror, how much they have invested in American companies, and which companies.
- Support the PATRIOT Act, and enact strict legislation that will protect us during this time of war.
- Ensure wide presidential powers to protect us during this time of war.
- Restrict visas granted to Islamic foreign nationals each year.
- Provide for U.S. energy security and reduce the importance of oil in the global economy—go to the Energy Security Policy Web site and learn.
- Create legislation that will lead to developing sources of energy other than oil.
- Pass laws that promote Western values and ideals and dismiss excessive political correctness.
- Secure the borders.
- Fight legislation that empowers all tax-exempt religious organizations with increased abilities for political influence.
- Enact laws to discourage excessive foreign funding for religious groups within the U.S.

- In dealing with Islamic countries, insist on reciprocation or no deal. If they want to build a mosque or Islamic school in our country, we should be able to build a church and a Christian school in theirs.
- Pursue all means available to uncover the plots of terror cell members and supporters living among us.

Monitor Your Local College or University

Another important way that you can make a difference is at your local college or university. Call the registrar's office and ask if they have a Middle Eastern studies program or a course in Islamic religion. If so, try to talk to some of the students taking the course to understand the nature and content of the professors' lectures. Better yet, just show up to class every day and monitor courses to see if they have any anti-American or anti-Semitic focus. See if the course covers material that you feel may present a threat to America's continued existence or include sentiments that could be construed as incitement to hate or murder. Make sure that you document everything that is said in class. Present your findings to the school administration, the media, the FBI, the local police, and the ACLU. (Wouldn't it be great if the ACLU did something for a change and really stood up against those who want to replace America's civil liberties with Sharia law?)

Report Suspicious Activity or Behavior

Speak out and fight against terror in our country by reporting any suspicious activity or individual. Homeland Security has reported that a number of suspects and known terrorists in this country have been apprehended thanks to the attentiveness of the American people. If you hear a person speak in a manner that can be construed as treasonous, or speak about an individual or group in such a way that it may promote violence against them, address that person. Let him/her know his/her vicious remarks are the result of ignorance and won't be tolerated in your presence. If you feel that this individual may be a threat to our communities, contact the authorities.

Raising awareness to the threat of radical Islam in our country is an excellent way to fight terrorism. Our job is to inform as many people as we can about the history and deceitfulness of Islam, and the inflammatory, hateful passages in the Koran toward non-Muslims. This knowledge can be disclosed to one individual during a casual conversation, or to a group of people invited into your home. The more people who are informed, the more voices there will be to place additional restrictions on organizations that preach radical Islamic idealism. This is an essential step in curtailing the flow of terrorism.

Join an Activist Organization Against Terror

Joining an organization whose mission is to expose and combat the threat of Islamic terrorism is an excellent way to become an informed activist. These types of organizations will expose you to accurate facts on issues related to terrorism and will bring like minds together to discuss concerns and solutions. Working together, we can provide each other with the comfort and strength needed to battle our enemies.

The group I founded, American Congress for Truth (ACT), is one such organization. ACT was formed to give a voice to Americans—Jews, Christians, and Muslims—who have lost their tongue to political correctness. ACT's mission is to inform, educate, inspire, motivate, network, and empower millions of uninformed Americans about the threat of militant fundamentalist Islam to America, Israel, and Western civilization. Through media, speaking engagements, and meeting with our elected leaders, ACT is working to bring change through an organized grassroots movement to oppose the terrorist threat to America.

We are informing concerned Americans using action alerts and a highly organized and informative Web site which deals with timely issues and legislation relating to our security. We are educating millions of uninformed Americans about our enemy and what they can do to protect themselves and our country. We are inspiring activists to get involved and take action. We are motivating Americans to become active in decisions affecting their security and way of life. We are networking with like-minded organizations to work together to bring about change. We are empowering average people to become a voice affecting their community and their nation.

Since its inception, ACT has created a membership of thousands of concerned Americans. We have given hundreds of presentations and numerous radio and TV interviews to educate the public about the Islamic threat facing our nation.

Join us today and become one of thousands of concerned Americans who have joined their hands with ours. Sign up at www.americancon gressfortruth.org. With the threat of radical Islam to our country and with so many of our citizens remaining silent and apathetic, President John F. Kennedy's words still apply today: "Ask not what your country can do for you; ask what you can do for country."

Lobby for Patriotic Education in America's Schools

Lobby for young people to be taught more in school about our founding documents, civics, American history and its heroes and participants, and America's place in the world. Without this, our children grow up ignorant of the awesome and truly unique nature of our country. Think long term, as our enemy does. Hold school systems accountable for providing nonpartisan education. Monitor this by asking your children about what political positions their teachers take, and whether they indoctrinate against our country. If so, organize the parents to protest in writing. Make it known that you will not tolerate the teaching of any anti-Americanism in your child's school, and enforce it.

Stay Informed and Speak Out

Stay informed—attend seminars in your local community about current issues. Many organizations, especially Jewish temples and community centers, host speakers on current affairs regularly. Read books, Web sites, and magazines. Watch political talk shows and listen to talk radio. There is so much information over the airwaves regarding what is happening in America and around the world. Do whatever you can to get the truth out. Write letters to your local newspaper expressing your opinion and letting journalists know that people are monitoring what they write. Speak up in your church, temple, or social group and inform others. If you can't do either, then financially support those who can and have dedicated their time, energy, and effort to educating the public, putting the facts out, and mobilizing average Americans to protect America. Support americancongressfortruth.org.

Promote Western Values in Your Home

Promote Western values and ideas in your own home. Plan family trips and take your children to Washington, D.C., and other historical sites to teach them to know and respect our culture and heritage. The White House Historical Society has games, toys, puzzles, and books which teach kids history in a fun way. Search the Internet for more information. Start instilling patriotic values in your children at a young age.

Important Things You Can Do

- Divest your own portfolio of investments in companies that do business with terrorist-sponsoring states. Go to the DivestTerror.org Web site and learn more.
- Learn which Muslim organizations have ties to terror (Hamas, Islamic Jihad, Hezbollah, Muslim Brotherhood, etc.) and work to allow them no support within the U.S. or around the globe.
- Learn about electromagnetic pulse attacks, and support the EMP Threat Commission.
- Defend and support all movements toward personal freedoms in the Middle East.
- Reduce your own fuel consumption.

Support Our Troops

Finally, one of the kindest ways to fight the threat of Islamic radicalism is to send cards and letters to our military men and women in the Middle East and the rest of the world. Search the Web for organizations supporting our troops through letter-writing campaigns. Write the troops and thank them for their service and courage in their battle to restore the world to order and eliminate the danger of Islamic terror.

So many times in history in the last hundred years, citizens have stood by and done nothing, allowing evil to prevail. As America stood up against and defeated Communism, now it is time to stand up against the terror of religious bigotry and intolerance. For the sake of our children and our country, we must wake up and take action. The longer we lie supine, the more difficult it will be to stand erect.

I wish to thank you for reading my book. I also thank you for doing your part in helping me protect America, the dream, that became my address.

NOTES

INTRODUCTION TO THE 2006 EDITION

1. Tony Blankley, *The West's Last Chance: Will We Win the Clash of Civilizations?* (Washington, D.C.: Regnery Publishing, 2005); Andrew G. Bostom, ed., *The Legacy of Jihad: Islamic Holy War and the Fate of Non-Muslims* (Amherst, NY: Prometheus Books, 2005); Mark A. Gabriel, *Islam and Terrorism* (Lake Mary, FL: Charisma House, 2002); Dore Gold, *Hatred's Kingdom: How Saudi Arabia Supports the New Global Terrorism* (Washington, D.C.: Regnery Publishing, 2003); Hal Lindsey, *The Everlasting Hatred: The Roots of Jihad* (Murrieta, CA: Oracle House, 2002); Robert Spencer, ed., *The Myth of Islamic Tolerance* (Amherst, NY: Prometheus Books, 2005); Serge Trifkovic, *The Sword of the Prophet: Islam—History, Theology, Impact on the World* (Boston: Regina Orthodox Press, 2002); "Al Qaeda's Intellectual Legacy: New Radical Islamic Thinking Justifying the Genocide of Infidels," Jerusalem Center for Public Affairs, Jerusalem Viewpoints no. 508, December 1, 2003, http://www.jcpa.org/jl/vp508.htm; "The Relationship Between International and Localized Terrorism," Jerusalem Center for Public Affairs, Jerusalem Issue Brief, vol. 4, no. 26, June 28, 2005, http://www.jcpa.org/brief/brief004-26.htm.

2. Daniel Pipes, *Militant Islam Reaches America* (New York: W. W. Norton, 2002); Kenneth R. Timmerman, *Preachers of Hate: Islam and the War on America* (New York: Crown Forum, 2003).

INTRODUCTION TO THE 2008 EDITION

1. UN Security Council Press Release, http://www.un.org/News/Press/docs/2006/sc8808.doc.htm.
2. CNN News, http://www.cnn.com/2006/WORLD/americas/06/03/canada.terror/index.html.
3. MSNBC News, http://www.msnbc.msn.com/id/13491653/.
4. CBS News, http://www.cbsnews.com/stories/2007/06/02/national/main2877931.shtml.
5. Daniel Pipes, *New York Sun,* September 6, 2005, http://www.danielpipes.org/pf.php?id=2920.
6. *International Herald Tribune,* May 1, 2007, http://www.iht.com/articles/2007/05/01/news/terror.php.
7. "Pope's Comments on Islam Incite Outrage and Protest," PBS, http://www.pbs.org/newshour/bb/religion/july-dec06/islam_09-18.html.
8. Olga Craig, "The People Who Cure You Will Kill You," *Sunday Telegraph* (UK), July 7, 2007, http://www.telegraph.co.uk/news/main.jhtml?xml=/news/2007/07/08/nrmuslim408.xml.
9. "Keelty Shocked at Suicide-Baby Bomb Plot," NEWS.com.au, http://www.news.com.au/story/0,23599,20115941-2,00.html.
10. Richard Esposito, "Six Arrested in Plot to Storm N.J. Army Base," May 8, 2007, http://abcnews.go.com/Blotter/LegalCenter/story?id=3150833.
11. "Radicals Wanted to Create Carnage at Fort Dix," CNN, May 9, 2007, http://www.cnn.com/2007/US/05/08/fortdix.plot/index.html.
12. "Unthinkable Terror Devastation Prevented," MSNBC, http://www.msnbc.msn.com/id/18999503/.
13. *Islamist Website Monitor,* Memri.org, http://memri.org/bin/articles.cgi?Page=archives&Area=sd&ID=SP165607.
14. WorldPublicOpinion.org, a project on the program on international policy attitudes at the University of Maryland, April 24, 2007, http://www.worldpublicopinion.org/pipa/pdf/apr07/START_Apr07_rpt.pdf; Bob Spencer, "Dhimmi Watch: Survey: 61 Percent of British Muslims Want Sharia Courts," JihadWatch.org, January 3, 2005, http://www.jihadwatch.org/dhimmiwatch/archives/004524.php; Hudson Institute, *Current Trends in Islamist Ideology, vol.4,* by Lorenzo Vidino, November 1, 2006.
15. Robert Spencer, "Fox News and Forced Conversions," *FrontPage* magazine, August 30, 2006, http://www.frontpagemagazine.com/Articles/Read.aspx?GUID={D8B967AE-2694-4F9B-A724-31F866DF06A5}.

1. PEACE BEFORE THE RAGE

1. Christopher B. Siren, "Canaanite/Ugaritic Mythology," http://home.com cast.net/~chris.s/canaanite-faq.html.

2. http://phoenicia.org/xtian.html#anchor133914.

3. Library of Congress Country Study—Lebanon, chap. 2—Religion, http://lcweb2.loc.gov/cgi-bin/query2/r?frd/cstdy:@field(DOCID+lb00502).

4. Itmar Rabinovich, *The War for Lebanon—1970–1985* (Ithaca, NY, and London: Cornell University Press, 1985), p. 24; http://phoenicia.org/christiansmea.html.

5. Rabinovich, *War for Lebanon,* p. 24.

6. http://phoenicia.org/christiansmea.html (see chap. 1, *supra*, no. 2).

7. Library of Congress Country Study—Lebanon, chap. 2—Living Conditions, http://lcweb2.loc.gov/cgi-bin/query/D?cstdy:1:./temp/~frd_nRSV::

8. Library of Congress Country Study—Lebanon, chap. 2—Education, http://lcweb2.loc.gov/cgi-bin/query/r?frd/cstdy:@field(DOCID+lb0076).

9. Rabinovich, *War for Lebanon,* p.40; Library of Congress Country Study—Lebanon, chap. 2—Population—the Palestinian Element, http://lcweb2.loc.gov/cgi-bin/query/r?frd/cstdy:@field(DOCID+lb0046).

10. Arlene Peck, "Dell and the New 'Huggy Feely' Attitude," *Newsbull.com,* March 21, 2005.

11. "Talk Show Host Fired for Linking Islam to Terrorism," *World Net Daily,* August 21, 2005, http://www.worldnetdaily.com/news/article.asp?ARTICLE_ID=45887.

12. Yashiko Sagamori, "The Mythical Muslim Extremist," *Isralert.com,* http://yashiko.middleeastfacts.com/MME_eng.html.

13. David Masci, "An Uncertain Road: Muslims and the Future of Europe," The PEW Forum on Religion and Public Life, http://pewforum.org/docs/index.php?DocID=60.

14. Alliance for Security, "What Defines the Muslim World?" http://www.allianceforsecurity.org/muslim_world.

2. MY 9/11

1. Rabinovich, *War for Lebanon,* p. 58.

3. LIFE UNDER TERROR

1. "Unforgotten Massacre: Damour," January 20, 1976, http://www.geocities.com/damour1976/index1.html; M. Kahl, "Yasir Arafat's Planned Christian

Genocide," http://www.chretiens-et-juifs.org/article.php?voir%5B%5D=594&voir%5B%5D=3532

4. HOPELESS EXISTENCE

1. Libya withdrew its token force in late 1976. Library of Congress Country Study—Lebanon, chap. 1—Historical Setting—"The Civil War, 1975–76," http://lcweb2.loc.gov/cgi-bin/query/r?frd/cstdy:@field(DOCID+lb0036). See also Rabinovich, *War for Lebanon,* pp. 55–56.
2. Rabinovich, *War for Lebanon.*

6. REBUILDING OUR LIVES

1. Library of Congress Country Study—Lebanon—the Siege of Beirut. See also Rabinovich, *War for Lebanon,* p. 122, http://lcweb2.loc.gov/cg-bin/query/r?/frd/cstdy:@field(DODID+1b0164).
2. Joel Himelfarb, "Hezbollah's Deadly Record," *Washington Times,* March 15, 2005.
3. N. C. Livingston and D. Halevy, *Inside the PLO* (New York: Quill/William Morrow, 1990), p. 265.
4. Ira Stoll, "Iraq's WMD Secreted in Syria, Sada Says," *New York Sun,* January 26, 2006.

7. CLASH OF CIVILIZATIONS

1. Dan Bahat, *The Illustrated Atlas of Jerusalem* (New York: Simon and Schuster, 1990), p. 118.
2. http://forums.lemonde.fr/perl/showthreaded.pl?Cat=&Board=terreur&Number=227519&page=3&view=collapsed&sb=5&part=.
3. Thomas Friedman, *From Beirut to Jerusalem* (New York: Farrar, Straus and Giroux 1989), p. 133.
4. Rory McCarthy, "Car Bomb Kills Lebanese Journalist as UN Attacks Syria over Hariri Murder Inquiry," *Guardian,* December 13, 2005.
5. Jeff Jacoby "Trading Truth for Access?" *Boston Globe,* April 17, 2003 www.boston.com/dailyglobe2/107/oped/Trading_truth_for_access_+.shtml
6. Eason Jordan, "The News We Kept to Ourselves," *New York Times,* April 11, 2003.
7. http://www.cpj.org/killed/killed_archives/1992_list.html.

8. http://www.answering-islam.org/Muhammad/Enemies/asma.html.
9. Stephen Young, "Colonel Bui Tin's Interview with Stephen Young," *Wall Street Journal,* August 3, 1995.

8. TERRORISTS AMONG US

1. Amir Taheri, *Nest of Spies: America's Journey to Disaster in Iran* (New York: Pantheon, 1988), p. 123.
2. Paul Marshall, "Saving Sudan—the State Department Should Stand Up to Sudan," Center for Religious Freedom/Freedom House, April 22, 2004, http://www.freedomhouse.org/religion/country/sudan/saving%20sudan.htm?article_id=170; John Eibner, "Suffering Sudan," *National Review,* April 27, 2004, http://www.nationalreview.com/comment/eibner 200404271122.asp.
3. Bill Berkeley, *The Graves Are Not Yet Full: Race, Tribe, and Power in the Heart of Africa* (New York: Basic Books, 2001), pp. 6, 196, and passim; Marshall, "Saving Sudan."
4. "Slavery and Slavery Redemption in the Sudan," Human Rights Watch, March 1999, http://www.hrw.org/backgrounder/africa/sudan1.htm; Richard Lobben, "Slavery in the Sudan Since 1989," *Arab Studies Quarterly,* Spring 2001, http://www.findarticles.com/p/articles/mi_m2501/is_2_23/ai_77384489/pg_1; "Slavery and Slavery Redemption in the Sudan," Human Rights Watch, updated March 2002, http://www.hrw.org/backgrounder/africa/sudanupdate.htm; Michael Coren, "Slavery Lives on in Sudan," *Toronto Sun Online,* www.defenddemocracy.org/research_topics/research_topics_show.htm?doc_id=199401 November 15, 2003.
5. John Eibner, "Suffering Sudan."
6. Gerard Prunier, *Darfur, the Ambiguous Genocide* (Ithaca, NY: Cornell University Press, 2005); "Darfur Destroyed—Ethnic Cleansing by Government and Militia Forces in Western Sudan," Human Rights Watch Report, May 2004, http://hrw.org/reports/2004/sudan0504/; Warren Hoge, "U.N. Aide Says Sudan Is Tolerating Ethnic Cleansing," *New York Times,* April 3, 2004, http://select.nytimes.com/gst/abstract.html?res=FA0F10 F7385D0C708CDDAD0894DC404482; Nicholas D. Kristof, "Ethnic Cleansing, Again," *New York Times,* March 24, 2004, http://www.nytimes.com/2004/03/24/opinion/24KRIS.html
7. Colum Lynch, "U.N. Report Details Rampant Sexual Violence in Darfur," *Washington Post,* July 30, 2005, http://www.washingtonpost.com/wp-dyn/content/article/2005/07/29/AR2005072901740.html?referrer=emailarticle;

"Darfur Destroyed—Ethnic Cleansing by Government and Militia Forces in Western Sudan," Human Rights Watch Report, May 2004, http://www.hrw.org/reports/2004/sudan0504/; Jon S. Corzine, "Darfur, the Nightmare Continues," *Jerusalem Post,* April 28, 2005, http://www.jpost.com/servlet/Satellite?pagename=JPost/JPArticle/ShowFull&cid=111465 4778910&p=1006953079865.

8. "UN's Darfur Death Estimate Soars," BBC News, March 14, 2005, http://www.news.bbc.co.uk/2/hi/africa/4349063.stm; Associated Press, "UN: Nearly 180,000 People Have Died in Darfur," *Jerusalem Post,* March 16, 2005, http://www.jpost.com/servlet/Satellite?pagename=JPost/JPArticle/ShowFull&cid=1110943123187&p=1078113566627.

9. Associated Press, "UN: Sudan Violated International Law in Darfur," *Jerusalem Post,* February 1, 2005, http://www.jpost.com/servlet/Satellite?pagename=JPost/JPArticle/ShowFull&cid=1107141484718&p=10781135 66627.

10. Associated Press, "Sudanese Leaders Sign Peace Agreement," *Jerusalem Post,* January 10, 2005, http://www.jpost.com/servlet/Satellite?pagename=JPost/JPArticle/ShowFull&cid=1105240993174&p=1078113566627; "South Sudan Peace Force Approved," BBC News, March 25, 2005, http://news.bbc.co.uk/2/hi/africa/4381323.stm; Associated Press, "UN Sends Peacekeepers to Sudan," *Jerusalem Post,* March 25, 2005, http://www.jpost.com/servlet/Satellite?pagename=JPost/JPArticle/ShowFull&cid=1111634310474&p=1078113566627.

11. Daniel Pipes and Jonathan Schanzer, "Militant Islam's New Strongholds," *New York Post,* October 22, 2002, http://www.danielpipes.org/article/491.

12. "Nigeria's Turmoil: Even Moderate Muslims Fear Shariah Push," *Dallas Morning News Online,* May 5, 2004, http://www.dallasnews.com/s/dws/dn/opinion/editorials/stories/050504dnedinigeria.9d41.html.

13. Paul Marshall, "Outside Encouragement—Sharia Rules Nigeria—with the Help of Foreign Islamists," Freedom House/Center for Religious Freedom, May 5, 2004, http://www.freedomhouse.org/religion/country/Nigeria/Outside%20Encouragement.htm.

14. Corine Hegland, "No End in Sight," *National Journal,* May 7, 2004, http://www.nationaljournal.com/about/njweekly/stories/2004/0507nj2.htm; Associated Press, "Indonesia Double Bombing Kills 20," *Jerusalem Post,* May 28, 2005, http://www.jpost.com/servlet/Satellite?pagename=JPost/JPArticle/ShowFull&cid=1117247287656; Associated Press, "Chronology of Recent Terrorist Attacks in Indonesia," *Jerusalem Post,* October 1,

2005, http://www.jpost.com/servlet/Satellite?pagename=JPost/JPArticle/ShowFull&cid=1128133158740&p=1078113566627.

15. Pipes and Schanzer, "Militant Islam's New Strongholds."

16. "Chronology of Recent Terrorist Attacks in Indonesia" (see chap. 8, n. 14); "Girls beheaded," *Gulf Daily News* (Bahrain), October 30, 2005, http://www.gulf-daily-news.com/arc_printnews.asp?Article=125637.

17. Associated Press, "Eight Dead in Indonesian Christian Market Bombing," *Jerusalem Post,* December 31, 2005, http://www.jpost.com/servlet/Satellite?cid=1135696368941&pagename=JPost%2FJPArticle%2FShowFull.

18. B. Rahman, "International Terrorism: Back to 9/10," South Asia Analysis Group Paper no. 1481, July 31, 2005, http://www.saag.org/papers15/paper1481.html.

19. Dean Nelson, "India Fences Off Bangladesh to Keep Out Muslim Terror," *Sunday Times* (London), November 13, 2005, http://www.timesonline.co.uk/article/0,,2089-1869575,00.html.

20. Pipes and Schanzer, "Militant Islam's New Strongholds"; Ruth Baldwin, "The 'Talibanization' of Bangladesh," *Nation,* May 18, 2002, http://www.thenation.com/doc/20020527/baldwin20020517; "Anti-Christian Rampage Features 2,000 Muslims," *WorldNetDaily,* November 13, 2005, http://www.wnd.com/news/article.asp?ARTICLE_ID=47380.

21. Hegland, "No End in Sight," *National Journal,* May 7, 2004, http://nationaljournal.com/about/njweekly/stories/2004/0507nj2.htm; Corine Hegland, "Global Jihad," *National Journal,* May 7, 2004, http://nationaljournal.com/scripts/printpage.cgi?/about/njweekly/stories/2004/0507nj1.htm; "Bomb at Pakistan Shrine Kills 20," *Guardian* (London), May 28, 2005, http://www.guardian.co.uk/pakistan/Story/0,2763,1494479,00.html.

22. Yvette Claire Rosser, *Islamisation of Pakistani Social Studies Textbook* (Delhi: Observer Research Foundation, 2003), p. 43.

23. James Rupert, "Bombings in Thailand—Muslim Insurgents Set Off Three Blasts at Same Time; Nature of Attacks Suggest Rebels Have New Technology, Ideas," *Newsday,* April 4, 2005, http://www.newsday.com/news/nationworld/world/ny-wothai0442030031apr04,0,606021.story?coll-ny-worldnews-headlines.

24. Associated Press, "Muslim Insurgents Hit Targets in Thailand; 6 Dead," *Jerusalem Post,* October 27, 2005, http://www.jpost.com/servlet/Satellite?cid=1129540609636&pagename=JPost%2FJPArticle%2FShowFull.

25. Associated Press, "Muslim Thai Separatists Strengthen in South," *Jerusalem Post,* July 4, 2005; B. Rahman, "International Terrorism: Back to

9/10," South Asia Analysis Group Paper no. 1481, July 31, 2005, http://www.saag.org/papers15/paper1481.html.

26. "India Mourns," *Jerusalem Post,* October 30, 2005, http://www.jpost.com/servlet/Satellite?cid=1129540633331&pagename=JPost%2FJPArticle%2FShowFull; Associated Press, "India: Suicide bomber kills six in Kashmir," *Jerusalem Post,* November 3, 2005, http://www.jpost.com/servlet/Satellite?cid=1130954354477&pagename=JPost%2FJPArticle%2FShowFull.

27. Dr. Nicholas Berry, CDI Terrorism Project, September 14, 2001, The International Islamic Terrorist Network.

28. Bob Newman, "Hezbollah: The Other Snake in America's Grass," *MensNewsDaily.com,* May 22, 2005, http://www.mensnewsdaily.com/archive/m-n/newman/2005/newman052205.htm; "Federal Judge Sentences Lebanese Man to 4½ years for Aiding Hezbolah," *Detroit Free Press,* June 14, 2005, http://www.freep.com/news/statewire/sw117167_20050614.htm.

29. Noreen S. Ahmed-Ullah, Sam Roe, and Laurie Cohen, "A Rare Look at Secretive Brotherhood in America," *Chicago Tribune,* September 19, 2004, http://www.chicagotribune.com/news/local/chi-0409190261sep19,1,3947993.story?coll=chi-news-hed.

30. Joseph Farah, "G2 Bulletin, Tancredo to Request Al-Qaida Nuke Briefing," *WorldNetDaily,* July 13, 2005.

31. Mark Silverberg, "Sleeper Cells in America: The Enemy Within," http://www.jfednepa.org/mark%20silverberg/sleeper.html.

32. "Administration Links Saudi Funds to U.S. Sleeper Cell Network," *World Tribune.com,* June 27, 2003, http://216.26.163.62/2003/ss_terror_06_27.html; Jerry Seper, "Briton Accused of Planning Terrorist Camp in U.S.," *Washington Times,* August 19, 2005, http://www.washingtontimes.com/national/20050808-093052-8094r.htm.

33. Mark Silverberg, "Sleeper Cells in America."

34. Steve Emerson, *American Jihad: The Terrorists Living Among Us* (New York: Free Press, 2002).

35. Ibid.

36. Ibid.

37. 1988 Hamas Charter, English translation at http://www.library.cornell.edu/colldev/mideast/hamas.htm.

38. Joseph Farah, "G2 Bulletin, Al-Qaida Nukes Already in the US," *World Net Daily,* http://www.worldnetdaily.com/news/article.asp?ARTICLE_ID=45203.

39. Robert Spencer, "Radioactive Mosques?" FrontPageMagazine.com, December 28, 2005.

40. Jerry Seper, "Terrorists Will Fail, Official Says," *Washington Times,* May 4, 2005, http://www.washingtontimes.com/national/20050503-114633-5129r .htm.

41. Evan McCormick, "Jihad in America," FrontPageMagazine.com, September 5, 2003, http://www.frontpagemag.com/Articles/ReadArticle.asp? ID=9706.

42. "Profile CAIR," *Investor's Business Daily,* August 8, 2005.

43. ADL, "Arab Leaders Glorify Suicide Terrorism," April 17, 2002, http://www.adl.org/israel/israel_suicide_terror.asp.

44. Treasury Department Fact Sheet on the Global Relief Foundation, http://www.ustreas.gov/press/releases/po3553.htm.

45. CAIR, "The Status of Muslim Civil Rights in the United States, 2002," http://www.cair-net.org/civilrights/2001_Civil_Rights_Report.pdf.

46. Daniel Pipes, Talk at York University, Campuswatch.org, http://www .campus-watch.org/article/id/455.

47. Evan D. McCormick, "Profile of Terror," FrontPageMagazine.com, February 15, 2005, http://frontpagemag.com/Articles/ReadArticle.asp?ID=16971.

48. Daveed Gartenstein-Ross, "Extremists Among Us!" December 11, 2005, www.dallasnews.com/sharedcontent/dws/dn/opinion/points/stories/DN-mas_11edi.ART.State.Edition1.3d859b9.html.

49. Hugh Fitzgerald, "Mahdi Bray: Just a Country Muslim from Norfolk, Virginia," JihadWatch.org, May 5, 2005.

50. Evan D. McCormick, "Profile of Terror."

9. THE TOXIC TSUNAMI OF HATE

1. Cameron S. Brown, "The Shot Seen Around the World: The Middle East Reacts to September 11," *Middle East Review of International Affairs Journal* 5, no. 4 (December 2001), http://meria.idc.ac.il/journal/2001/issue4/ jv5n4a4.htm.

2. "Saudi Publications on Hate Ideology Fill American Mosques," Freedom House/Center for Religious Freedom, Washington, D.C., January 2005.

3. Ibid., pp. 11, 19.

4. Ibid., p. 23.

5. Ibid., pp. 11, 20.

6. Ibid., pp. 11, 19, 28, 57.

7. Ibid., p. 43.

8. Ibid., p. 58; see also p. 44.

9. Ibid., p. 59.

10.   IAD Web site, "Why Do We Pray?"

11.   IAD Web site, "Negative Qualities of Mankind in the Holy Koran."

12.   IAD Web site, "Rights Dictated by Nature: Rights Due to Non-Muslims."

13.   IAD Web site, "Why Do We Pray?"

14.   Alex Alexiev, "Wahhabism: State-Sponsored Extremism Worldwide," Testimony before the U.S. Senate Subcommittee on Terrorism, Technology and Homeland Security, June 26, 2003, http://www.centerforsecurity-policy.org/index.jsp?section=static&page=alexievtestimony; "Huge Saudi Efforts in the Field of Establishing Islamic Centers, Mosques and Academies All Over the World," *Ain-Al-Yaqeen,* March 1, 2002, http://www.ain-al-yaqeen.com/issues/20020301/feat3en.htm; "Saudi Publications," p. 3; Steven Stalinsky, "Preliminary Overview—Spreading Saudi Education to the World," MEMRI Special Report no. 12, December 20, 2002, http://www.memri.org/bin/articles.cgi?Page=archives&Area=sr&ID=SR01202.

15.   Richard P. Bailey, "Jihad—the Teaching of Islam from Its Primary Sources—the Quran and Hadith," Answering Islam—a Christian Muslim Dialogue, http://www.answering-islam.org.uk/Bailey/jihad.html.

16.   Bernard Lewis, *The Political Language of Islam* (Chicago: University of Chicago Press, 1988/91), pp. 72–73. See also, Bernard Lewis, *The Crisis of Islam: Holy War and Unholy Terror* (New York: Modern Library, 2003), pp. 29–37.

17.   Douglas E. Streusand, "What Does Jihad Mean?" *Middle East Quarterly* 4, no. 3, (September 1997), http://www.meforum.org/article/357, citing Muhammad ibn Isma'il Bukhari, *The Translation of the Meaning of Sahih al-Bukhari,* trans. Muhammad Muhsin Khan, 8 vols. (Medina: Dar al-Fikr: 1981). See also Andrew G. Bostom, ed., *The Legacy of Jihad: Islamic Holy War and the Fate of Non-Muslims* (Amherst, NY: Prometheus Books, 2005); Ibn Warraq, *What the Koran Really Says* (Amherst, NY: Prometheus Books, 2002); Bailey, "Jihad"; Vernon Richards, "Islam Undressed—a Critical Analysis of 'Real Islam,'" chap. 2, "'Real Islam' from the Religious Texts," February 13, 2005, http://islamundressed.com/; James M. Arlandson, "Legal Jihad in the Quran and Early Islam," Answering Islam—a Christian Muslim Dialogue, http://www.answering-islam.org.uk/Authors/Arlandson/jihad.htm; Hugh Fitzgerald, "Islam for Infidels, Part One," JihadWatch.org, January 13, 2005, http://www.jihadwatch.org/archives/004628.php; Ernest Hahn, "Jihad in Islam: Is Islam Peaceful or Militant?" Answering Islam—a Christian Muslim Dialogue, http://www.answering-islam.org.uk/Hahn/jihad.htm; Sheik Muhammed Salih Al-Munajjid, "Ruling on Jihad and Kinds of Jihad,"

www.islam-qa.com and http://63.175.194.25/index.php?n=eng&ds=qa&lv
=browse&QR=20214&dgn=4.

18. "Taqiyya and Kitman—Lying for the Sake of Islam," Faith Freedom International Forum, http://www.faithfreedom.org/forum/viewtopic.php?t=
178; Timothy W. Dunkin, *10 Myths About Islam,* 4th ed., http://www
.studytoanswer.net/islam_myths.html, "Myth #8—Islam Is a Tolerant Religion," http://www.studytoanswer.net/myths_ch8.html; Carl Cantrell, *The Koran and the Bible* (London and New York: Penguin, 1956), http://
www.hauns.com/%7EDCQu4E5g/koran.html#Koran, "Al-Taqiyya," http://
www.hauns.com/%7EDCQu4E5g/koran5.html; Joel Richardson, *Will Islam Be Our Future—A Study of Biblical and Islamic Eschatology,* chap. 16,
"Understanding Dishonesty and Deceit in Islam," Answering Islam—a Christian Muslim Dialogue, http://answering-islam.org.uk/Authors/
JR/Future/ch16_understanding_dishonesty.htm (http://answering-islam.org.
uk/); Fitzgerald, "Island for Infidels"; Richards, "Islam Undressed."

19. Ahmad ibn Naqib al-Misri, *The Reliance of the Traveller—A Classic Manual of Islamic Sacred Law* trans. Nuh Ha Mim Keller (Beltsville, MD:
Amana Publications, 1997), section r8.2, p. 745.

20. Amir Taheri, *Holy Terror: The Inside Story of Islamic Terrorism* (Bethesda,
MD: Sphere Books, 1987).

21. Abdullah al:Araby, "Lying in Islam," *Islam Review,* http://www.islamreview
.com/articles/lying.shtml.

22. See notes 18 and 19, above.

23. Yashiko Sagamori, "The Mythical Muslim Extremist," Freedom Center for
Strategic Studies, http://yashiko.middleeastfacts.com/MME_eng.html.

24. Ibn Warraq, *What the Koran Really Says,* p. 67–75; Sam Shamoun, "Abrogated Verses of the Quran—Evidence from Islamic Sources," Answering
Islam—a Christian Muslim Dialogue, http://answering-islam.org.uk/Quran/
abrogatedverses.html; Bailey, "Jihad"; Richards, "Islam Undressed," chap. 2.

25. Ibn Warraq, *What the Koran Really Says,* p. 69, citing Ibn Salama, *Al Nasikh wa'l-mansukh* ["The Abrogator and the Abrogated"] (Cairo,
1899), p. 184, referred to by D. Powers, "The Exegetical Genre nasikh
al-Qur'an," in *Approaches to the History of Interpretation of the Quran,*
ed. A. Rippin (Oxford: Oxford University Press, 1988), p. 130; Richards,
"Islam Undressed," chap. 2.

26. Alex Alexiev, "Wahhabism: State-Sponsored Extremism Worldwide," Testimony before the U.S. Senate Subcommittee on Terrorism, Technology and
Homeland Security, June 26, 2003, http://www.centerforsecuritypolicy
.org/index.jsp?section=static&page=alexievtestimony; "Huge Saudi Efforts

in the Field of Establishing Islamic Centers, Mosques and Academies All Over the World," *Ain-Al-Yaqeen,* March 1, 2002, http://www.ain-al-yaqeen.com/issues/20020301/feat3en.htm; Saudi Hate Report, p. 3; Steven Stalinsky, "Preliminary Overview—Spreading Saudi Education to the World," MEMRI Special Report no. 12, December 20, 2002, http://www.memri.org/bin/articles.cgi?Page=archives&Area=sr&ID=SR01202.

27.   Michael S. Doran, "Intimate Enemies," *Washington Post,* February 18, 2004; Nimrod Raphaeli, " 'The Sheik of Slaughterers': Abu Mus'ab Al-Zarqawi and the Al-Qa'ida Connection," MEMRI Inquiry and Analysis Series no. 231, July 1, 2005, http://memri.org/bin/opener.cgi?Page=archives&ID=IA23105.

28.   Raphaeli, " 'The Sheik of Slaughterers' "; Loretta Napoleoni, "Profile of a Killer," *Foreign Policy,* November–December 2005, http://www.foreignpolicy.com/story/cms.php?story_id=3264.

29.   Fouad Ajami, "Heart of Darkness," *Wall Street Journal,* September 28, 2005, http://www.opinionjournal.com/editorial/feature.html?id=110007326.

30.   Thomas L. Friedman, *From Beirut to Jerusalem* (New York: Farrar, Straus and Giroux, 1989), p. 77. Rifaat Assad, brother of Hafiz and commander of the Hama slaughter, was insulted by low death-toll estimates. He insisted that the number of deaths was closer to thirty-eight thousand. Ibid., p. 90.

31.   Lenny Ben-David, "Sunni and Shiite Terrorist Networks: Competition or Collusion?" JCPA Jerusalem Issue Brief, vol. 2, no. 13, December 18, 2002, http://www.jcpa.org/brief/brief2-13.htm; Dore Gold and Jonathan D. Halevi, "Zarqawi and Israel: Is There a New *Jihadi* Threat Destabilizing the Eastern Front?" JCPA Jerusalem Issue Brief, vol. 15, no. 12, December 15, 2005, http://www.jcpa.org/brief/brief005-12.htm; Stephen F. Hayes, "Saddam's Terror Camps," *Weekly Standard,* January 16, 2006, http://www.weeklystandard.com/Content/Public/Articles/000/000/006/550kmbzd.asp.

10. THE IVY-COVERED FIFTH COLUMN:
Islamic Influence Alive and Well on American Campuses

1.   Office of Postsecondary Education, http://165.224.220.253/about/offices/list/ope/iegps/title-six.html.

2.   Joel Mowbary, "Saudis Behaving Badly," *National Review Online,* December 20, 2002, http://www.nationalreview.com/mowbray/mowbray122002.asp.

3. Alexiev, "Wahhabism: State-Sponsored Extremism Worldwide," http://www.centerforsecurity.org/index.jsp? section= static & page=alexievtestimony.

4. Robert Spencer, "The Missing Link in the War on Terror: Confronting Saudi Subversion," Center for Security Policy, http://www.centerforsecuritypolicy.org/index.jsp?section=static&page=alexiev.

5. Hamid Algar, "Wahhabism: A Critical Essay," in *Islamic Values in the United States,* ed. Yvonne Yazbeck Haddad and Adair T. Lummis (Oxford, UK: Oxford University Press, 1987), p. 124.

6. http://www.frontpagemag.com/ReadArticle.asp? ID=5101; http://www.wrmea.com/backissues/1188/8811050.htm; http://Kyl.senate.gov/legiscenter/subdoes/091003 epstein.pdf.

7. http://www.meforum.org/article/208; http://www.campus-watch.org/article/id/740.

8. John L. Esposito, *Unholy War: Terror in the Name of Islam* (Oxford, UK: Oxford University Press, 2003).

9. Ariel Beery, "Wherefore Columbia?" *Columbia Spectator,* September 25, 2005.

10. Jane Glickman, public affairs officer for the United States Department of Education, personal interview on September 4, 2003, with Lee Kaplan of *FrontPage Magazine.*

11. George Livadas, "Harvard's 'Inner Struggle,'" Accuracy in Academia, June 6, 2002, http://www.academia.org/news/struggle.html.

12. Chris Beam, "Is the MEALAC Department Balanced?" *Columbia Spectator,* April 28, 2003.

13. Joseph Massad, "Curriculum Reform Should Start in the United States and Israel," *Electronic Intifada,* August 18, 2003, http://electronicintifada.net/v2/article1825.shtml.

14. Francis Bok, *Escape from Slavery* (New York: St. Martin's Press, 2002).

15. http://www.dafka.org/NewsGen.asp? S=4 & Page ID= 57.

16. Michelle Gabriel, "Campuswatch.org's Founder Says Key to Peace in Israel is Palestinian ''Change of Heart,'" *Daily Northwestern,* October 22, 2002, http://www.dailynorthwestern.com/vnews/display.v/ART/2002/10/22/3db500ff1394f.

17. Student comments about Joseph Massad, Columbia University, Spring 2002, http://www.columbia.edu/~msd39/; Campuswatch.org, http://www.campus-watch.org/article/id/63.

18. Roger Kimball, "The Intifada Curriculum," *Wall Street Journal,* May 9, 2002.

19. Personal interview with student accepted in spring 2001, Campuswatch.org, http://www.campus-watch.org/about.php.

20. Jane Glickman, interview on September 4, 2003.

21. Lee Kaplan, "Jihad at Georgetown," *FrontPage Magazine,* December 29, 2005, http://www.frontpagemag.com/Articles/ReadArticle.asp?ID=20716.

22. http://www.mtsu.edu/~baustin/holokron.html.

23. David Dalin, "Hitler's Moffti." *First Things,* 155, August–September, http://www.firstthings.com/ftissues/ft0508/opinion/dalin.html.

24. Chuck Morse, "The Nazi Connection to Islamic Terrorism: Adolf Hitler and Haj Amin al-Husseini," iUniverse, Inc., September 11, 2003, http://www.amazon.com/gp/product/0595289444/102-4975513-5296100?v=glance&n=283155.

25. "CU Professor Compares 9/11 Victims to Nazis," Denver Channel, January 28, 2005, http://www.frontpagemag.com/Articles/ReadArticle.asp?ID=16812.

26. Vincent Stevens, "Jews and Honkeys Need Not Apply," *FrontPage Magazine,* April 8, 2005, http://www.frontpagemag.com/Articles/ReadArticle.asp?ID=17635.

27. Francis Bok, *Escape from Slavery*.

11. BULL'S-EYE OF THE MIDDLE EAST

1. See all reference materials cited in Introduction, n. 1.

2. Robert S. Wistrich, *Muslim Anti-Semitism: A Clear and Present Danger* (American Jewish Committee, 2002) pp. 13–15; Raphael Israeli, *Poison: Modern Manifestations of a Blood Libel* (New York: Lexington Books, 2002); Arieh Stav, *Peace: The Arabian Caricature—a Study of Anti-Semitic Imagery* (New York: Gefen Publishing House, 1999); "Anti-Semitism in the Syrian Media," Middle East Media Research Insitute (MEMRI), Special Dispatch Series no. 66, December 22, 1999; "Leading Egyptian Newspaper Raises Blood Libel," MEMRI, Special Dispatch Series no. 150, November 6, 2000; "The Blood Libel Again in Egypt's Government Press," MEMRI Special Dispatch Series no. 201, April 2, 2001; Raphael Israeli, "Poison: The Use of Blood Libel in the War Against Israel," Jerusalem Center for Public Affairs, Jerusalem Letter/Viewpoints no. 476, April 15, 2002, http://www.jcpa.org/jl/vp476.htm; "The Damascus Blood Libel (1840) as told by Syria's Minister of Defense, Mustafa Tlass," MEMRI Inquiry and Analysis Series no. 99, June 27, 2002; "Syrian Ramadan Series on Hizbullah's Al-Manar: 'Diaspora,' Episode I," MEMRI

Special Dispatch Series no. 598, October 29, 2003; "Egyptian Government Weekly Magazine on 'The Jews Slaughtering Non-Jews, Draining Their Blood, and Using It for Talmudic Religious Purposes," MEMRI Special Dispatch Series no. 763, August 17, 2004; Matthias Kuntzel, "National Socialism and Anti-Semitism in the Arab World," Jerusalem Center for Public Affairs, *Jewish Political Studies Review* 17, no. 1–2 (Spring 2005).

3.   "Egyptian Government–Sponsored Scientific Journal: On American and Israeli Biological Warfare and Jews Spreading AIDS to Africa and Asia," MEMRI Special Dispatch Series no. 332, December 28, 2001; Raphael Israeli, "The New Muslim Anti-Semitism: Exploring Novel Avenues of Hatred," Jerusalem Center for Public Affairs, *Jewish Political Studies Review* 17, no. 3–4 (Fall 2005); Roee Nahmias, "Israel Using AIDS Against Us," YNetNews.com, October 17, 2005, http://www.ynetnews.com/articles/0,7340,L-3156094,00.html.

4.   Barton Gellman, "Pop! Went the Tale of the Bubble Gum Spiked with Sex Hormones," *Washington Post,* July 28, 1997; see also Israeli, "Poison: The Use of Blood Libel in the War Against Israel."

5.   Gellman, "Pop!"

6.   Itamar Marcus and Barbara Cook, " 'Kill a Jew—Go to Heaven': A Study of the Palestinian Authority's Promotion of Genocide," Palestine Media Watch, 2005, http://www.pmw.org.il/KAJ_eng.htm, citing and quoting from Palestinian Authority Television, May 25, 2004.

7.   "Iranian TV Drama Series About Israeli Government Stealing Palestinian Children's Eyes," MEMRI Special Dispatch Series no. 833, December 22, 2004, http://memri.org/bin/articles.cgi?Page=archives&Area=sd&ID=SP83304.

8.   Ibid. This series, originally produced in Farsi, has been dubbed into Arabic for consumption by the whole Arab world.

9.   "Producer of Anti-Semitic TV Series 'Zhara's Blue Eyes': A White Zionist Ship Sails Around the World, Kidnapping Babies to Use Their Organs," MEMRI TV Monitor Project, Clip no. 538, February 8, 2005, http://www.memritv.org/Transcript.asp?P1=538.

10. "Saudi Government Daily Accuses U.S. Army of Harvesting Organs of Iraqis," MEMRI Special Dispatch Series no. 834, December 24, 2004, http://memri.org/bin/articles.cgi?Page=archives&Area=sd&ID=SP83404; see also Jonathan Gurwitz, "Inquiring Minds in Saudi Arabia Know All About Evil America," *San Antonio Express-News,* January 23, 2005, http://www.mysanantonio.com/opinion/columnists/jgurwitz/stories/MYSA012305.3H.gurwitz.299d5ea8.html.

11. *Jomhouri-ye Islami* (Iran), December 19, 2004; *Teshreen* (Syria), December 19, 2004.

12. "Terror in America (4): Arab Columnists: The Perpetrators of the Attacks Are Not Arabs or Muslims," MEMRI Special Dispatch Series no. 270, September 20, 2001, http://memri.org/bin/articles.cgi?Page=archives&Area=sd&ID=SP27001; Cameron S. Brown, "The Shot Seen Around the World: The Middle East Reacts to September 11th," *Middle East Review of International Affairs (MERIA) Journal* 5, no. 4 (December 2001), http://meria.idc.ac.il/journal/2001/issue4/jv5n4a4.htm; "Arab League Think Tank Hosts Event: U.S. Military Behind September 11," MEMRI Special Dispatch Series no. 383, May 23, 2002, http://memri.org/bin/articles.cgi?Page=archives&Area=sd&ID=SP38302; "A New Antisemitic Myth in the Middle East Media: The September 11 Attacks Were Perpetrated by the Jews," MEMRI Special Report no. 8, September 10, 2002, http://memri.org/bin/articles.cgi?Page=archives&Area=sr&ID=SR00802.

13. Robert Spencer, "Ending the Saudi Double Game," *FrontPage Magazine*, June 23, 2005, http://www.frontpagemagazine.com/Articles/ReadArticle.asp?ID=18520.

14. "Saudi Minister of the Interior, Prince Nayef Ibn Abd-Al-Aziz: 'Who Committed the Events of September 11 . . . I Think They [the Zionists] Are Behind These Events. . . . It Is Impossible That 19 Youths, Including 15 Saudis, Carried Out the Operation of September 11,' " MEMRI Special Dispatch Series no. 446, December 3, 2002, http://memri.org/bin/articles.cgi?Page=archives&Area=sd&ID=SP44602.

15. "MEMRI TV Special Report: 9/11 Conspiracy Theories on Arab and Iranian TV Channels 2004–2005," MEMRI Special Report no. 38, September 9, 2005, http://memri.org/bin/articles.cgi?Page=archives&Area=sr&ID=SR3805.

16. United Nations, *Arab Human Development Report (AHDR 2002)*, p. 51.

17. For a discussion of the Merneptah Stele, see Hershel Shanks, William Dever, Baruch Halpern, and P. Kyle McCarter, *The Rise of Ancient Israel* (Washington, D.C.: Biblical Archaeology Society, 1992), pp. 17–19, 54–55. See also Yohanon Aharoni, *The Land of the Bible: A Historical Geography* (Philadelphia: Westminster Press, 1979), pp. 183–84, 195; H. H. Ben Sasson, ed., *A History of the Jewish People* (Cambridge, MA: Harvard University Press, 1976), pp. 42, 50–52; Jack Finnegan, *Archaeological History of the Middle East* (New York: Dorset Press, 1979), pp. 312–313; Michael Grant, *The History of Ancient Israel* (New York: Charles Scribner's Sons,

1984), pp. 37; Baruch Halpern, *The Emergence of Israel in Canaan* (Chico, CA: Scholars Press, 1983), pp. 93, 216.

18. Amihai Mazar, *Archaeology of the Land of the Bible—10,000–586 B.C.E.* (New York: Anchor Bible Reference Library/Doubleday, 1990); Ephraim Stern, *Archaeology of the Land of the Bible vol. 2; The Assyrian, Babylonian and Persian Periods (732–332 B.C.E.)* (New York: Anchor Bible Reference Library/Doubleday, 1990); Ephraim Stern, ed., *The New Encyclopedia of Archaeological Excavations in the Holy Land* 4 vols. (New York: Israel Exploration Society/Simon and Schuster, 1993); Thomas E. Levy, ed., *The Archaeology of Society in the Holy Land* (New York: Facts on File, 1995); Yohanan Aharoni, *The Archaeology of the Land of Israel* (Philadelphia: Westminster Press, 1982); Avraham Negev, ed., *The Archaeological Encyclopedia of the Holy Land* 3rd ed. (New York: Prentice Hall Press, 1990); Amnon Ben Tor, ed., *The Archaeology of Ancient Israel* (New Haven, CT: Yale University Press, 1992).

19. Parliament, *Report by the Royal Commission on Palestine* (Peel Report), Cmd. 5479 (1936–37), p. 7, para. 14; p. 11, para. 23.

20. In an effort to fabricate a more ancient connection, the Arab world has claimed that "Palestinian" Arabs are descended from the Philistines, from whom the name "Palestine" is derived. However, there is no historical or cultural connection between the Philistines and the "Palestinian" Arabs. The Philistines were one of the "Sea Peoples"; they originated in Cyprus, Crete, or southwest Asia Minor. They spoke a proto-Greek language, and were related to the Phoenicians and Carthaginians. The "Palestinian" Arabs of today bear no cultural or ethnic relationship to the ancient Philistines, who were wiped out by the Assyrian and Babylonian conquests (eighth century B.C. and sixth century B.C., respectively). See, e.g., Trude Dothan and Moshe Dothan, *People of the Sea—The Search for the Philistines* (New York: Macmillan, 1992); Michael Grant, *The History of Ancient Israel* (New York: Charles Scribner's Sons, 1984), pp. 67–68. It is critical to note that the Philistines are not mentioned in either Philip K. Hitti, *History of the Arabs,* 10th ed. (London: Macmillan/St. Martin's Press, 1970); or Albert Hourani, *A History of the Arab Peoples* (Cambridge, MA: Belknap/Harvard, 1991). If "Palestinian" Arabs were descended from or related to the Philistines, it surely would have been mentioned in at least one of these comprehensive histories of the Arabs. Since the myth of "Palestinian" descent from the Philistines has been debunked, the "Palestinians" have claimed that they are descended from the Canaanites. Recently, the Saudis have asserted that the Jebusites migrated

to Jerusalem from the Arabian Peninsula in 3000 B.C. However, as with the claim of "Palestinian" descent from the Philistines, there is no historical or archaeological evidence to support these assertions. Neither of these theories is mentioned in Hitti, *History of the Arabs,* or Hourani, *A History of the Arab Peoples.*

21. Between ca. 925 B.C. and 586 B.C., a succession of Jewish kings ruled the independent kingdoms of Israel and Judah. During the second and first centuries B.C., the independent state of Judea was ruled by the Hasmonean dynasty, descendants of the Maccabees. During the rest of that three-thousand-year period, the land was a tiny sliver ruled from a distance by a succession of empires: the Assyrians, the Babylonians, the Persians, the Greeks, the Romans, the Byzantines, the Arabs, the Crusaders, the Mamluks, and finally the Ottoman Turks.

22. Yohanan Aharoni, Michael Avi-Yonah, Anson Rainey and Ze'ev Safrai, *The Macmillan Bible Atlas, 3rd ed.* (New York: Macmillan, 2002); Meir Ben-Dov, *Historical Atlas of Jerusalem* (New York: Continuum, 2002); Hitti, *History of the* Arabs; Hourani, *A History of the Arab Peoples;* Bernard Lewis, *The Middle East: A Brief History of the Last 2,000 Years* (New York: Touchstone/Simon and Schuster, 1995); Bernard Lewis, "The Palestinians and the PLO, a Historical Approach," *Commentary,* January 1975, pp. 32–48; Joan Peters, *From Time Immemorial: The Origins of the Arab-Jewish Conflict Over Palestine* (New York: Harper and Row, 1984) p. 139; James B. Pritchard, ed., *The Times Atlas of the Bible* (New York: Crescent Books/Random House, 1996).

23. *Peel Report* (see chap. 11, n. 19).

24. United Nations General Assembly Resolution 181, November 29, 1947, http://www.yale.edu/lawweb/avalon/un/res181.htm.

25. United Nations Security Council Resolution 242, November 22, 1967, http://www.yale.edu/lawweb/avalon/un/un242.htm.

26. See, e.g., Khaled Abu Toameh, "Abbas Vows to Bring 'Saboteurs' to Trial," *Jerusalem Post,* February 27, 2005; Itamar Marcus and Barbara Cook, "Saboteur or Shahid," *Jerusalem Post,* March 2, 2005 (Tel Aviv nightclub suicide bombing, February 25, 2005); Khaled Abu Toameh, "Palestinians: Thorns in His Side," *Jerusalem Post,* July 15, 2005 (Netanya shopping mall suicide bombing, July 12, 2005); Khaled Abu Toameh, "Abbas Condemns Kissufim Shooting," *Jerusalem Post,* July 24, 2005 (Kissufim border crossing shooting attack, July 12, 2005); Khaled Abu Toameh, "Tensions Build Between PA and Hamas," *Jerusalem Post,* August 28, 2005 (Beersheba suicide bombing, August 28, 2005); David Rudge, "Hadera Victictims Buried,"

Jerusalem Post, October 27, 2005 (Hadera market suicide bombing, October 26, 2005); "An Absence of Morality," *Jerusalem Post,* December 5, 2005 (Netanya shopping mall bombing, December 4, 2005); Khaled Abu Toameh, "Abbas Criticizes Rocket Attacks," *Jerusalem Post,* December 10, 2005 (continuing rocket and mortar barrages from Gaza); Tom Gross, "Yasser Abbas," *Wall Street Journal,* December 22, 2005 (Netanya shopping mall bombing, December 4, 2005).

27. *CNN World,* "Arafat Condemns Bombing, Calls for Cease-Fire," http://transcripts.cnn.com/2001/WORLD/meast/06/02/israel.explosion .03/index.html.

28. See, e.g., Khaled Abu Toameh, "Female Terror Bomber Becomes a Palestinian heroine," *Washington Post,* August 4, 2005; Marcus and Cook, "Saboteur or Shahid"; Toameh, "Abbas Condemns Kissufim Shooting"; Gross, "Yasser Abbas"; Itamar Marcus and Barbara Cook, "PA on Terror: 'Condemns' on Paper, Praises in Practice," Palestine Media Watch, December 5, 2005, http://www.pmw.org.il/Latest%20bulletins%20new.htm# b051205.

29. Michael Matza, "Gunmen Become Lawmen to Avoid Israeli Want List," *Philadelphia Inquirer,* March 27, 2005; Khalid Amayreh, "Joining Forces," *al-Ahram* (Egypt), no. 736, March 31–April 6, 2005; Khaled Abu Toameh, "Abbas Adds Fugitives to Security Forces," *Jerusalem Post,* April 10, 2005; "Palestinian Gunmen Join Police Force to Keep Weapons," *Khaleej Times Online* (Dubai, UAE), May 10, 2005, http://www.khaleejtimes.com/aboutus .asp; Khaled Abu Toameh, "PA-Sponsored Gunmen Abet Anarchy," *Jerusalem Post,* June 14, 2005; Khaled Abu Toameh, "PA to Grant Gunman Zubeidi Rank of Sergeant," *Jerusalem Post,* July 5, 2005; Khaled Abu Toameh, "PA Criticizes Hamas Refusal to Join," *Jerusalem Post,* July 6, 2005; Mortimer B. Zuckerman, "Alone at the Dance," *U.S. News and World Report,* August 15, 2005, http://www.usnews.com/usnews/opinion/ articles/050815/15edit.htm; Khaled Abu Toameh, "PA Rejects Call to Disarm Militias," *Jerusalem Post,* September 22, 2005.

30. United Press International, "Abbas Denies Seeking End to Armed Struggle," *Washington Times,* December 15, 2004, http://washingtontimes.com/ upi-breaking/20041215-083516-2665r.htm.

31. Charles Krauthammer, "Arafat's Heir," *Washington Post,* January 2, 2005, http://www.washingtonpost.com/wp-dyn/articles/A54851-2005Jan6.html.

32. Evelyn Gordon, "Terrorism Works," *Jerusalem Post,* July 14, 2005, http:// www.jpost.com/servlet/Satellite?pagename=JPost/JPArticle/ShowFull&cid= 1121221100927&p=1006953079865.

33. *Wikipedia,* S.V. "Sbarro Restaurant Suicide Bombing," http://en.wikipedia
.org/wiki/Sbarro_restaurant_suicide_bombing.
34. Larry Collins and Dominique LaPierre, *O Jerusalem!* (New York: Touch-stone/Simon and Schuster, 1988), pp. 190–95.
35. Although there were anti-Jewish riots in 1921 and 1922, the beginning of the Arab terror war against Jewish nationalism can be traced to 1929, when Arabs destroyed the centuries-old Jewish community of Hebron, the site of the tomb of the Jewish Patriarchs. Sixty-four Jews were murdered and the remainder were expelled. At the same time there were Arab riots against Jews in Jaffa, Safed, Acre, and other communities. Hundreds more Jews were murdered. There were numerous other outbreaks of violence against Jews throughout the British Mandatory period.

12. SOCIETIES ARE NOT CREATED EQUAL

1. *Arab Human Development Report 2003—Building a Knowledge Society (AHDR 2003)* (New York, 2003: United Nations Development Programme), p. 137.
2. *AHDR 2003,* pp. 35–37, 144.
3. *AHDR 2003,* p. 51.
4. *AHDR 2003,* p. 151.
5. *AHDR 2003,* p. 51.
6. *AHDR 2003,* p. 71.
7. *AHDR 2003,* p. 78.
8. *AHDR 2003,* p. 157. All three patents were granted to residents of Morocco.
9. *AHDR 2003,* p. 71.
10. Brian Whitaker, "Islamic Leaders Unveil Action Plan to Rescue a 'Nation in Crisis'," *Guardian,* December 9, 2005.
11. Ghani Jafar, "Makkah Tidings," *News International,* December 18, 2005.
12. Sharon Lapkin, "Palestinian Honor" *FrontPage Magazine,* January 28, 2000.
13. Hillel Newman, "The Worst Exploitation," *Boston Globe,* June 7, 2004.
14. Hillel Newman, "Recruiting Women for Terror," *Boston Globe,* June 14, 2004.
15. Itaman Marcus and Barbara Cook, "PA Course Honors Terrorist Wafa Idris," *Palestinian Media Watch,* July 7, 2005.
16. Hillel Newman, "The Worst Exploitation," *Boston Globe,* June 7, 2004.

13. IS ISLAM A PEACEFUL RELIGION?

1. *Online News Hour with Jim Lehrer,* Osama bin Laden videotape, http://www.pbs.org/newshour/bb/terrorism/july-dec01/video_12-13a.html.
2. Sahih Al-Bukhari, *Hadid vol.1, no. 24.*
3. "The Mind of an Islamic Terrorist, Terrorism," Muhammadanism.org, http://www.muhammadanism.org/Terrorism/Terrorist_Mind.htm.
4. Itamar Marcus and Barbara Cook, "Religious War Against 'Infidels' Inherent to PA Religious Ideology," Palestinian Media Watch, http://www.pmw.org.il/Latest%20bulletins%20new.htm.
5. Ibrahim Mudayris, PA TV, May 13, 2005. Palestinian Media Watch, http://www.pmw.org.il/ and *World Net Daily,* July 15, 2005, "Global Jihad: Palestinian TV Sermon Calls for Genocide; After London Attack, Cleric Urges: 'Annihilate Infidels.'" http://www.worldnetdaily.com/news/article.asp?ARTICLE_ID=45277.
6. "Arab Americans Speak Out," *USA Today,* February 6, 1991.
7. Excerpts from Daniel Pipes, "The Danger Within," http://www.danielpipes.org/article/77.
8. Daniel Pipes, "The Danger Within: Militant Islam in America," *Commentary,* November 2001, http://www.danielpipes.org/article/77.
9. Daniel Pipes, "Fighting Militant Islam Without Bias," http://www.city-journal.org/html/11_4_fighting_militant.html.
10. Steven Emerson, *Jihad in America,* produced for PBS, 1994.
11. Joel Mowbray, "Islamic Hall of Shame," www.frontpagemagazine.com, May 30, 2005.
12. CNN.com, The situation room, February 8, 2006, http://transcripts.cnn.com/TRANSCRIPTS/0602/08/sitroom.03.html.
13. Jill Lawless, "Police Reject Critics of Cleric Case," Associated Press, February, 8, 2006, http://newszine.jou.ufl.edu/index.php?id=97.
14. David Stout, "American is Sentenced to 30 Years in Terror Case," *New York Times,* March 30, 2006.
15. "Global Jihad, U.S Muslims Desecrate American Flag," WorldNetDaily.com, June 8, 2005, http://www.worldnetdaily.com/news/article.asp?ARTICLE_ID=44664.

14. POLITICAL CORRECTNESS GONE MAD

1. Homeland Security: Testimony by Deputy Secretary of Homeland Security Admiral James Loy Before the Senate Select Committee on Intelligence, Washington, D.C., February 16, 2005.

2. http://www.townhall.com/columnists/calthomas/ct2005022.shtml-27K.

3. http://www.washtimes.com/national/20040928-123346-3928r.htm-69K.

4. http://www.wnd.com/news/article.asp?Article_ID=42985-34K.

5. "Al-Qaida Nukes Already in the US," http://www.worldnetdaily.com/news/article.asp?ARTICLE_ID=45203.

6. Federation for American Immigration Reform, "The Cost of Illegal Immigration," http://www.fairus.org/site/PageServer.

7. Donna Leinwand, "Foreigners Linked to Terror Tricked INS," *USA Today,* May 22, 2002, http://www.usatoday.com/news/sept11/2002/05/22/terrorists-ins.htm.

8. Center for Immigration Studies, Securing the Homeland Through Immigration Law Enforcement, Testimony prepared for the U.S. House of Representatives Committee on the Judiciary, "Department of Homeland Security Transition: Bureau of Immigration and Customs Enforcement," April 10, 2003, statement of Mark Krikorian, Executive Director of the Center for Immigration Studies, http://www.cis.org/articles/2003/msktestimony410.html.

9. Testimony before the U.S. House of Representatives, Committee on the Judiciary March 11, 2004, http://www.cis.org/articles/2004/cutlertestimony031104.html.

10. Charles Babington, "Bill Would Allow Warrantless Spying," *Washington Post,* March 17, 2006.

11. Lebanese Information Center, Press release, LIC statement on the - Arab-American position on Homeland Security, January 5, 2006, by Dr. Joseph Gebeily, President, http://cedarmailer.com/americancongress/pages/archive/messagedetails.asp?ID=360.

12. Energy Information Administration (EID), Country Analysis Briefs, Saudi Arabia, August 2005 report, http://www.eia.doe.gov/emeu/cabs/saudi.html.

ACKNOWLEDGMENTS

Writing a book is a daunting task that involves hundreds of hours, and much energy and research. I would like to highlight and mention those individuals who were directly instrumental in the writing and publishing of this book.

I begin by thanking my dear friend Mark Leslie, who dedicated hours, days, and months to research and writing from beginning to end. I am forever grateful to have been so fortunate to have a knowledgeable, passionate, and dedicated friend like you. Jerry Gordon, my dear friend, mentor, confident, advisor, and the anchor that keeps me grounded in the storms of attacks and hate from my enemies. Karen Freeman, my dear friend, whose research has been invaluable. Without her help I wouldn't have made my deadline. Dr. Joseph Gebeily, my friend who is also a survivor of the Lebanese war, was always there to help answer any question I had about the war. Susan Smith and Liz Black for their help in editing the proposal. My agent Lynne Rabinoff, whose effort made this book see the light. She is not only one of the most professional people I have worked with, Lynne is also a beautiful human being inside and out who became my very dear and wonderful friend. Nichole Argyres, my editor at St. Martin's Press, who kept everyone in line throughout the whole process. Working with her was a pleasure. Charles, who worked by my side and wiped my tears during the day and held me through my bouts of PTSD at night, reassuring me that everything is okay, as I relived my experiences to write this book. I am forever grateful for his love and kindness.